ABOUT THE AUTHOR

Victor (Vic) Ient was born in army quarters at 9 Nicholson Terrace, Aldershot, Hampshire in 1946. This was the home of his parents after they were reunited when Albert Ient returned home after the War. Albert Ient had returned from Japan in November 1945 and his mother and Vic's two brothers had returned to England from Australia earlier in that summer.

He retired from a career of over 40 years in telecommunications and IT in 2008. In his retirement Vic specialises in voluntary and public service work. He is now a blogger, climate change activist, hiker and cyclist, a supporter of the underdog and fair play. A onetime politician and avid student of history. He is keen to understand what really happened in decades and centuries past. Vic has spent many years researching his family history with its roots in London, Oxfordshire, Wales and Germany.

He has a Master of Science degree in the Management of Technology (1992) from the Universities of Brighton and Sussex. His dissertation was written on the subject of virtual and remote networking.

THESE VALIANT MEN

THE STORY OF EIGHT BRITISH SERVICEMEN IN WORLD WAR II IN THE FAR EAST

VICTOR S. IENT

Copyright © 2020 Victor S. Ient

The moral right of the author has been asserted.

Apart from any fair dealing for the purposes of research or private study, or criticism or review, as permitted under the Copyright, Designs and Patents Act 1988, this publication may only be reproduced, stored or transmitted, in any form or by any means, with the prior permission in writing of the publishers, or in the case of reprographic reproduction in accordance with the terms of licences issued by the Copyright Licensing Agency. Enquiries concerning reproduction outside those terms should be sent to the publishers.

Matador
9 Priory Business Park,
Wistow Road, Kibworth Beauchamp,
Leicestershire. LE8 0RX
Tel: 0116 279 2299
Email: books@troubador.co.uk
Web: www.troubador.co.uk/matador
Twitter: @matadorbooks

ISBN 978 1838594 954

British Library Cataloguing in Publication Data.
A catalogue record for this book is available from the British Library.

Printed and bound by CPI Group (UK) Ltd, Croydon, CR0 4YY
Typeset in 11pt Adobe Caslon Pro by Troubador Publishing Ltd, Leicester, UK

Matador is an imprint of Troubador Publishing Ltd

This book is dedicated to all of those who served to preserve our freedom and liberties during World War II in the Far East.

A POEM BY A PRISONER OF WAR:

Barbed Wire! Barbed Wire! Barbed Wire!
To the North, South, West and East
Will it always hold me captive
Without hope or joy or peace
Must I ever curve this eager flame
That burns within my chest
Or know once more the joy of home
With pleasant hours of rest
Such questions to my mind do crowd
When deep in thought I sit
But ever with it comes the cry
It won't be long, don't quit
And so it goes from day to day
A never changing scene
But someday soon I will leave it all
As though it were a dream.

Unknown – from http://www.merkki.com/poetry.htm

Contents

	Foreword	ix
	Introduction	xi
	Author's note	xxi
1.	World War II in the Far East	1
2.	Albert Ient	18
3.	Maynard Skinner	49
4.	Harold Bates and Monty Truscott	57
5.	William (Bill) Alfred Butler	74
6.	Terence (Flash) Kelly	113
7.	Philip (Chick) Henderson	129
8.	Wilfred Batty	173
9.	Visits to the Far East	195
	Postscript	207
	Acknowledgements and Thanks	210

Foreword

DR TONY BANHAM

The window is almost closed. Very few of the wartime generation are left as I write this, and by the time you read it they may all be gone. None will be left to answer our questions, tell their stories, or share an experience that – in truth – we could never really grasp.

All that remains are notes and diaries, remembered conversations (for those of us fortunate enough to speak to them) and a few faded photographs and documents. So it is left to books like this to serve as memorials to a generation who did their bit, and more, to stop the spread of fascism in the East. Many lost their lives in the conflict, and none came home unchanged. Few spoke much about what they did, never seeing themselves or their comrades as heroes; they just got on with life when they returned, worked, raised families, carried on. But they never forgot.

They stayed in touch with each other, valuing the opportunity to talk with those who shared experiences which neither their children nor today's generations could ever quite understand.

Two very different experiences link the men described in this book. The first was service in the Hong Kong Signal Company when the Colony was invaded by Japan in December 1941, along with service with the RAF in what was the Dutch East Indies, now Indonesia and Singapore, and the second was internment in POW camps in the Japanese homeland.

They were lucky to survive the first, a battle in which 10 per cent of the defenders died, lucky to survive transportation across the seas to Japan (the draft prior to theirs was torpedoed and a thousand men died) and lucky to survive the diseases and docks of Innoshima. Some prisoners of war even endured all that but perished after liberation, dying on their way home. The eight men described here were more fortunate: they lived, they came home. But they never forgot.

Dr Tony Banham
Hong Kong, May 2019

ABOUT DR TONY BANHAM

Tony is the founder of the Hong Kong War Diary Project, which studies and documents the 1941 defence of Hong Kong, the defenders, their families, and the fates of all until liberation. His published books are considered to be examples of some of the best research on the Hong Kong experience during the Second World War.

His published books include:

Not the Slightest Chance
(Hong Kong University Press, 2003) ISBN 962-209-615-8

The Sinking of the Lisbon Maru
(Hong Kong University Press, 2006) ISBN 962-209-771-5

We Shall Suffer There
(Hong Kong University Press, 2009) ISBN 978-962-209-960-9

Reduced to a Symbolical Scale
(Hong Kong University Press, 2017) ISBN 978-988-839-087-8

Tony graduated from Herefordshire University, England, with a degree in computer science. At the age of 30 his business career took him to Hong Kong, which is now his permanent home. He received his PhD in history from the Australian Defence Force Academy (ADFA), Canberra, Australia.

Introduction

This book is set in the Far East during World War II and describes the lives and experiences of eight servicemen including my father. Five of them were based in Hong Kong in the run-up to the outbreak of war in the Far East at the end of 1941. These five, including my father, were all signalmen in the Hong Kong Signal Company and fought in the brief but fierce Battle for Hong Kong, which started on 8 December 1941 and finished with the British surrender on Christmas Day, 25 December 1941. The signalmen's accounts include the story of the fall of Hong Kong, life in the prisoner of war camp in Hong Kong, the terrible journey to Japan and their imprisonment in prison camps there.

This book also tells the story of three other servicemen, members of the RAF, who were captured in Java, in the Dutch East Indies (now Indonesia) in February 1942. They have been included because all three were imprisoned in the same POW camp as my father in Habu, Japan. The capture of the Dutch East Indies by the Japanese ran in parallel to the fighting in the Malay peninsula and was finally complete a few weeks after the fall of Singapore, which was on 15 February 1942. As in Hong Kong and Singapore, thousands of Allied troops were captured in the Dutch East Indies.

The desperate situation in Singapore was of course linked with that of the Dutch East Indies but since these servicemen were not based in Singapore I have not tried to delve too deeply into the background military situation in the Malay peninsula or Singapore. Also, I have not tried to cover events leading up to the conquest of the Dutch East Indies by the Japanese since RAF serviceman had only arrived in the Far East, in Singapore and the Dutch East Indies, a few months before their capture. Such events are more expertly covered in other books and publications. However, in the case of Hong Kong, my father and his colleagues had a longer experience of this outpost of the British Empire over a number of years before their capture and because of that I had a great desire to understand the situation leading up to the fall of Hong Kong. Indeed, Hong Kong was where my mother, father and brothers lived before the war. In summary, I am attempting to present the reader with a picture of what life was like before the war in Hong Kong.

As a child, I was surrounded by military life in one way or another. My father had served in the army. We lived in Aldershot, which was an army town, and my father was a member (later president) of the Royal Signals Association, Aldershot Branch. He was also a member of the Hong Kong Signal Company Veterans Association. Military and ex-military servicemen, often with their wives, were frequent visitors to our house. Also, I went with my father sometimes to pay social visits on ex-servicemen. When I was about four my eldest brother, John, aged 15, joined the Boys Regiment. Two years later, my brother George joined the Army Apprentice Corp. Their return in uniform when they got leave was a reminder of the army. So, it was no wonder that there was much talk of military matters in the house.

I remember my father opening his desk and showing me some items that he had from his time as a prisoner of war. These included a pair of handmade rims for his glasses, a bamboo razor holder and a bamboo name tag. I discovered in our garden shed the rubber-soled shoes he wore as a prisoner. I asked him about the war and I remember snippets from his description of the Battle for Hong Kong and his capture. He was my hero. To me, even from this early age, Hong Kong and that whole region of the world seemed full of mystery. My imagination also took me to Australia, where my mother and two brothers had been throughout the war period. There was a picture on our wall at home – that of my mother and my two brothers, George and John. She told me that it was taken in the Philippines, at Baguio,[2] high up in the hills north of Manila on the main island of Luzon, as that was where they had been evacuated to from Hong Kong in 1941 before they were evacuated again to Australia. There were stories of Australia, of George and John walking barefoot on days out, of going to Manly Beach and swimming in the sea.

---

2   Baguio was presumably chosen by the Allies as an 'evacuee' location as it had been loaned by the family of the American newspaper magnate William Randolph Hearst. Fortunately for the families it has a cool climate due to its altitude in the otherwise tropical climate of the Philippines. It is 1,540 metres (5,050 feet) above sea level. Under American rule it was the summer capital of the Philippine Islands.

INTRODUCTION

At my home in Aldershot, on the wall in the lounge was a black-and-white drawing of a set of hutments on a quayside, which I was told was where my father was imprisoned as a POW during the war in Japan. As a boy I used to look at this picture and I would transport myself there in my imagination, thinking of how it was for my father. This drawing, made by Geoffrey Coxhead, who was a fellow POW, was sent to my father after the war. On the back of this drawing, as I found out many years later when I was clearing the house after my mother's death, was the word 'Habu'. This was the name of the place in Japan where my father was held captive as a POW. So it was no wonder that I picked up lots of information about the army and my father's role in it. Little snippets came out about it all the time. For instance, as a child I understood all the ranks in the army, from private to general, and I could piece together the main events of the war without being directly told. It became obvious that there was a great camaraderie among my father and his fellow soldiers, and especially with those with whom he served in Hong Kong. The Hong Kong Signal Company was obviously a close-knit group. After all, they served together, fought together and became POWs together.

So, it was quite an easy step for me to take to try to record more formally the events surrounding my mother and father's pre-war life and what happened to them during the war. As a child I wanted to know more, and I asked questions, putting away in my memory those important little snippets. In my teenage years my interest waned but as I got into my early twenties I began to promise myself that I had to record my parents' history. However, my busy career diverted me away from this task. It wasn't until my father died, in 1988, that I began. There were so many strands to bring together. I spent a number of years as time allowed investigating my family history and that still goes on today.

In the ten years that followed, on my visits to my mother until she died in 1999, I brought up the subject of life before the war and in wartime in terms of her experiences. I did this in an informal way to try to get her to expand on the subject. Sometimes it worked. Although I'd started to write quite a bit about our family history including the war, there was still more I needed to know.

In 1999 I had to travel to the Far East on business. This gave me the opportunity to visit Hong Kong, probably the most significant place in my parents' lives. This was where their lives were shattered by the outbreak of war in the Far East. My mother briefed me, so I was able to visit many of the places she and my father had mentioned. I reported back to Mum on the success of my trip. She was delighted to have news of my visit and to see the photos of places in Hong Kong. Sadly, later on that year, in 1999, she died. As I cleared the house, I gathered together for the first time all the papers and memorabilia to do with my parents' lives. This is what really started me on the journey to discover the wartime history of my father and his colleagues and research their experiences in World War II in the Far East.

Firstly, after Mum died I spoke to my eldest brother, John. I had given him the drawing of the POW camp at Habu. On a label on the back it simply said 'HABU'. Some months later John sent me a black-and-white photo of six servicemen photographed outside a large hut. One of the men was my father. The hut looked very similar to the hut in the drawing. I telephoned John and asked him how he had got hold of the photo. John and his wife had looked for books relating to Habu Camp, and John had spoken to one of the authors to get a copy of his book. The upshot of the conversation was John being sent not only a copy of the book but also a copy of the photo. After reading the book I wanted to meet the author and find out how he got hold of the photos. The author was Terence Kelly.

Terence Kelly's book *Living with the Japanese* (recently republished under a new title, *By Hellship to Hiroshima*) gives a very detailed account of life in Habu POW camp, which was where my father was imprisoned. Habu POW camp was on the south-west coast of Innoshima, which sits within the 'Inland Sea' (The Seto Inland Sea), a body of water separating Honshu, Shikoku and Kyushu, three of the four main islands of Japan (see the endnotes for details of the location). Its calm waters stretch over 400 kilometres from Osaka to Kitakyushu. It has a mild climate and serves as a waterway, connecting the Pacific Ocean to the Sea of Japan, and contains some 3,000 islands. In the period before WWII many small shipyards had developed on the shores of the island. Habu Camp was near one of these many shipyards. POWs were used as labour in many of these yards.

I felt it was important to meet Kelly and find out more about him and life in the POW camp that my father served in. There were so few POWs left alive, over 70 years after the start of the war in the Far East. Any survivor alive today would have to be at least 94! Also, to meet the author of a book who had WWII experience in the Far East as a POW would be not only enormously helpful but a privilege. I met Terence in 2007 and we had a very interesting and productive discussion, which he allowed me to record. This was my first big step forward. I am deeply grateful for the opportunity to have spoken to Terence. The conversations we had ranged over many topics and provided me with factual and anecdotal evidence about life as a Far East Prisoner of War (FEPOW) that I would never have found elsewhere. And so, importantly for me, he answered some of the questions I wish I had asked my father but never had.

My second lucky break came as a result of my parents' address books. Dad was good at keeping in touch with past friends and military and wartime comrades, so I was able to go through their address books and Christmas card lists to see who served with my father and knew Mum and Dad in the Far East.

I sent letters to my father's old comrades. Although I had a number of disappointments because some had sadly passed away, one came back with a positive reply and as a result I was able to visit and interview Maynard Skinner, who was a close friend of Mum and Dad and had served with my father in Hong Kong.

With Terence Kelly's, Maynard Skinner's and my father's stories, I felt I was beginning to record something quite significant about the experiences of our servicemen who had been captured in the Far East during World War II.

I was lucky with the next few events. At Maynard Skinner's funeral a few years ago (in 2013), and quite by accident, I got into conversation with a brother and sister, Lizzie and John, who had come to pay their respects because their father (Harold Bates) had served with Maynard in Hong Kong. Through this chance meeting I was able to record the story of three other members of my father's regiment, the Hong Kong Signal Company, all of whom knew him. Alongside this, a fellow researcher, Adrian Batty, who had contacted me through my website, recommended I attend the annual meeting of the 'Java Club'. This was formed from the RAF veteran survivors who had been captured in Java, in the Dutch East Indies (now Indonesia). I had thought that there would be little or no chance of meeting anyone who had been imprisoned at the same POW camp as my father. I couldn't have been more wrong. I finally decided to book for the 'reunion weekend', saying to myself that, if the conference was no good, at least I could enjoy Stratford-upon-Avon. So, one weekend in August 2013, I walked into the lounge of the Falcon Hotel and within a few minutes I saw two veterans (easily distinguishable as they were wearing name badges), so I thought I would introduce myself. I told them the reason why I was there and to my amazement I found out both of them had been imprisoned in Habu prisoner of war camp! I could not believe my luck: the chance of finding anyone from that period in the war was remote to say the least and then to actually meet servicemen who had been in the same POW camp, from what was effectively a chance meeting, at this reunion was astounding. There were literally hundreds of Japanese POW camps. The Japanese captured about 140,000 Allied troops[3] and something over 36,000 of these were transported to Japan to be imprisoned in over 80 POW camps. The two men I met on this day could have been sent to any of the hundreds of POW camps across South East Asia and Japan. I felt very lucky! So, here I was with 'Chick' Henderson and his colleague Ted Read, both of whom had been transported to the RAF section of Habu POW camp, where my father had also been held. Amazing luck to meet servicemen who were still alive after all these years! I sat down with these great guys and Chick led the discussion. We began an interview, which must have lasted over three hours. He took me through his time as an RAF serviceman, leaving England in 1941, being captured and imprisoned and returning to England in 1945. Ted was obviously a much quieter person and just nodded or confirmed a point or two during the afternoon. It was a very jovial meeting but punctuated with anecdotes from their time as prisoners of war. I hope I'll be able to carry on a conversation at the age of 94 in the same way as Chick had done that day!

We met again during the weekend of the reunion and on parting I said I would like to go and see him at his home in Hampshire to follow up on the meeting. That was not to happen, though. He died a few weeks later on 5 September 2013. However, before he died he sent me a video of a talk he had given a few years earlier in his hometown of Sunderland about his experiences some years earlier. In the attached note he said that he would be delighted if I could make use of his video lecture. The lecture gave a comprehensive account of his experiences in the RAF and as a POW. You could say it was his filmed biography.

As I said, I had gone to Maynard Skinner's funeral, in Bournemouth in 2013. I knew by now that Maynard had not only existed in my parents' address books but had been a friend since before World War II and, like my father, had been captured in Hong Kong. It seemed fitting to go to Maynard's funeral and pay my respects, not only because of my mother and father but because he had been so open and helpful in opening a window into the past. On this occasion, though, I was not attending to further my investigations into WWII, but just as a mark of respect and thanks. This

---

3 During World War II, the Japanese Armed Forces captured nearly 140,000 Allied military personnel (Australia, Canada, Great Britain, India, the Netherlands, New Zealand and the United States) in the South East Asia and Pacific areas. From Forces War Records: https://www.forces-war-records.co.uk/prisoners-of-war-of-the-japanese-1939-1945

visit to Bournemouth was to provide me with another lucky break. After the funeral ceremony, I chatted to some of the other mourners, a brother and sister, Lizzie Spink and her brother John. They said that, like me, they weren't related to Maynard but had also had come to pay their respects because their father, who had died some years ago, had been a military colleague of Maynard's in Hong Kong. This immediately sparked my interest. We exchanged contact details and agreed to be in touch at some future date. Then, just as we were parting, Lizzie Spink mentioned that she thought there was another Royal Signals WWII veteran still alive. Her father, Harold Bates, had kept in touch with this veteran, Bill Butler, who lived in Lincolnshire. Some weeks later Lizzie phoned and confirmed that she had spoken to Bill. He was still alive! In the past I had delayed following up with World War II ex-servicemen only to find that they had sadly passed away. I wasn't going to delay on this one, so a few weeks later I got the train up to Lincolnshire, Lizzie picked me up from the station and we went off to interview Bill at his bungalow in Mablethorpe.

We found Bill at his small bungalow, not far from the seafront. The bungalow was in a poor state of repair and looked a little sad. His wife had died a few years earlier and he lived alone, surrounded by pictures of his wife, wartime photos and memorabilia and photos of the Royal Signals reunion meetings. However, we found Bill in good spirits and very pleased to see us. We chatted to him throughout the morning, using the photographs on the wall to prompt our discussions. Within a short time, we were laughing with him over some of his wartime antics. At one point he showed us what looked like a baggy pair of underpants made of a single sheet of cotton. He explained that this was a replica of what was worn under the POW workmen's clothing and used to smuggle things into the POW camp from the nearby docks where they had worked. Some time into the conversation he mentioned that his story had been written up by volunteers in the British Legion and he produced a full booklet of over 30 pages which described his story. It was his autobiography. He said we could use it to write up his story as part of my book and mentioned that the British Legion had extra copies. Finally, it was time to go. We felt so privileged at having met such a jolly ex-serviceman who had enjoyed his life in the Royal Signals, endured his incarceration with equanimity and had returned to civilian life to enjoy many years of happiness with his wife. While we were there in Mablethorpe we took the opportunity to catch up with the British Legion and they quickly produced some spare copies of Bill's story, which has been used as part of this book recording our valiant men's experiences in World War II.

On the way back to the railway station, Lizzie mentioned that she had a recording of a BBC interview carried out in the 1970s with her father (Harold Bates) and another colleague of my father's, Monty Truscott. They were being asked to recount their wartime experiences during the joint services veterans' visit, including Royal Signals veterans, to Hong Kong. My mother and father were longstanding friends of Mr and Mrs Truscott, having first met them in Hong Kong before the war. I was excited and amazed that, quite by chance, through the visit to Maynard's funeral I had uncovered three more of my father's fellow ex-servicemen! It was wonderful to listen to the interview and complete the picture by hearing these two men speak of their military service and their imprisonment as POWs.

I mentioned how Adrian Batty had got in touch with me through my website in January 2013. He had been writing his father's story just in the same way as I had written my father's story. I helped him with a bit of research at the Imperial War Museum and through 2013 he updated me with later versions of his father's wartime biography and agreed that I could add it to my website. I felt this was important as, although as far as we know Adrian's father had not known my father, he had been imprisoned in the same POW camp in Japan. This further biography would, I hope, complete the story, as far as I'm able, of how World War II not only changed the course of world history but also changed the lives of these men.

Looking back, I never thought that I would ever get this far in piecing together what life was like for my father in those wartime years. I knew I hadn't asked my mother and father enough questions when they had been alive. However, I've been very lucky in finding and meeting or recording those other ex-servicemen who have helped me piece together the story of capture and imprisonment during those terrible wartime years. I hope this record of these valiant men, who doggedly survived the vicissitudes of the degrading life as a POW and went on to return to their families and loved ones and lead a normal life after the war, will serve as my tribute to them and especially my mother and father.

It must have been awful for my mother and father to have their family life wrenched apart in 1940, with my father remaining in Hong Kong to face the consequences of World War II, for my mother not to know what had happened to my father throughout those wartime years, and for her to have received that awful telegram from the War Office stating that my father had been 'lost presumed missing in action'.

This book is only part of my father and mother's story and primarily focuses on the lives of the POWs in World War II. In addition to piecing together my mother's and father's wartime experiences, I feel extremely lucky and privileged to have actually met four of the ex-servicemen and heard the recorded voices of two others. Also, I'm thankful to Adrian Batty for allowing me to include his father's wartime story.

This book therefore presents you with the biographies of those eight valiant men who survived the war allowing me to tell their tale as best I'm able. Like my mother, they bravely and steadfastly survived the wartime years, leaving them able to rebuild their lives afterwards.

In this book I present you with the biographies of these eight men. It's not all doom and gloom, as you will see. Of course, they describe some of the horrors, but their characters are strong, and they have been able to open a window into the past for us, punctuated with their factual and sometimes humorous accounts. Their own personal accounts, which are recorded in this book, I hope bring into focus what life was like in those terrible years for these eight men. Here is a summary of the biographies you will find contained in the chapters of this book:

My father, Albert Ient, Army, Royal Signals, stationed in Hong Kong, who fought in the Battle for Hong Kong in 1941, was captured and became a prisoner of war and was eventually shipped to Japan.

Maynard Skinner, Army, Royal Signals, stationed in Hong Kong, who served with my father in Hong Kong, fought in the Battle for Hong Kong, was captured, became a prisoner of war and was sent on the infamous *Lisbon Maru* during his journey to a POW camp in Japan.

Harold Bates, Army, Royal Signals, stationed in Hong Kong, who served with my father in Hong Kong and fought in the Battle for Hong Kong in 1941, was captured, became a prisoner of war and was then transported to Japan.

Monty Truscott, Army, Royal Signals, stationed in Hong Kong, who served with my father, fought in the Battle for Hong Kong, was captured, became a prisoner of war and was then shipped to Japan, also on the *Lisbon Maru*.

Bill Butler, Army, Royal Signals, stationed in Hong Kong, who served with my father there and fought in the Battle for Hong Kong. He was captured, became a prisoner of war and was then shipped to Japan, also on the *Lisbon Maru*.

Terence Kelly, RAF, stationed in Java, who was captured and became a prisoner of war at Boei Glodok, Batavia (modern-day Jakarta). He was one of those who had to undergo the terrible journey to Japan on the SS *Dainichi Maru*. He published a book about life with the Japanese in the Habu POW camp where my father was held captive.

Philip ('Chick') Henderson, RAF, originally stationed in Singapore, who escaped to Java and was captured, becoming a prisoner at Boei Glodok, Batavia (modern-day Jakarta). He was one of those who had to undergo the terrible journey to Japan on the SS *Dainichi Maru*. I met him by chance at a Far East POW meeting of the Java Club in August 2013, finding out he was in the same POW camp (Habu) as my father.

Wilfred Batty, RAF, stationed in Java, who was captured and became a prisoner of war at Boei Glodok, Batavia (modern-day Jakarta). He was one of those who had to undergo the terrible journey to Japan on the SS *Dainichi Maru* and was then imprisoned in the same POW camp (Habu) in Japan as my father.

All were POWs in Japan. I've recorded all of the information and interviews I have for these valiant men and have published their stories on my website but feel it's only right to finish the job off and hence I decided to publish this book. I want their stories to live on and this book is my small contribution to that end.

This book is also a tribute to all the men who served to preserve our liberty and freedom in WWII and to those who served with my father in Hong Kong and who were incarcerated in Habu POW camp in Japan. This book is a tribute both to my parents and to all of those who served, suffered or died in the war in the Far East.

I hope you find this window into the past and the experiences of our WWII heroes of interest.

Author's Note

I have not tried to alter the way in which the servicemen told their stories or the form in which I received the information. Adrian Batty told his father's story and I have told my father's story. I interviewed Terence Kelly, Maynard Skinner, Chick Henderson and Bill Butler and have set down their stories as close as possible to the way they told them. I have referred to Terence Kelly's book and Bill Butler's story is documented by the Royal British Legion. I also refer to the BBC recording of Harold Bates and Monty Truscott. You will therefore see that the experiences recounted in places like Hong Kong and on the *Lisbon Maru* are repeated in different people's accounts. I felt this was the best way to proceed, for reasons of authenticity. I hope you won't find it too frustrating.

I have had permission from the POWs and Adrian Batty to use their photos and images. All other photos and images are mine or are from my family archive unless stated otherwise.

CHAPTER 1

World War II in the Far East

World War II in the Far East spread over a vast area including South East Asia, the Philippines, the Dutch East Indies and Borneo. Conflict began on 8 December 1941, including the invasion of Hong Kong, where my story starts. Hostilities officially ended on 9 September 1945, preceded by Emperor Hirohito giving a radio address to the Japanese nation on 15 August regarding their surrender. Just before this, the United States Air Force dropped atomic bombs on Hiroshima on 6 August and on Nagasaki on 9 August 1945.

BRITISH HISTORY OF HONG KONG

Hong Kong was a British colony from the middle of the nineteenth century until it was handed back to China on 1 July 1997. Hong Kong Island was ceded to the British in 1841 in a settlement following the First Opium War. Eventually, in 1898, a 99-year lease was granted for their New Territories, which added to the colony, as illustrated on the following page.

JAPANESE EMPIRE EXPANDS

On 7 December 1941, the Japanese attacked Pearl Harbor. That same day, six hours later, at 0800 hrs, they attacked the British crown colony of Hong Kong.

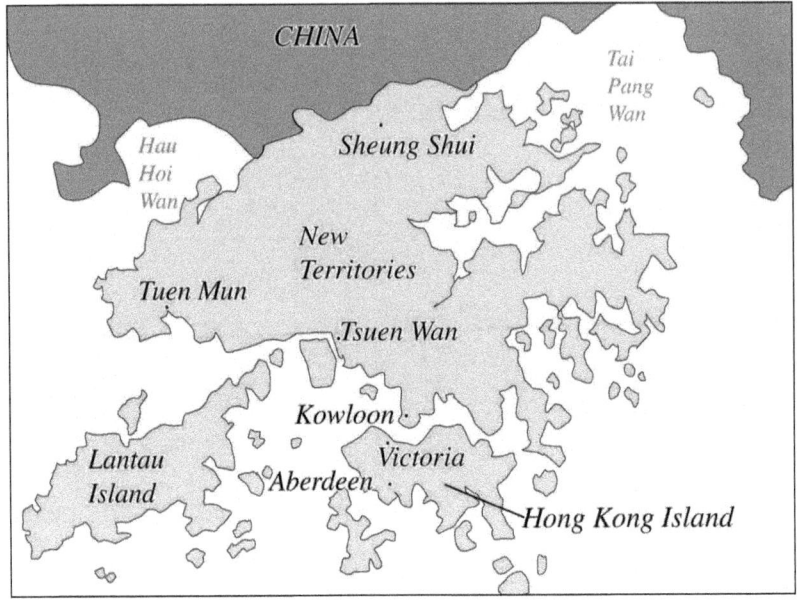

Figure 1.1 Hong Kong.

Figure 1.2 The location of Hong Kong in the Far East.

The world took little notice of that 'incident'. For those of us who had family members in Hong Kong, like my mother (who was by then in Australia), and family members in England, it was a different matter. It was a day and month never to be forgotten. My mother and my brothers had been evacuated from Hong Kong in 1940 owing to concerns about the military threats in the area. Before December 1941 the Japanese had made no threats to the British Empire, though they had, following their invasion of Manchuria, also taken over various ports and towns on the coast of China nearer to Hong Kong.

The defenders of Hong Kong fought a valiant fight. It was a hopeless effort from the beginning, but they fought on anyway. After 18 long, cruel days of non-stop struggle they were finally defeated on Christmas Day 1941. Those who survived began their period of captivity as prisoners of war, which lasted nearly four years.

The Japanese first took mainland Hong Kong (the New Territories) from their newly conquered positions in mainland China.

Figure 1.3 shows the extent of the Japanese Empire by the end of 1942.

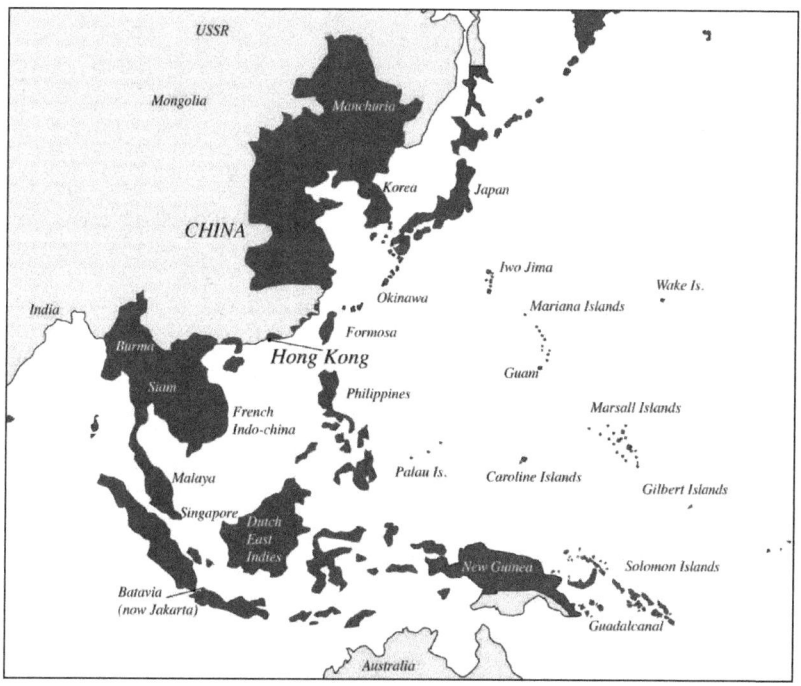

Figure 1.3 The Japanese Empire.

THE BRITISH VIEW OF THE JAPANESE

At the time of the fall of Hong Kong, Japan had not attacked Singapore – the other major centre of the British Empire in the Far East. The military and government in England were focused on the war with Hitler in Europe. I suspect their intelligence was sketchy, to say the least, when it came to the Japanese. One account given to the newly arrived Canadian troops in Hong Kong, in 1941, reportedly said that, even if the Japanese did attack, British intelligence had information that 'there were only 5,000 poorly-trained, poorly-equipped troops, who could not fight at night because of the shape of their eyes, and besides they were prone to sea sickness'. British intelligence's assessment was that the Japanese were not much to contend with.

KEEP THE BRITISH FLAG FLYING

At the height of the Battle for Hong Kong, on 21 December 1941, Churchill sent this message to the troops in Hong Kong:

> There must be no thought of surrender. Every part of the Island must be fought for and the enemy resisted with the greatest stubbornness. The enemy should be compelled to expend the utmost life and equipment. There must be vigorous fighting in the inner defences and, if need be, from house to house. Every day you maintain your resistance you help the Allied cause all over the world, and by prolonged resistance, you and your men can win the lasting honour which we are sure will be your due.[4]

My dad referred to this message in my conversations with him. I can't remember his exact words, but they went something like this: 'We were there to keep the flag flying for as long as possible – that's what Mr Churchill wanted us to do. We knew we were likely to be captured or die.'

---

[4] This was probably part of a series of messages sent by Churchill. For example, on 12 December Churchill sent a telegram to Hong Kong governor Mark Young: 'We are all watching day by day and hour by hour your stubborn defence of the port and fortress of Hong Kong. You guard a link long famous between the Far East and Europe... Every day of your resistance brings nearer our certain victory.'

FURTHER RESEARCH ABOUT THE BATTLE FOR HONG KONG

In my research about my father I have come across others who are investigating their father's wartime experiences. In this respect I would like to refer you, the reader, to a website dedicated to the commanding officer of 'D' Company of the Royal Rifles of Canada, Major Maurice A. Parker, http://battleofhongkong.com. You will find details of the heroic battle they fought and other historical information.

THE PHASES OF THE BATTLE FOR HONG KONG

For this account, I decided to base my summary on Tony Banham's website records and the following are extracts from the 'Battle of Hong Kong Background and Hong Kong War Diary' there (http://www.hongkongwardiary.com).

Tony has also published a number of books about the subject. Further details can be found at https://en.wikipedia.org/wiki/Tony_Banham and in the foreword to this book.

Tony's account helps us understand how Hong Kong was viewed by the British Army in 1941 and gives details of the events as they unfolded during the 18 days from the Japanese invasion to the capitulation of Hong Kong by the British Forces. The map overleaf shows the situation.

THE GARRISON AT FORTRESS HONG KONG[5]

In the first half of 1941, Hong Kong's garrison was commanded by General Grasset. It consisted of three infantry battalions – the 2nd Battalion the Royal Scots, the 5/7th Rajputs and the 2/14th Punjabis – plus one machine-gun battalion: the 1st Battalion, Middlesex Regiment. These were supported by a large number of Royal Artillery Batteries, the Hong Kong Volunteer Defence Corps (HKVDC), and all the supporting units that an isolated garrison needed. The British government had depleted the Royal Navy resources in Hong Kong and only one destroyer, HMS *Thracian*, several gunboats and a flotilla of motor torpedo boats remained. Altogether, the garrison consisted of some 10,000 men at this time.

---

5   Fortress Hong Kong was how Hong Kong was known at the time by the British military.

NEW CANADIAN BATTALIONS ARRIVE

In mid-July, Grasset was replaced by Major General Christopher Maltby. When Grasset left the colony, he – himself a Canadian – suggested that it be reinforced by two Canadian battalions. Somehow, he persuaded Churchill's advisors to ask for these battalions, and he also made his case to the Canadian government. Canadian forces ('C Force', as they were dubbed) finally arrived in Hong Kong just three weeks before the Japanese attacked. The Hong Kong Signal Company was only a small part of the 12,000-strong British Forces (made up of British, Indian, Canadian, HK Defence Force, Royal Navy and RAF), which, when police – who had been sworn in as militia – and front-line nurses are included, now numbered some 14,000. This was, of course, too small a number to have a hope of stopping the Japanese. The combined forces were outnumbered nearly 4:1 by the Japanese forces, whose strength was over 52,000.

PHASES OF THE BATTLE IN DECEMBER 1941

The 18 days of fighting can be neatly broken down into these phases:

- The loss of the mainland (New Territories)
- The siege of Hong Kong Island
- The invasion of the island
- The forcing of Wong Nai Chung Gap
- Pushing the line west
- Formal surrender
- Encircling Stanley

The Loss of the Mainland, 8–13 December
Beginning in the early hours of 8 December, the Japanese slowly but irresistibly moved south towards Kowloon, in the New Territories on the mainland. A small force of 2/14th Punjabis and Field Engineers, supported by infantry of the HKVDC, delayed their progress by sabotage until the 'Gindrinkers Line' was reached.

At the Shing Mun Redoubt was the first skirmish, in which the 2nd Battalion the Royal Scots were pushed out of their position and fell back to

Golden Hill. Golden Hill was very exposed, and in a far bigger battle the next day it was given up. From then until the evacuation of the mainland to Hong Kong Island, of all military personnel there was only one other significant engagement, at the Ma Yau Tong line, as the Indian rearguard defended their retreat.

The Siege of the Island, 13–18 December
With all defending forces now tied up on the island, the Japanese started a concerted effort to bomb and shell all significant military areas on Hong Kong Island. 'The Peak' and the fixed defences (naval installations, gun batteries and pillboxes) were the major targets, though civilian areas in Central, Mid-levels, Causeway Bay and Wan Chai were also hit, with many casualties. My father, Sgt Albert Ient, was captured at Mount Austin (in older documents it is spelt Austen) in the area of the Peak on Christmas Day.

The Invasion of the Island, 18 December
Hong Kong is a small island with an irregular coastline containing a number of bays and its main feature is its peaks or mountains. The British, under the command of General Maltby, arranged the defence of the island into east and west zones. The map below shows the movement of Japanese troops during the capture of the island.

On the evening of 18 December, the invasion began. Japanese landings commenced between North Point and Shau Kei Wan (or Shaukiwan), in conditions made all the more confusing for the defenders by poor weather and thick smoke from bombed industrial sites. The Rajputs, with elements of the Middlesex, HKVDC, Royal Artillery and Royal Rifles (in particular, C Company) put up initial resistance but by midnight almost the whole north-eastern corner of Hong Kong was in Japanese hands, with the line as far south as the northernmost point of Jardine's Lookout and as far west as the North Point power station.

The Forcing of Wong Nai Chung Gap, 19 December
In the centre of the island is Wong Nai Chung Gap. One could say that the Battle for Hong Kong was lost once the Japanese had taken the New Territories since that was where the main water reservoirs were. The possibility of surviving by just holding Hong Kong was an unrealistic prospect. However, at this stage of the battle the option of capitulation was not acceptable to the

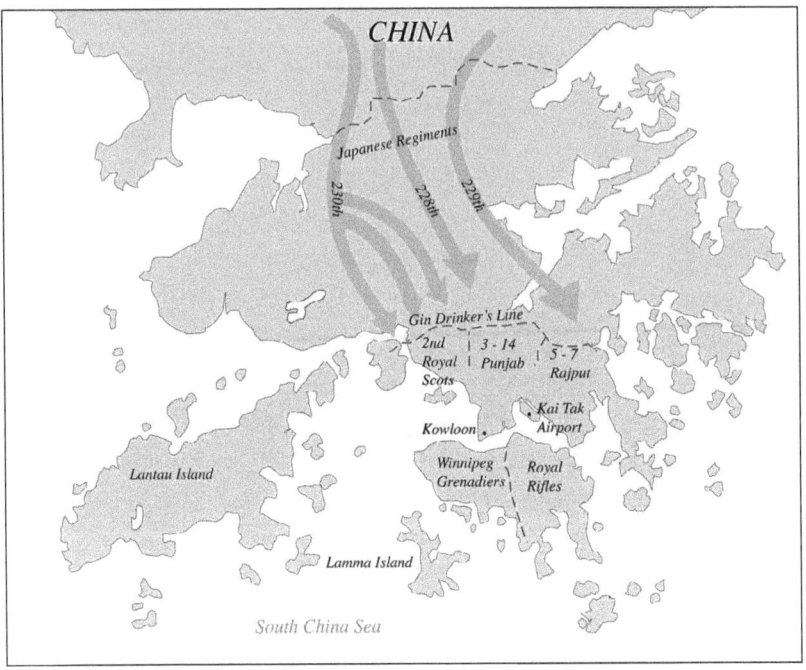

Figure 1.4 The Battle for Hong Kong, 18-25 December 1941.
This figure is my sketch version of the diagram.

British governor of the island. As far as the defence of the island itself was concerned, it was crucial that Wong Nai Chung Gap should not be lost.

The Japanese strategy was simple: take Wong Nai Chung Gap and continue south along Repulse Bay Road to split the island in two. This necessitated keeping East Brigade busy so that they could not organise any useful counter-attack, while other Japanese forces concentrated on knocking out defences on Jardine's Lookout and Mount Nicholson (overlooking the Gap from the east and west, respectively), and at the bottom of the Gap itself. Once this was done, and the strategically important police station at the south of the Gap was captured, the fighting moved south along Repulse Bay Road. In 1941 it was relatively sparsely populated, thus the skirmishes on this and later days were generally named after the isolated houses at or around which they occurred: (from north to south) Postbridge, Altamira and the Ridge, Twin Brooks, Overbays, Repulse Bay Hotel and Eucliffe.

This was by far the hardest day's fighting, with the defenders losing in 24 hours approximately one-third of the total fatalities incurred in the whole

18-day battle. By midnight, although there were still pockets of resistance, the Gap and the majority of Repulse Bay Road were, in all practical terms, in Japanese hands.

How far south Japanese forward patrols advanced along the road that day is uncertain, but there is a distinct possibility that a few small groups or individuals reached the south coast itself.

Pushing the Line West, 19–25 December

As early as the night of the 18th, the defenders had the genesis of a line running south from the power station through the developed north coast to the hills, preventing the Japanese from advancing to Central. Over the next few days, this 'northern sector' was pushed steadily west by the Japanese, with the northernmost anchor moving quickly from Caroline Hill back to Leighton Hill (which was defended energetically by the Middlesex Regiment) and finally Morrison Hill and Mount Parrish (now spelt Parish), while street fighting was intensive in Wan Chai. The defenders' southern anchor moved from Wong Nai Chung Gap to Mount Nicholson, then Mount Cameron, and finally Wan Chai Gap and further west.

Further south was the 'central sector'. Here Mount Nicholson was taken with ease by the Japanese, but Mount Cameron was a hard struggle, with Wan Chai Gap being held almost to the end. Finally, the 'southern sector' fell back in stages from Shouson Hill, to Brick Hill, to the stoutly defended Bennet's Hill before being taken.

It was this relentless western progress of the Japanese forces that prompted the surrender on the 25th, by which time it was felt that Wan Chai could not be held any longer. Central was already within the range of small arms fire from the central sector.

Formal Surrender

By the afternoon of 25 December 1941, it was clear that further resistance would be futile and British colonial officials headed by the governor of Hong Kong, Sir Mark Aitchison Young, surrendered in person at the Japanese headquarters on the third floor of the Peninsula Hong Kong hotel. This was the first occasion on which a British crown colony had surrendered to an invading force, and the day is known in Hong Kong as 'Black Christmas'.

Encircling Stanley, 19–26 December
When East Brigade HQ at Tai Tam withdrew towards Stanley on the 19th, fighting on two fronts became impossible to avoid. Delaying actions at Red Hill and Bridge Hill could not prevent the Japanese advance from the north-east, and the Repulse Bay Hotel area could not be held against their advance from the north-west. The circle tightened around Stanley Mound and Stone Hill, where Canadians and Volunteers fought it out with the invaders in particularly tough country, and finally squeezed them into the Stanley Peninsular itself. By the time of the official surrender on Christmas Day, the first two of three defensive lines had fallen. However, the defence of the final line was maintained until the early hours of 26 December, when written orders to surrender were finally delivered to Brigadier Wallis.

SHAMSHUIPO POW CAMP, HONG KONG

Most people imagine that, at surrender, the garrison was taken prisoner en masse. In fact, prisoners were taken from the very start of the fighting and the Japanese had to find different places to intern them. In January 1942 they rationalised their camp system. North Point became the Canadian and Royal Navy camp; Shamshuipo became the British Army and HKVDC camp; Ma Tau Chong was opened as the British Indian Army camp, and 'enemy civilians' (as titled by the Japanese administration) were sent to Stanley Internment Camp, Rosary Hill and Ma Tau-wai.

Shamshuipo (also spelt Sham Shio Po, which means 'Deep Water Pier' in Cantonese), where the British were held, is situated in the north-western part of the Kowloon Peninsula in Hong Kong. Descriptions of this camp invariably focus on the different diseases suffered by POWs interned there, in particular epidemics of diphtheria and outbreaks of malaria.

This was the situation until early September 1942, when the first transportation of POWs to Japan took place. In total, nearly 2,500 men were removed by ship, primarily from Shamshuipo.

Reactions among the prisoners of war were mixed. After the initial shock of the surrender on Christmas Day 1941 had been absorbed, hopes had run high for an early release, but it soon become apparent that no relief was to be expected from the Chinese Army to the north. Singapore and the Philippines had fallen to the Japanese and the news from the European theatre was bad.

On 25 September 1942, 1,816 British prisoners of war were assembled on the parade ground of Shamshuipo Camp, Hong Kong, and addressed by Lieutenant Hideo Wada of the Imperial Japanese Army through his interpreter, Niimori Genichiro.

'You are going to be taken away from Hong Kong,' he said, 'to a beautiful country where you will be well looked after and well treated. I shall be in charge of the party. Take care of your health. Remember my face.'

Some prisoners argued that a move to Japan, which seemed the obvious destination, would be an improvement since (they believed) the Japanese would not wish to display in their own homeland their inhumanity to prisoners of war and, consequently, better treatment might be expected. The more cynical scorned these ideas and would have preferred to stay in Hong Kong, where, they felt, perhaps the chances of rescue and escape were slightly greater. But discussion was futile, for a prisoner of war has no choice of action.

THIRD DRAFT: FROM SHAMSHUIPO TO THE JAPANESE MAINLAND

Tony Banham, of FEPOW (Far East Prisoner of War Community – an association of survivors, their families and descendants who have a common interest in WWII in the Far East) advised that my father was among the servicemen in the third draft[6] (this refers to the third shipment of POWs to Japan) sent from Shamshuipo to the Japanese mainland; their destination was Habu, the principal township on Innoshima Island,[7] and Hiroshima No 5 prisoner of war camp. In an email dated 19 March 2007 Banham explained where he got this information from:

> The Japanese employed Chinese clerks in various functions. These clerks had no love for the Japanese, but it was that or starve. The Camp maintained lists of all POWs. One clerk decided, on his own initiative, to take a sheet of this list home each night, copy it with his own typewriter, then smuggle it back next morning. He did this until he had copied all 8,000 names, and then he put it

---

6   A.V. Ient, my father, was a member of the third draft, as confirmed by Tony Banham of the FEPOW Community.
7   Innoshima is a 'ken' (the English equivalent is a county) in the Hiroshima Prefecture. It is an island in the 'Inland Sea' off the southern island of Honshu.

Figure 1.5 Colonel Levett's diary.

in a briefcase, escaped to China, and handed it to British authorities there. The daughter of the man he gave it to kept a copy which she passed to me. By many names such as A V Ient, there is a number indicating which draft they were on. In Ient's case it is a 3.

WAR DIARY OF CHIEF SIGNAL OFFICER, CHINA COMMAND, HONG KONG 1941

After my mother died in 1999 (my father, Albert Ient, having died in 1988) I saw for the first time copies of two diaries which my father had been given by the Royal Signals. The diaries were written by Lieutenant Colonel Levett OBE, chief signal officer, China Command. He led the Hong Kong Signal Company from 1938. These have given me considerable detail about the Battle for Hong Kong.

The first entry in the diary starts on 7 December 1941 and it finishes on 10 February in Shamshuipo POW camp. The events during the Battle for Hong Kong are described from a telecommunications point of view. Also, Levett tries to record accurately the casualties and the state of the men under his command.

The second diary starts in POW camp and finishes in 1945. In this diary Levett tries to record the location, status and casualties of all prisoners in Hong Kong (he remained in Hong Kong throughout the war) as well as outstanding events and details of food rations issued to the POWs.

In order to complete the story of my father's (Sgt Albert Ient's) life in the Far East, I make use of some details from these diaries below.

Record of Casualties

Overleaf is the suffix to both of these documents, which summarises the casualties of the Royal Signals from the outbreak of hostilities to 1945:

Company strength before the battle:	185
Killed in action	15
Died in Shamshuipo Camp	7
Drowned on the *Lisbon Maru*	50
Died in POW camps	19
Killed on a flight to freedom	2
Total dead	93 (over 50%)

Maintaining Communications

Lieutenant Colonel Eustace Levett's principal task was to prepare and put into operation plans covering trunk and radio communications for the defence of Hong Kong. This must have been the work that my dad was engaged in on the island before the outbreak of war.

Levett reports in some detail the Royal Signals Company's actions and fierce fighting in the Battle for Hong Kong as they endeavoured to keep communication lines open; however, at about 1530 hours on 25 December, Levett received instructions from the GOC (general officer in command, i.e. the head of the armed forces) to order the Hong Kong Signal Company to display the white flag at the entrance to their barracks and lay down their arms. This order was passed by telephone to his men. Later Levett addressed the men of the company. He said:

> It is, I consider, a matter of pride and to the greatest possible credit of the Hong Kong Signal Company that communications worked as long and as efficiently as was humanly possible... During the Mainland retirement on 11/12 and 12/13, they worked in their entirety right up to the end, and undoubtedly, by permitting detailed instructions to be given to the commanders direct, saved many lives. On the Island, despite difficulties due to enemy action, shortages of field cable due to loss of dumps, and fatigue of men due to continuous bombardment, the essential communications were working up to within three hours of the order for capitulation, and even then most of the G.O.C.'s direct concentrator circuits were through (this means that the cables and telephone exchanges has been repaired by the Royal Signals), enabling him to give his instructions direct to commanders.

The diary covers the communications problems encountered by Levett and the Signal Company during the 18 days of heavy fighting, heavy shelling and bombing and their continuous struggle to repair damaged communication routes and maintain wireless communication.

Colonel Levett talks about maintaining communications during the battle for Hong Kong in some detail in his diary. This sketch map, thankfully preserved by Harold Bates, shows graphically the extent of the problem he faced!

Sgt Albert Ient's Experiences

It is impossible to say exactly where my dad fits into the action on a day-to-day basis, but we do know from what he told me that he was captured at Mount Austin in an area called 'the Peak', which was about 1,000 yards west of Magazine Gap. Passages from the diary which refer specifically to this area have, therefore, been selected in the hope that they correctly portray some of what my dad experienced.

Lt Colonel Levett's diary details work carried out by two Brigades covering

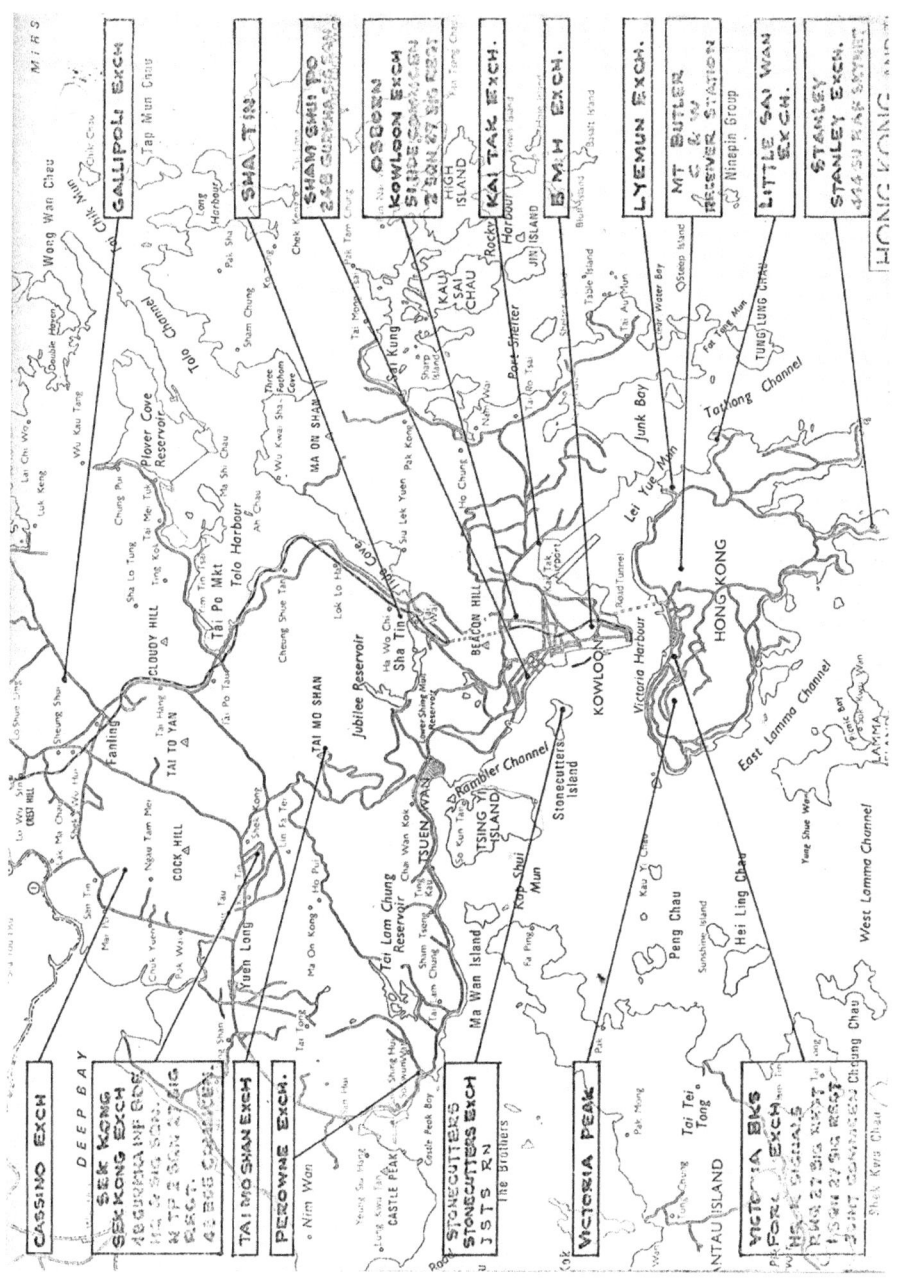

Figure 1.6 1941 sketch map showing the deployment of telephone exchanges in Hong Kong.

different parts of the island. Mount Austin and the Peak were covered by the Western Brigade Group. I assume therefore that Dad was a member of this group.

Western Brigade Group

> 20th – An attempt was made to break through the surrounding enemy, some succeeded... The main route between Victoria Gap and Magazine Gap suffered severely, especially in the former area. Magazine Gap area, though continually shelled, fortunately suffered less and little damage was done to the cables, though subsidiary routes suffered... Victoria Peak... Mt Austen Barracks and Peak Mansions were heavily shelled and bombed, several breaks occurred and frequent bombing raids in that area made repairs difficult.
>
> 24th – By the afternoon of the 24th, the situation along the route VICTORIA GAP – WAN CHAI GAP was extremely serious. The main route had been cut in many places and communications to batteries and O.P.s were being maintained by field cable, of which there was now a very great shortage, the main cable dump at the Ridge now being in enemy hands.
>
> 25th – It seemed likely that retirement from Wan Chai Gap was probable as the enemy were occupying Mt Nicholson and Mt Cameron. Arrangements were therefore made for exchanges to be established at Magazine and Victoria Gaps and for battery positions and O.P.s and any necessary infantry H.Q. to be linked up to whichever exchange was the nearer... This communication was through [meaning communicated to Royal Signals engineers] by early morning on the 25th but was again cut by enemy action. By noon it had become practically impossible to keep the route though [meaning connected], and at one o'clock, under the orders of the West Brigade Commander (who was then at No. 500 The Peak, about 1,000 yards west of Magazine Gap), attempts to do so were abandoned... The final order to surrender came before any further steps could be taken to repair the route. This would, in any case, have been difficult owing to the shortage of cable, as at one o'clock a stick of bombs had been dropped near Brigade H.Q. and the undergrowth around was on fire, burning the field cables laid out on the ground.

Hong Kong Command Compliments the Royal Signals
A senior staff officer is reported to have commented to Levett at the end of the battle, 'Signals at any rate did their stuff, and you should be proud of your fellows.'

CHAPTER 2

Albert Ient

Dad had four older brothers, all of whom served in the army, including in WWI. Luckily, they all survived. I guess there was plenty of talk about the army around the house so it's not surprising my father joined up as a regular soldier in 1921. The difficult economy may have been another reason for joining.

ABOUT ALBERT (VIC) IENT

Albert Victor Ient, my father, was born on 5 December 1905, the youngest child of Charles (formerly Karl Gottlob) Jent and his second wife, Julia Ann Thurley Hemmings. Dad's birth certificate originally recorded his name as Albert Herbert Jent but this was corrected to Albert Victor Ient. Albert was named after the Victoria and Albert Museum by his father, Charles, who at the time was a senior stone mason working on the museum's construction. The family lived at 5 Warsill Street, Battersea, London.

I talked to Dad about his life but clearly not enough, so I only have a sketchy history of his life before I was able to remember him (from the age of about four) in 1949/50. By that time, he was already nearly 50 years old and had gone from being a boy in London to various postings with the army, including camps in England and postings in Malta, Egypt and Hong Kong. He finally came home in 1945 after three and a half years as a POW in Japan.

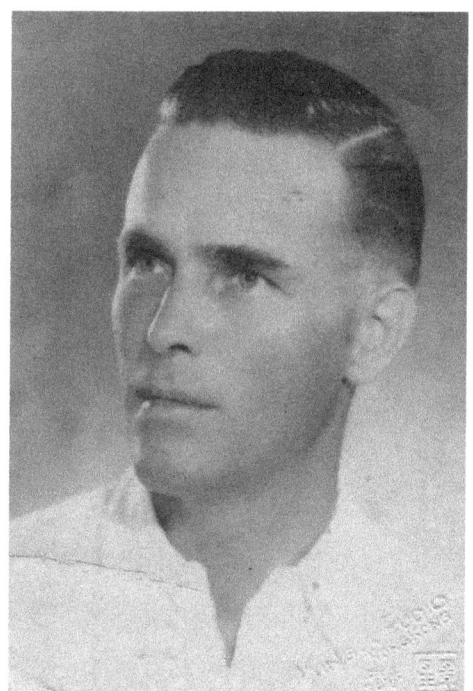 

Left: *Figure 2.1* Albert Ient in Hong Kong in about 1940.
Right: *Figure 2.2* Albert Ient was a soldier in the Royal Signals and afterwards a key figure in the Royal Signals Association. This is a copy of a plaque presented to him when he was president of the Aldershot Royal Signals Association.

LONDON

Dad grew up in Battersea. We only have three photos of Dad as a young boy (overleaf).

Dad was a choirboy at Southwark Cathedral and this must have been between the ages of around eight or nine and 14 or 15. Certainly, I remember him telling me that his voice broke and he could no longer sing. His ultimate accolade was to be chosen as lead choirboy in the Southwark Cathedral Choir. He was clearly of some significance in terms of the choir, because there are apparently recordings on cylindrical disks of him singing at Westminster Abbey. He was very proud of this; he sang standing on the grave of Lady Jane Grey in the Chapel of St Peter ad Vincula at Westminster Abbey.

(Left to right)
Figure 2.3 Albert Ient in 1910, when he was about four.
Figure 2.4 An earlier picture shows him sitting on his father Karl's knee in around 1908 or 1909, when he was about three.
Figure 2.5 Albert in 1917, at the age of about 12.

Dad recalled going to Southwark Cathedral twice on Sundays, journeying first to attend the morning Mass, returning home, presumably for lunch, then going back again for evensong. It is quite a distance from Battersea to Southwark Cathedral. I think I remember him saying he usually walked. Dad could read Latin and I assume he learnt this because it was taught at Southwark Cathedral. He also sang at St Saviour's in Battersea.

THE ARMY – IN ENGLAND

Dad enlisted with the 13th London Regiment (TA) on 13 September 1921. This was known as the Kensington Regiment.

His army number was 6653403. Whatever regiment or rank you attain when you join the army, this number stays with you throughout your military career. Two years later, on 28 December 1923, he transferred to the Regulars and the Royal Corp of Signals. The next six years were spent at Signal Training Centres in Maresfield or Aldershot and for most of that time he was a mounted linesman with D Troop Cavalry Division Signals. In those days,

(Left to right)
Figure 2.6 In the post-WWII years Dad was very keen to keep up with army contacts. This is a front cover of the Regimental magazine of his original regiment, *The Kensington Regiment's Magazine*. He had originally enlisted with them in 1921.
Figure 2.7 Dad on his horse.

being a linesman meant providing the telecommunications for the army; a linesman was usually required to erect and construct telegraph lines, which would connect the headquarters through to the main divisional army unit in the battlefield.

Maresfield gave Dad his first experience of being a horseman. He loved horses from then on. Unfortunately, I only have the briefest insight into his life at this time. When I first moved to Sussex I took him on a tour of the area and as we came down into Lewes, where I now live, we passed The Volunteer pub, which he pointed out, explaining it was the first pub he'd gone to as a young soldier, using an evening pass from the army training camp at Maresfield. In those days, you could get a train from Maresfield directly through the Sussex countryside to Lewes, getting off at the station behind the old library, just off Cliffe High Street, Lewes. The Volunteer pub is nearby. The rail line and station are now gone.

As you can see in Figure 2.8, the Signals troops, whose job it was to lay cable on the battlefield and behind the lines, were still mounted in the 1920s.

Figure 2.9 and 2.10 (see p. 23) are other military photos in England pre-WWII.

MALTA

On 13 November 1929 Dad was posted abroad to Malta, where he met his wife, Myfanwy Edwards from Abertridwr, Caerphilly. One of Dad's jobs was to collect signals (like telegrams) from the Signals HQ and take them to the home of officers on the island. My mother, at the age of 18 years, was a servant working at this officer's house, which also served as a military office. She noticed Albert coming and going and eventually, because my father said nothing, she broke the ice and spoke to him, which started their romance.

ROMANCE IN MALTA

Myfanwy Edwards (nicknamed 'Toby' because she was a tomboy as a child and did the heavy work in the family) arrived in Malta in about 1931. She had been working for the officer and his wife in North London and went out with the family when he was posted to Malta. At that time, it was the headquarters of the British Military Command in the Mediterranean. She and Albert Ient were married on 10 September 1932 in St Paul's Anglican Cathedral in Valletta.

After this, they stayed on the island and lived in army rented quarters in Valletta. They were on the island together for three years. Both my brothers, Tommy (who died in an accident in Hong Kong in 1940) and John, were born there.

Albert was an NCO in the Royal Signals and was in charge of installing telegraph and telephone lines across Malta. He had a team of locally employed

Figure 2.8 Albert Ient (centre, front) as a young soldier in about 1922. This photo was probably taken at Maresfield, Sussex.

Figure 2.9 This is from Albert's collection, though we don't know which soldier is him. The picture is named and dated on the back as 'Tidworth 1929'. Tidworth is in Wiltshire and is part of a number of military bases which were developed around Salisbury Plain military training area. The British Army started training exercises here in 1898.

Figure 2.10 Dad was a crack shot with a rifle and this picture from the 1930s shows him (front row, far right) with the winning team after an army competition at Bisley Camp in Surrey.

(Top left) *Figure 2.11* Albert (left) and Toby (centre, rear) with friends at Rinella beach, Malta.
(Bottom left) *Figure 2.12* Toby (left) and a friend in the sea at Rinella.
(Top right) *Figure 2.13* Albert and Toby in Malta.

labourers to erect telegraph poles across the island. After marriage, Toby was able to stop being a servant.

I think they had a wonderful time in Malta – the best years of their life. There was a good climate, it was peacetime and they had friends from families who were similarly placed. Also, they had the island to explore in those pre-tourist days!

Just before leaving Malta they witnessed one of the last times the British Navy was seen in all its glory. In talking about those days of British imperial might, Dad said that, in the lead-up to King George V's Golden Jubilee review of the fleet, looking out from the harbour wall at Valetta, you could not see the horizon for British warships, and at night the glittering lights of the ships lit up the ocean. The review in Malta was probably in 1934 as Dad was posted back to England in 1935. The official review of the British Fleet took place in July 1935 at Spithead, Portsmouth, and included 160 warships.

My two eldest brothers were born in Malta. Tommy was born on 1 April 1933 and John on 2 September 1934. The family returned to England on 29

January 1935, Dad's posting back to England was possibly associated with the 1935 Jubilee celebrations. Their home for the next few years was in army quarters (a rented house) in Frimley Green, Surrey, not far from the army town of Aldershot; the review of troops was carried out on nearby Laffan's Plain, which was the headquarters of the British Army at the time.

EGYPT

But Dad was not long at home. On 14 September 1935 he disembarked in Alexandria, Egypt, for service with 'Bare Defences Mediterranean'. This is how my father described the military mission, though my further research under this heading has not succeeded in revealing anything. I believe the reason for a British military mission to defend Egypt was to do with the second Italo-Abyssinian War. This colonial invasion by Mussolini's Italian Army was fought from 3 October 1935 until 19 February 1937. The British government was probably taking precautions in case the Italian colonial expansion spilled over into Egypt from neighbouring Libya which was already a colony of Italy. In 1936 Egypt and Britain signed a treaty giving the right to Britain to defend the Suez Canal and station 10,000 troops there. Dad's work involved putting up telegraph and telephone lines in the desert. He was away from his family until 7 August 1936.

Figures 2.14 and 2.15 are pictures from Egypt.

Top to bottom
Figure 2.14 In Egypt
Figure 2.15 This picture is dated Christmas Day 1936. Albert Ient is in the centre.

However, the family's world was soon to change dramatically, as back in England a new posting for the Far East was coming up.

POSTING TO THE FAR EAST

In 1938, after the birth of their third son, George, on 24 July 1937, Dad was posted to Ceylon, but he swapped the posting with a friend and went to Hong Kong instead. He departed for Hong Kong on 14 December 1938. It was a decision he lived to regret; Ceylon (later renamed Sri Lanka after independence) never saw action during the war. Mum and the boys followed sometime later.

HONG KONG

The pre-war period in Hong Kong saw the peak of Dad's military career. He was a senior NCO and well-respected and liked in the Royal Signals. The future looked good. When Mum and the three boys joined him in 1939 it was an almost perfect situation – one of the best postings in the army and with his family too!

The first months in Hong Kong must have seemed wonderful to Albert and Toby; it was an exotic place and they had a seemingly idyllic lifestyle.

This all came to a terrible end on 21 February 1940

Figure 2.16 This is the apartment block in Happy Valley, Hong Kong, where Mum and Dad lived in 1939/1940. It was from the top of this block that my brother Tommy Ient fell to his death in a tragic accident in February 1940. This picture was taken by my brother John Ient on his visit to Hong Kong from Singapore in 1962, where he was based during his army service with the Royal Signals Regiment. The date has been added by my father.

(Top Left) *Figure 2.17* Albert at the grave of his son Tommy in Happy Valley Cemetery, Hong Kong. He is in crutches because of a broken leg.

(Top Right) *Figure 2.18* Albert and Toby with George (L), Tommy (M) and John (R). However, before this the family had a wonderful time in this magical oriental outpost of the British Empire. Albert enjoyed military life and the camaraderie of the sergeants' mess.

(Bottom) *Figure 2.19* The family in 1939.

when, very sadly, my brother Tommy (the eldest) died while playing with other boys. He was eight. I guess my brother George was too young to remember, and John was only six. It was only recently on a visit to my brother John in Yorkshire, in 2014, that I found out what really happened. Some 60 years after the event, John and I were looking at the photograph of the apartment block where the family used to live in Happy Valley, Hong Kong. Assuming what I'd always been told, that Tommy had fallen from a balcony, I asked him if he would point out the apartment. His answer was completely surprising. He said that, while it was to the left side and not visible, Tommy had actually been playing on the roof with his friends, and in a game of 'Cowboys and Indians' had decided to hide behind the parapet on the edge of the roof. He apparently stood up at one point, upon which another boy saw him and said, 'Bang, you're dead,' and in surprise Tommy fell backwards down to the road below. I never knew my brother Tommy, but the emotions rose and it brought tears to my eyes to hear of this tragic accident.

Fifty-four years after WWII ended, in 1999, I would visit Hong Kong. But before I went I asked Mum where I should go, and she clearly enjoyed directing me to places like the Wan Chai Ferry, the Peak, Aberdeen, Stanley Bay and Temple Street market. 'You must go across to the New Territories by the ferry – the waterway is always busy with junks and the view of Hong Kong is lovely. Visit Temple Street market – they sell everything; you can even have a suit made!' she said. It was good to see Mum in her mid-80s remember so much and be enthusiastic about a place she lived in so long ago. It was clear to me that she had vivid memories of Hong Kong. A lot happened to her and Albert – with the wonder of this new place, Tommy's death, her subsequent evacuation and Albert's capture.

Though the war began in Europe in September 1939, the Far East remained at peace, albeit uneasily. Japan would not strike for over two years later, in December 1941.

The death of my brother Tommy set the scene for 1940, because later that year, in July, Mum had to be evacuated with John and George. At the time of their departure, Dad was in hospital with a broken leg, following an incident at work on 25 May 1940.

Evacuation from Hong Kong
Toby and the boys were evacuated when it became clear that the war was about to reach the Far East. From Hong Kong all the evacuees were taken by liner to Manila, on the island of Luzon in the Philippines.[8] After docking at Manila, they were transferred to Baguio up into the highlands – a long journey of

---

8   My mother's story of evacuation to the Philippines is corroborated by someone else writing about their parents' wartime history. On the BBC website World War II People's War a lady writes about being evacuated from Hong Kong with her mother in July 1940. She says:
    We were evacuated in July 1940. Mum was only able to take a suitcase and a pram! We went first to the Philippines to Manila and up to Baguio where we stayed at the Loretto Hospital. We were there for five weeks. Then we sailed from there on HMT Awatea for Australia.
    Contributed by Annmarie. People in story: Annmarie Leslie. Location of story: Far East and York Article ID: A2045611 Contributed on 15 November 2003
    The HMT *Awatea* was a British troopship during WWII. It had been converted from an ocean liner.

Figure 2.20 Albert Ient in an army group photo, second from the left in the front row. The embossed name on the photo says 'King Studios Hong Kong'. Dad was a crack shot with a rifle, so my guess is the trophies were from an army shooting competition. I would say it was taken before May 1940, which was when he broke his leg.

Figure 2.21 Pines Hotel – Island of Luzon, Philippines 1,400 metres (4,600 feet) above sea level, about 150 miles from Manila – the port of arrival for my mum and other evacuees. Source: unknown.

about 130 miles. Here they were first billeted at the Red Cross headquarters, at the Pines Hotel.[9]

They were able to take very little from Hong Kong with them owing to government restrictions, but also there was the thought of returning. Their

---

9   Baguio, in mountainous, wooded Northern Luzon, became the 'Summer Capital of the Philippines'. The Americans established it as a place for all to escape the intense April/May/June summer heat. By the mid-1930s, Baguio City and its surroundings reached its pre-WWII peak in popularity and facilities. Baguio had become a year-round attraction.

ship was hit by a typhoon and Toby remembered everyone being very sick. At Baguio Mum said that the hotel they stayed in was owned by the American William Randolph Hearst, the newspaper magnate. They were all evacuee women and children together. Mum recalled that she loved it when walking back to the hotel from the village in the afternoon, when it almost always rained, and it was so refreshing and amazing that by the time she got back her dress was dry. Part of the time it must have been a little chilly, as she said that the women chopped their own wood and lit fires in the open-hearth fireplaces. This may just have been at night. However, they weren't there long – Toby and the children were evacuated again to Australia.

The Letters and Cables/Telegrams

During the latter part of 1940 and the first months of 1941, Mum and Dad were able to exchange letters and cables (telegrams). From November 1941 it became impossible to send letters or cables to and from Hong Kong.

It's very clear that Dad missed his family enormously and he wrote frequent letters. Between 7 July 1940 and 30 December 1940, he wrote 31 letters. That's more than one letter a week! And it's clear he longed for replies and information about how they were and how the two boys were (my brothers George and John). He sometimes got frustrated that he hadn't received a reply and while he didn't get angry he did point this out in his letters. The situation must have been very stressful; after all, he was holed up in Hong Kong for month after month, with no idea of how long their separation would be, and the government couldn't give any guidance. He was not the only one and it must have been frustrating for all of the married servicemen.

On the other hand, we don't seem to realise it must have been very difficult for my mother. First of all, she was evacuated to the Philippines with the ship encountering a dreadful typhoon on the way. All the evacuees and children arrived in a dreadful state in Manila and then they had to undergo a long journey up into the hills to reach their temporary accommodation. Shortly after this she was evacuated to Australia and it's clear from the addresses that my dad had to write to that in those early months of the evacuation she was constantly being moved from house to house. Dad writes very well, with beautiful handwriting, but it must have been difficult for Mum with two children to keep up the responses. Mum didn't have the same quality of schooling as Dad and spent much of her time in South Wales helping the family, including daily walks over the hills to get provisions from a relation's

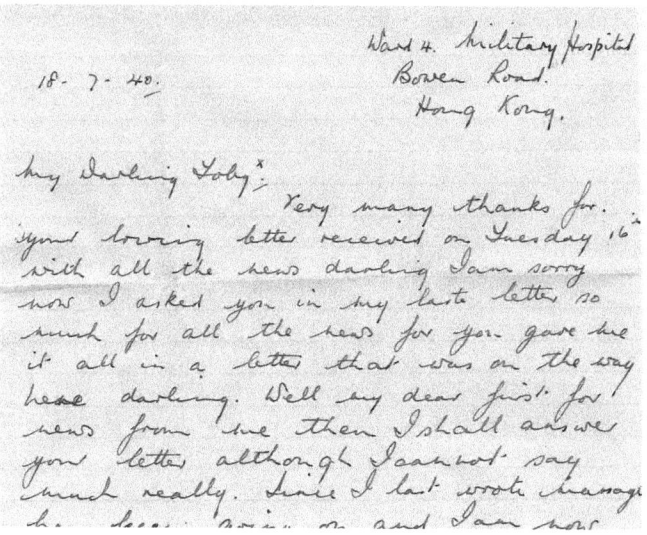

Figure 2.22 Letter from Dad to Mum
(Toby as she was known to him) on 18 July 1940.

farm. Her writing abilities and spelling were not good, and it must have been stressful for her to keep up the correspondence with Dad.

The following are the notes I made during my research, as I read the many letters my father sent my mother from Hong Kong, firstly when she was in the Philippines and then when she lived in Australia in 1940–45. I assume that letters from my mother were lost when my father was captured in Hong Kong in 1941. The notes reveal both the narrative of the next events and how I was increasingly piecing the story together.

On 20 January 1942, the War Office wrote to my mother in Australia saying that Dad was 'missing presumed lost'. It was not until July 1944 that my mother had further news. She received a letter from the Red Cross saying that my father had been found in a Japanese POW camp.

1940

A letter from Albert to Toby, dated 7 July 1940, addressed to '2 Happy Glen Loop c/o Red Cross Headquarters', confirms Toby had left Hong Kong for Manila on the previous Monday.

A letter from Albert to Toby, dated 10 July 1940, from the Military Hospital, Bowen Road, Hong Kong, confirms that the plaster on Albert's leg had been removed that day, but he had been ordered to take strict bed rest.

29 July 1940 – letter from Albert to Toby confirms her imminent departure from Manila and journey to Australia.

17 August 1940 – first letter from Albert to Toby in New South Wales, Australia. By this time, she is at 35 Denham Street, Bondi, near Sydney.

29 August 1940 – letter from Albert to Toby in which he says how sorry he was to hear that Toby's lodgings were 'no good', but he was pleased to hear that the journey had gone well and that the boys 'were so good'. He commented on the poor reception the evacuees had received in NSW.

7 September 1940 – Albert wrote to Toby from the Victoria Barracks, Hong Kong, to confirm that he was out of hospital. His letter was addressed to 244 Allison Road, Randwick, in Sydney.

18 September 1940 – Albert wrote to 18 Alexander Street, Manly, near Sydney.

7 October 1940 – Albert's letter responds to comments Toby had obviously made about her evacuation. She was clearly very upset about it. Albert wrote, 'You seem to be in a rage about it all dear and I only hope it won't be much longer'. Albert agreed that it was silly that younger, single women had been able to remain in Hong Kong when the married women had been evacuated. He said, 'If you couldn't find a better nurse than some they have left behind here, I'll eat my hat.'

27 November 1940 – Albert acknowledged Toby's move to Windsleigh, Pacific Parade, 'Dee Why' (yes, that's the name of the town) and the need for her to have taken this step for 'economic reasons'. In the same letter he confirmed that doctors had passed him A1 fit and that he was going back to work. He also commented on the continuing commotion caused by compulsory evacuation of the servicemen's families; he advised Toby that the Husbands' Committee, of which he was not a member, was putting together a fresh petition to allow the families to be repatriated to Hong Kong. Obviously asked what he was doing with himself, Albert commented, 'Life here is much the same and work goes on steadily. Pip Badge and myself play snooker and billiards until we look

like them and we have taken to listening to the wireless in the bunk [*in the army barracks*] at nights.'

6 December 1940 – Albert wrote to 56 Fairlight Street, Manly.

12 December 1940 – Albert wrote to Toby and confirmed that he had signed a petition requesting the repeal of the compulsory evacuation order. He said, however, that he did not feel that it would do much good.

30 December 1940 – Albert's letter was addressed to 18 Beach Road, Harboard. He wrote, 'I hope you like your new address, darling and… that you won't have to move again and be satisfied with this one, darling.'

1941
9 January 1941 – Albert's letter was addressed to 18 Alexander Street, Manly. He expressed surprise at her 'moving separately'. The impression gained from the letter is that Toby had decided to move independently, away from other army wives.

21 January 1941 – Albert's letter was addressed to No 1 Flat, Seaview, Beach Street, Harboard.
20 February 1941 – Albert's letter was addressed to 18 Alexander Street, Manly. He acknowledged Toby's decision to move back here.

26 June 1941 – Albert commented on what he called the 'evacuation scandal' and told Toby that 'the husbands are holding a big meeting at the Peninsular Hotel on Friday, I don't know what they can do of course, but let's hope for the best, dear.'

10 August 1941 – Albert described his life as 'pictures [*cinema/movies*] – work – mess and tombola. Work is still plentiful. Life here is about the same – very dull as it has always been since you left, darling'.

Undated letter, August 1941 – Albert thanked Toby for the parcel he had received from her containing socks, soap and creams. This suggests that shortages were being experienced in Hong Kong and that Toby had easier access to such items in Australia.

The Last Letter
27 November 1941 – the last letter between Albert and Toby before the fall of Hong Kong.

The evacuation question was still at the front of both their minds. Toby had obviously told Albert about action taken by wives in Australia and Albert responded by confirming that, in Hong Kong, the committee 'had been hard at work. They hope to get some ruling on the situation'. He went on to say, 'You ask me, my dear, my opinion about the whole situation. This I wouldn't dare put on paper my dearest, all I can say is, it's LOUSY.'

Censorship
Throughout this period Albert's letters were subject to censorship. He answered Toby's questions and responded to her news as best he could. He repeatedly said he had little news himself to impart, and he told her very little about life in Hong Kong at this time. Major themes throughout all the letters were: news relating to their sons, George and John; the continuing improvement in Albert's leg; his regular visits to Tommy's grave; and their joint unhappiness over compulsory evacuation. Delays in sending and receiving post caused concern for both parties, in particular the long gaps in correspondence which occurred between February and April 1941. On several occasions during these weeks, they sent each other reassuring cables to confirm all was well.

The Capture
On Christmas Day 1941, the British Army in Hong Kong surrendered to the invading Japanese forces. This marked the beginning of Albert's internment as a prisoner of war in the hands of the Japanese.

The War Office Cable
On 20 January 1942, the War Office wrote to Toby at 244 Allison Road, Randwick, Australia, informing her that her husband, Albert, had been posted 'missing'.[10]

Here is a copy of the telegram cable just prior to receiving the official letter:

---

10 The British War Office in Liverpool, England, notified my father as 'missing' in a letter dated 20 Jan 1942. The letter did not reach my mother in Australia until 25 Feb 1942.

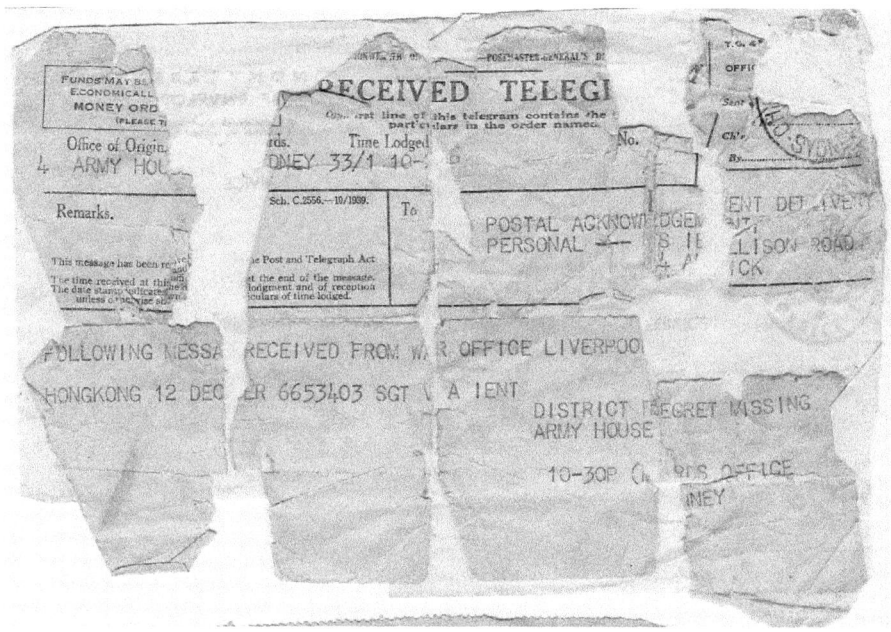

Figure 2.23 The telegram sent by the UK War Office to my mum (in Australia) giving the last news from Hong Kong on 12 December 1941. Mum and my brothers had been separated from Dad since July 1940 for nearly 18 months when she received this message.

Two and a half years later, on 14 July 1944, the Red Cross notified Toby that her husband was a POW in 'Zentzuiji' Camp (spelt elsewhere as Zentsuji).

Albert had sent numerous pre-printed, formal cards provided by his captors, and we know that Toby didn't receive them until sometime in 1944. She had heard nothing for two and a half years. The Japanese did not forward these until nearly the end of the war. The first card Albert sent said:

> I am interned in Fukuoka, Japan (Nippon). My health is usual. I am working for pay. Please see that George and John are taken care of. My love to you, Albert.

Here is a copy of one of the cards:

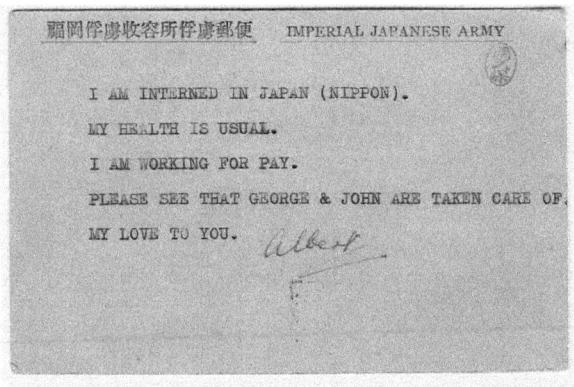

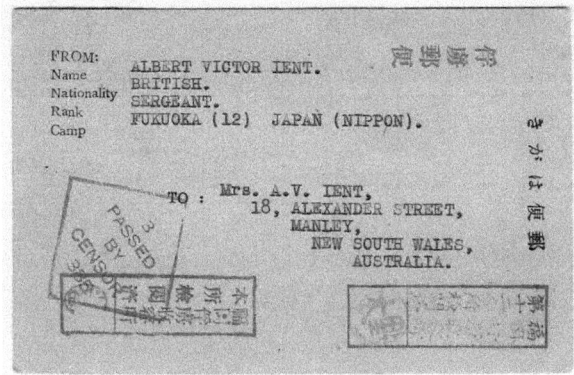

Figure 2.24 Dad's Japanese 'official' postcards to Mum sent from the POW camp - none of these arrived until 1944.

Subsequent cards were marked Zentsuji and Hiroshima. Both Zentsuji and Fukuoka are among the names the Japanese used for Habu Camp.

Like the other prisoners, Dad received no Red Cross parcels or letters until sometime in 1944 (over two years after his capture) but he wrote regularly to Mum on these pre-printed cards.

JAPANESE ATTACK ON HONG KONG

I asked Dad about the battle and capture. He recalled the military situation in Hong Kong in the period leading up to the capture of Fortress Hong Kong (the military name for Hong Kong in the immediate pre-war years) by the

Japanese, as that of a vastly outnumbered army holding an outpost in the Far East, keeping the Union Jack flying until the very last moment before final defeat and capture.

CHRISTMAS DAY 1941 – THE FALL OF HONG KONG

Dad fought in the Battle for Hong Kong when the Japanese attacked on 8 December 1941, following their earlier bombing of Pearl Harbor on 7 December. The Japanese swept down from the mainland and occupied the New Territories and bombarded the island itself. Dad was captured at Mount Austin in an area called 'the Peak'. He had been guarding the installations at the top of that mountain, leading a small platoon of men. They were told to lay down their arms and he had to surrender to a group of Japanese soldiers who were led by a young lieutenant. Dad said he was like a boy of 15. The average height of Japanese men was much shorter than Europeans and indeed the young Japanese officer was probably only about 20 or 21, therefore could easily have appeared much younger. The young officer's revolver hand was shaking as the British soldiers came out of their bunker; this was Christmas Day 1941. He confided to me that this was the most frightening part of the war; it was then that he could have lost his life. Dad remembered at this time seeing many of the civilian European population, the men who knew that they would be killed by the Japanese if they were not in uniform, donning uniforms, even of dead soldiers, in order to survive into capture, to avoid being immediately shot by the Japanese.

PRISONER OF WAR

After the surrender, Dad along with many other soldiers from this part of Hong Kong were at first confined in Victoria Barracks for a week. They were then force-marched to a place called Shamshuipo, in Kowloon, in the New Territories on the mainland, probably via the Wan Chai Ferry, for internment as prisoners of war. From there he was among the third draft of Allied soldiers to be transferred to Japan.

Dad travelled on board the *Tatsuta Maru*, an ex-cruise liner, for the three-day journey, which included crossing the Inland Sea to Innoshima.[11]

---

11 War Diary of Chief Signal Officer, page 1 – foreword by Lt. Col. Truscott.

Figure 2.25 Japanese soldiers in Queens Road, Hong Kong, in 1942.

On 23 January 1943, he disembarked in the village of Mitsunosho, on the western side of the island of Innoshima, and, along with 99 other prisoners (probably all Hong Kong Volunteer Defence Corps (HKVDC[12])), marched half a mile to Habu, the principal township on Innoshima Island, where the prisoner of war camp was located. This is where he spent the remainder of the war. At the time of Dad's arrival the camp was called Fukuoka 12. It was subsequently renamed Zentsuji 2 and again later as Hiroshima No. 5. The island of Innoshima is located on the Inland Sea, 45 miles east-south-east of Hiroshima at the southern end of Japan.

This information is verified by Terence Kelly in his book *By Hellship to Hiroshima* (p. 57) and a POW internal form, completed by Japanese authorities and used to monitor the movement of their prisoners. This document provides the following information:

23 Jan 1943 – Fukuoka Prisoner Camp (name of camp changed to Section 12)

20 July 1943 – Transferred to Section 2, Zentsuji Prisoner Camp (1 December 1943, name changed to Dispatch Unit 2)

14 April 1945 – Transferred to Section 5, Hiroshima Camp

15 Sept 1945 – Handed over to RAF WO Pritchard Harold Alfred[13]

---

12 Date confirmed by Japanese POW card and by log kept by T. Kelly, who advised that the number of HKVDC prisoners was 100.
13 On the form completed by A. V. Ient on his release, he stated that he had been liberated on 15 Sept 1945 into the hands of WO Pritchard, RAF.

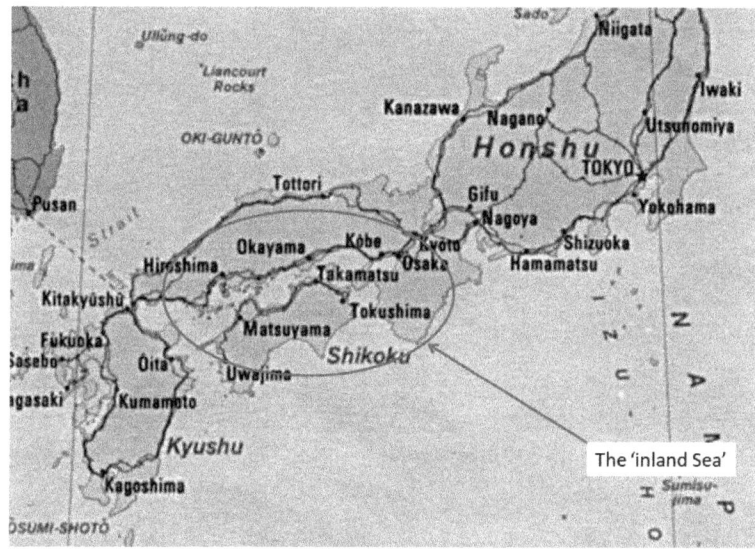

Figure 2.26 Map of the southern main island of Honshu showing the location of the 'Inland Sea'.

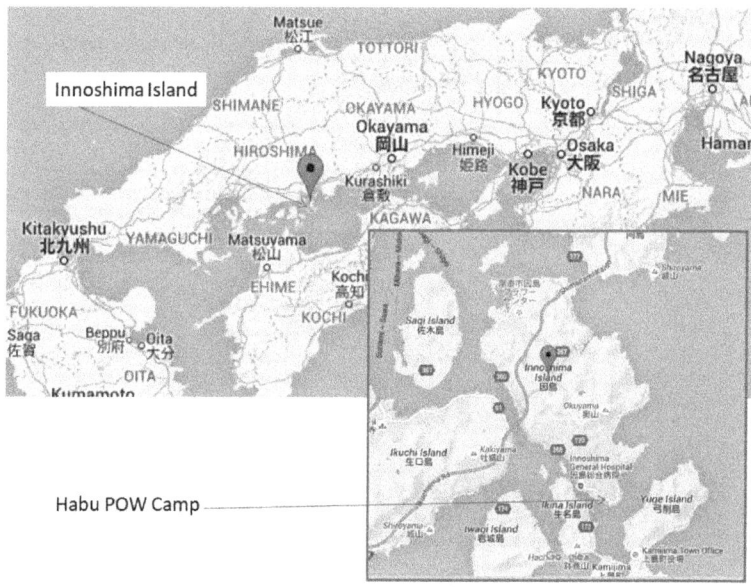

Figure 2.27 Sketch map based on a Google map showing the location of Innoshima Island within the 'Inland Sea'. The inset shows the approximate location of the Habu POW camp.

The Red Cross notified my mother on 14 July 1944 that her husband was a POW in Zentzuiji Camp. Dad had sent numerous pre-printed, formal cards provided by his captors on which the prisoners could put words like 'I am well', 'I am being fed', which were not received until 1944!

On 15 September 1945 a boat came and took the prisoners to Onomichi, where they boarded a train to Osaka and then boarded HMS *Ruler*, a British aircraft carrier, which took them directly to Sydney, Australia.

JAPANESE PRISON CAMP

In little snippets, Dad told me of his experiences as a POW, which are relayed below.

Prisoners worked on the repair and building of ships alongside Japanese workers. Dad said that in the cold winters, if you touched the metal of the ship, your hand could be frozen to the metal and strip your skin. Work was monotonously routine, starting with reveille at 5.15 am and finishing at 6 pm, and towards the end of the war it ended as late as 7 pm.

On one occasion he recounted to me that they were all marched into the sea and told to stand to attention in the rising tide. This was all over a missing bag of rice. I forgot to follow up with my father as to who 'owned up' and what the punishment was but if you read Chick Henderson's account in a later chapter in this book you will get a good idea of typical punishments!

The biggest problem Dad faced during the war and immediately after was

Figure 2.28 HMS *Ruler*.

suffering from beriberi. This is a condition caused by a lack of vitamin B1. Its symptoms include, among others, weight loss and bloating of the body. This bloating could happen very quickly – in a matter of an hour. After the war Dad suffered from boils. I remember these being quite ugly things. I think they went on until about 1952. All of this was because of a lack of proper food during captivity. An example of this is that the POWs often had to eat cooked soya bean husks rather than the beans themselves.

Things were improvised in the camp. Opposite are two items: one, a razor, was made and used by Dad, while the other (glasses and a case) probably came from bargaining with a prison guard, but I am not clear.

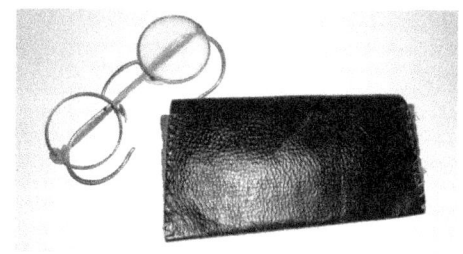

Figure 2.29 Razor.
Figure 2.30 Glasses and home-made case.

Dad recalled that towards the end of the war the Americans started heavy bombing, and many of the bombs landed very near the POW camp. Hiroshima was only 35 miles away over the hills but no one, either the POWs or the Japanese at the camp, knew about the dropping of the atomic bomb when it happened in August 1945, even though it happened so close by. This was probably because there was a range of hills between Innoshima and Hiroshima, and because there had already been so much bombing in the weeks leading up to that day. It was many weeks later that they were to learn what happened. The end of the war was confirmed for Dad and the other prisoners when a pinnace[14] flying the Royal Ensign came around the headland and docked at the quayside near the camp. In the pinnace was a small party of Royal Navy seaman. The officer leading the party announced to the POWs that the war was over, and they would be rescued and repatriated. However, he said that he could do nothing for them at that moment and Dad recalled: 'as quickly

---

14 A ship's boat, the pinnace is a light boat, carried by war vessels and lowered into the water to serve as a tender when a larger ship can't dock in shallow waters.

as he came, he went, and the pinnace disappeared around the headland'. Dad recalled the first army troops he saw arrive some weeks later were African-American. He said, 'They were all black.' This comment was not based on prejudice. I think Dad was just surprised. It's not corroborated by the other POWs but there are references to African-American troops being deployed in the Pacific theatre of war during World War II.[15]

Unfortunately, my father passed away before I had had the opportunity to dig out further wartime anecdotes from him. My research into my father's experience in WWII began. Early on my brother John and his wife, Dolly, helped me take a big step forward. Their research gave them a reference to Terence Kelly's book *Living with the Japanese* (recently republished under a new title, *By Hellship to Hiroshima*), which gives a very detailed account of life in Habu POW camp. John spoke to Terence Kelly and as a result Kelly sent John a photo of my father as he arrived at the POW camp. Amazing luck! Here is a copy:

Figure 2.31 Prisoners were photographed in groups of six on arrival. This photo is taken at Habu Camp on the island of Innoshima (Hiroshima camp #5). Albert Ient is on the far left in the front row.

---

15 Here is one such reference by Bernard C. Nalty on his web page entitled THE RIGHT TO FIGHT: African-American Marines in World War II 'When hostilities ended on 15 August, after the dropping of atomic bombs on Hiroshima and Nagasaki, the III Marine Amphibious Corps received orders to proceed to North China. Meanwhile, the V Amphibious Corps, which had conquered Iwo Jima, would participate in the occupation of Japan.'

Another fellow prisoner of war was Geoffrey Coxhead, who drew detailed pictures of the camp and the inland sea around Innoshima. He sent Dad a copy of this drawing after the war (Figure 2.32).

This drawing hung on the wall of my home in Aldershot and it was the very origin of my fascination with the war in the Far East.

Figure 2.32 This drawing shows the camp hut in Habu Camp, where Albert Ient lived for three and a half years, with the damaged bridge in front. This bridge was bombed by the US Air Force in 1945. (The reverse of the print is shown below the drawing.)

END OF WWII

Imperial Japan surrendered unconditionally on 15 August 1945, shortly after the atomic bombs were dropped on Hiroshima (6 August) and Nagasaki (9 August), but it was not until the 23rd that the Japanese High Command ordered a ceasefire and not until the 28th that the preliminary surrender document was signed in Rangoon and the Japanese Commander agreed to assist and obey the order of Admiral Lord Mountbatten, the supreme Allied commander of South East Asia.[16]

38 POWs died in Habu Camp (Hiroshima Camp No. 5), 33 of them British, from Hong Kong, all except two (L.M. Knight and William Charles) from the third draft. Of the 176 Hong Kong Signal Company men captured by the Japanese following the capitulation of Hong Kong, only 85 returned home.[17]

ALBERT IENT LEAVES POW CAMP

On his release Dad was taken by a short ferry journey to Onomichi (an industrial town between Hiroshima and Okayama), where he and many other POWs boarded a train to Osaka.

Terence Kelly's log confirms that he, and therefore we, can presume all the ex-POWs of Hiroshima Camp 5 left Japan on 17 September on board the British aircraft carrier HMS *Ruler* and arrived in Sydney on 27 September 1945 after spending three and a half years as a prisoner of war in the hands of the Japanese, firstly in Hong Kong and then Japan. On the form completed by my dad following his release, he stated that he left Hiroshima Camp No. 5 (Habu) on 15 September – which ties in with Kelly's date of leaving Japan, 17 September. However, the Royal Navy Archives say that HMS *Ruler* departed Tokyo Bay on 13 September, bound for Sydney and carrying POWs. The Far East Prisoner of War Community (FEPOW) website is rather vague, stating: 'It was HMS *Ruler*'s privilege to pick up 445 happy men, women and children who had assembled in Tokyo, to take them to Sydney in September 1945.'

Terence Kelly's book *By Hellship to Hiroshima* (p. 225) includes a picture of the Hong Kong Volunteer Defence Corp ex-prisoners on HMS *Ruler*. Terence confirmed to me, during our meeting in March 2007, that there was no picture taken of men from the Royal Signals or the RAF. He confirmed that men from the Signals Corps were on board.

On 29 September 1945, we know that Albert was at the HMS *Golden Hind* (shore base) at Royal Navy Barracks, some 20 miles outside Sydney. A copy of a confidential War Office form confirms that on this date Albert was 'briefly

---

16   B. MacArthur, *Surviving the Sword* (Time Warner, 2005), p. 420.
17   Figures confirmed by Lt. Col. Monty Truscott, Defence Army Data Processing Centre, Blandford Camp.

interrogated by an Intelligence Officer of HMS *Golden Hind*, RN Barracks, Sydney'. On arrival in Sydney, Albert found that his family had already left for England in June 1945. On 29 September 1945, Albert wrote to Toby, 'I was bitterly disappointed to find you not at home and I was at a loss as to what to do.'

Figure 2.33 Small card from SS *Dominion Monarch* (found in my father's desk).

ALBERT IENT RETURNS TO ENGLAND IN OCTOBER 1945

On 17 October 1945, Dad boarded the *Dominion Monarch*. Coincidentally, this was the same ship as the one Mum and my brothers had sailed back to England on a few months before. The original embarkation date had been set for 15 October but was delayed; he eventually set sail for home on 18 October 1945. The journey took him via Fremantle and Suez. Letters written by Albert to Toby during his journey confirm that he was in Aden on 3 November and Port Said on 7 November and that he hoped to arrive in Southampton on 15 November 1945.[18]

TOBY AND THE BOYS RETURN TO ENGLAND IN JUNE 1945

On 18 May 1945 Toby received notification from the welfare and administration officer of British Services Families that she was to prepare to leave New South Wales, Australia, for England and the departure would be some time during the second or third week of June. Her time as a military evacuee had come to an end.

The *Dominion Monarch* (Shaw Savill Line, 27,000 tons, advertised as the world's most powerful motor vessel) left Sydney for the UK, via the Panama Canal, at the end of June 1945 (exact date unknown) with my mum and my brothers, George and John, on board.

---

18 Source: letters from Albert to Toby – 17 and 20 October 1945.

ALDERSHOT – FROM 1946 ON

Dad was given family quarters at 9 Nicholson Terrace, Aldershot. I was born there on 9 September 1946. I asked my brother John why Dad left the army in 1946. He said it was all to do with the POWs being sent to, in Dad's case, an army camp at Pocklington Yorkshire. The men who had been in POW camp for four years were sent there for 'retraining' to get them used to life back in the army. John said there was a sergeant, George Rockall, who John met some years later in the mid-1950s when John was in the army serving at NATO headquarters at Fontainebleau in France. George Rockall was in charge of drilling the men on the parade ground at Pocklington in 1945/46. It was all to do with Dad's reaction to this overzealous sergeant, who John said looked very much like Captain Mainwaring of *Dad's Army*. Apparently, Dad, together with some other soldiers, walked off the parade ground in the middle of being drilled as if he was a private soldier having just joined the army and asked for the papers so that he could resign from his service career.

After what Dad went through in the war I'm not surprised. Especially as Dad was a senior warrant officer in Hong Kong before he had been captured. He was an experienced soldier, having 20 years in the army before capture. I believe it was an insult to redrill such men. However, as John says, it was a decision which he believes Dad regretted. If he had stayed in the army, he would almost certainly have been made up to a senior warrant officer very quickly and probably would have got a commission as a major and served out another 15 years before leaving the army.

Sadly, Dad left the army and had to find a job. Things weren't good after the war as there were lots of men looking for jobs as most of the service people had been conscripted into the services just for the war period and they were all on the jobs market as well. Dad had to start all over again in telecommunications. He joined the GPO telephone engineering department and began life all over again as a labourer digging holes and putting up telegraph poles. What must have added insult to injury was that he had to work through one of the worst winters in living memory in 1947, when he spent months repairing the telephone overhead wires and telegraph poles in the Basingstoke area in freezing weather and deep snow! Dad's decision meant that our family didn't have much money and Mum had to go out to work. Luckily, being an ex-serviceman, our family was given a council house in Aldershot. In the end Dad did make the grade and became a manager in the GPO Guildford Telephone Area and was a very well-respected engineer and manager.

This new career with the Post Office Engineers was to last 23 years. He worked his way up to foreman and then area inspector in the Guildford Telephone Area.

He was a life member of the Royal Signals Association and he devoted much of his time and considerable energy to the Royal Signals Association (former members of the Corps of Signals). For many years he was secretary of the very active Aldershot Branch, and in 1981 took on the role of president. His enthusiasm and interest in corps matters were well known. In Dad's eyes, the bond of comradeship figured prominently: he was a soldier all his life, in and out of uniform.

MEDALS

Sergeant Albert Victor Ient was awarded the Long Service and Good Conduct and Military Medals on 14 November 1946:

Figure 2.34 L to R: The 1939–1945 Star, the Pacific Star, the Defence Medal, the 1939–1945 War Medal, the Meritorious Services Medal, and the Good Conduct and Long Service Medal.

EPITAPH

Albert Ient died on 9 February 1988 in Farnham Hospital, Surrey, of prostate cancer. He was 83. Until a few years beforehand he had had very good health.

He is greatly missed.

It was his wish to be cremated and his ashes are buried at Aldershot Crematorium along with those of my mother, who died in 1999.

Below is a copy of his epitaph, as published in the *Royal Signals Journal* (please note: he was known as Vic to his army colleagues and indeed to everyone except Mum and the family).

> Ient – ex-Sgt Albert Victor Ient. Vic died peacefully at the Farnham Hospital Surrey on Tuesday, 9 February 1988. Born into a large family in 1905, he spent his early years in London. Following his brothers' lead he enlisted with the 13th London Regiment (TA) on 13 September 1921. Two years later at Whitehall he transferred to the regulars and the Royal Corps of Signals. The next six years were spent at the Signal Training Centre Maresfield or Aldershot and most of that as a mounted soldier with 'D' Troop Cavalry Division Signals. Posted to Malta in 1929, he met and married Toby in 1932. In the following nine years, Vic saw service in the Near East, Middle East and at home before moving to Hong Kong as the Line Sergeant to the Hong Kong Signal Company in December 1938. On Christmas Day 1941 he became a Prisoner-of-War and for the next four years was forced to work in a dockyard near Osaka on the mainland of Japan. Liberated by the Americans in November 1945, he was ordered to Sydney, Australia, only to find his family had been repatriated a few weeks early. In 1947 having settled in Aldershot, Vic decided on a new career with the Post Office Engineers. Over the following 23 years he rose to Area Manager Telecoms for the Guildford and Basingstoke district. A life member of the Royal Signals Association, Vic devoted much of his time and considerable energy to the old comrades. For many years he was Secretary of the very active or Aldershot Branch where his enthusiasm and interest in Corps matters was well known; many serving and past members have paid tribute to his expertise and ever-willing support. In Vic's eyes this bond of comradeship figured prominently, he was a soldier all his life, in and out of uniform, and will always be remembered with great affection by his many friends, a memory that will be cherished most dearly. To Toby, his sons and their family go our heartfelt sympathy.

CHAPTER 3

Maynard Skinner

After my mother died in 1999 I decided to try to contact some of those who knew her and my father, Albert Victor Ient, during World War II. I started by searching through my parents' address books and letters and there I came across the name of Maynard Skinner, who I know had been a close ex-serviceman colleague of my father in the Royal Signals Association through the post-war years. Not only had Maynard kept in touch with Dad continually after the war but when Dad died, in 1988, he carried on writing to Mum until she died. I wrote to Maynard and asked him if I could go and see him. He was delighted, and we arranged for me to visit him and his second wife, Dulcie, at their house near Poole in Dorset.

On a lovely sunny day in late August 2005, Maynard and I sat in his lounge and he talked to me about his life as a soldier; he recalled the excitement of travelling to Hong Kong, how he was called up on a charge in front of my father and what happened to him when the British Forces capitulated to Japan on Christmas Day 1941. Although his memory may have been clouded in some respects and events reordered by the intervening years, I found the interview intriguing and absorbing. This note is a summary of the discussions that took place on that summer afternoon.

JOINING THE ARMY

Maynard's story begins when he joined the British Army in July 1940, on 4 July, in fact! He joked with me that he lost his independence that day! Like

Figure 3.1 Maynard and me on my second visit in August 2008.

most people who enlisted or were conscripted into the Royal Signals at the time, he was sent to Catterick, in Yorkshire, for training. From there he started a three-month journey out to Hong Kong. Maynard vividly described the holiday-like atmosphere of his journey aboard *The Duchess of York*, part of a convoy leaving Liverpool in March 1941. Their first port of call was Freetown, but the next was Cape Town and Maynard spoke passionately about how he fell in love with this place. He said, 'It was glorious, because after the blackout it was just full of life and blazing colour, plenty of everything, plenty of beer, plenty of food and whatever, and I was lucky enough to get ashore for four days. I had a very nice time there; I loved it.'

The next leg of the journey took in Bombay, where Maynard celebrated his twenty-first birthday, and then Singapore. The Royal Signals were based in Singapore, in what became the infamous Changi Prison, but at the time of Maynard's arrival this was a British training camp and the place Maynard most remembers for the games of football he played with his friend, Harold Bates, and the Royal Signals soccer team.

HONG KONG

In May 1941, Maynard arrived in Hong Kong and found the pre-war atmosphere almost dreamlike. In retrospect, Maynard viewed his perception of freedom and ease as youthful naivety and felt that, had he been trained as a professional soldier in the same way as my father and not been a green national serviceman, he would have had more idea about what was going on and what to expect. As it was, he did run foul of army discipline on one occasion, when he was put 'on a charge' for going out of camp to a social event wearing his best formal uniform 'dress' trousers. This abuse of regulations landed Maynard 'on the carpet' in front of my father, who, despite the seriousness of the charge, let him off with no punishment. Maynard recalled Sergeant Albert Ient as a smart soldier in his tropical uniform, a very fair man, different from other sergeants in that he did not shout at his men. Maynard said: 'He was older than me; he was "old" school. I mean, your father was a very nice man, I liked him very much because he was ever so straightforward, not a complicated man at all, and so everything he did was always straight up, he was what he was.'

CAPITULATION

Questioned about when he became aware of the reality of war in the Far East, Maynard explained that this did not happen until the Japanese started to bomb Hong Kong immediately after they had hit Pearl Harbor on 7 December 1941. At first it was token, sporadic bombing; they didn't declare war; they just started. The Japanese bombing soon increased in severity and, when the Japanese came down through China into the New Territories, members of the British Army began to be captured. Maynard was not among the first to be detained, and he described the uncertainty of the period and the long retreats from Tai Tam to Stonehill Telephone Exchange and then to Stanley, saying, 'They were coming on all the time.'

IMPRISONMENT – SHAMSHUIPO

Hong Kong capitulated to Japan on Christmas Day 1941, but, because of lack of communication and the fact that he was on another part of the island, remote from the centre, Maynard was not immediately aware of the surrender. In some ways, the beginning of his period of imprisonment was, he felt, an anti-climax:

All I remember is a truck coming through; on it was this white flag, and in the vehicle were some of our people, you know, officers, and that was it. The Japanese then didn't do anything at all, I witnessed no atrocities or anything like that; they left us for a few days, and then they came back, and they marshalled us all together and then we had to march from there back down into town, into Northpoint Camp, in a place called Causeway Bay.

From Northpoint, where Maynard suffered a bout of dysentery, he and his fellow captives were taken to Shamshuipo, on Kowloon mainland. When Maynard first arrived at this camp he was hospitalised and, from this point onwards, lost all contact with my father, but he believes that his experiences as a Japanese POW in both Hong Kong and Japan were probably similar to those of my dad's. In Shamshuipo there was a Japanese Army officer named Genchi Nemori, as Maynard spelt it (other records show this name as Niimori Genichiro), of whom Maynard could only say: 'He was a terrible, terrible man, Genchi Nemori, yes, he was a horrible man, he ran the camp.'

The 10,000 or so prisoners were put to work refilling the holes left by the constant bombings, building a new road for the Japanese Army, cleaning the camp, clearing and burying dead bodies. The work was both physically exhausting and an enormous psychological strain, as the prisoners never had sufficient food and constantly had to adhere to public displays of submission, which were designed to inflate the captors' status while degrading their captives. Maynard recalled: 'We just had rice with nothing else for literally about three months; just on a couple of occasions we might have some sort of dark vegetable stew, it was just vegetables and flowers, probably chrysanthemums or something like that and that's what caused us to get so much illness.' Disease was rife, with overworked and underfed soldiers plagued by dysentery, beriberi and diphtheria. Maynard was without doubt lucky to have survived.

LISBON MARU

On 25 September 1942, after nine months of imprisonment in Hong Kong, Maynard and 1,816 British prisoners of war boarded the *Lisbon Maru* (see figure 3.2 on p. 54) bound for Japan. Fortunately, my father was not on the same ship as Maynard. He went directly to Japan without any major incidents. However, for

Maynard and his fellow servicemen aboard the *Lisbon Maru*, the journey turned into a nightmare, of not only disease and deprivation but also sheer horror. On 1 October 1942, an American submarine, the *Grouper*, fired torpedoes at the *Lisbon Maru*, believing it to be a Japanese troop ship. They severely damaged the ship in the stern and brought her to a standstill. A Japanese patrol boat took off the 700 Japanese soldiers, but left the prisoners in the ship's hold, below battened-down hatches. Fortunately, the ship did not sink immediately, owing to its positioning in shallow water on a sand bank. Maynard described how they went through that night and all the next day before somebody forced a means of escape through the hatch in No. 2 hold through which they could break out:

> We'd have probably gone down with the ship if we had been in deeper water but fortunately we did eventually get out. While in the hold I thought, well, I'm going to die anyway, but I don't want to die down here in the hold. There were masses of people about after we broke out and then gradually they started dropping off [the ship], drowning and whatever, because no attempt was made to save us. Then they [a Japanese gun boat] started shooting at us in the water.

Through what must have been sheer determination and a great deal of luck, Maynard, with fellow Signals comrade Reg Biggs, survived the sinking of the *Lisbon Maru* and the shooting. He did not know how many died, but records show that only 970 survived the ordeal at sea. This was not, however, the end of Maynard's trial, as he was picked up by the Japanese and taken firstly to Shanghai and then to Osaka.

The American submarine attacked on 1 October 1942, between Formosa (Taiwan) and Shanghai. A Japanese destroyer escort took Maynard and the other survivors to Shanghai, where they were left standing on the wharfside almost naked for long periods. A number developed pneumonia and died. Survivors were taken to Osaka Camp in Japan.[19]

---

19 Tony Banham, FEPOW Community, *The Sinking of the Lisbon Maru*. I came to hear about the Lisbon Maru from my dad, Albert Ient, when I was a child. He told me of the terrible (and, for many, fatal) journey a number of his fellow prisoners of war had on the ship when they were transported to Japan, following the fall of Hong Kong, to be interned in POW camps for the rest of World War II.

My dad was lucky in the lottery of allocation not to have been drafted onto this doomed ship. However, a number of his friends and fellow servicemen were. In this book I record the experiences of four of them: Terence Kelly, Maynard Skinner, Monty Truscott and Bill Butler.

JAPAN – OSAKA PRISONER OF WAR CAMP

Maynard arrived in Japan in October and, like many prisoners of war, indeed the same as my father, was taken to a shipyard. From 1942 through to the end of hostilities in 1945, Maynard remained in the Osaka prisoner of war camp. He was set to work in Osaka's dockyards with other POWs and Japanese civilians. In Maynard's case the work mainly consisted of loading and unloading ships; the prisoners were woken at 5.15 am and worked through until five or six in the evening, month after month and year after year. Initially they were granted a *yasumi* day (a day off), but towards the end of their captivity they tended to work seven days a week. Maynard was never in good health and at one point badly injured his back but was still required to work. As in other camps, the prisoners only had a meagre, restricted diet,

---

To help get an overall picture I recommend researching the BBC website WWII People's War. They tell the story of the *Lisbon Maru*, based on accounts from Martin Weedon in his book *Guest of an Emperor*; the newspaper accounts of the war crimes trials of the Japanese responsible; extracts from the log of USS *Grouper*, which torpedoed the *Lisbon Maru*; newspaper accounts from the *Japan Times Weekly* dated 20 October 1942; *The Knights of Bushido*, by Lord Russell of Liverpool; and personal accounts written at the time and personal reminiscences. I also recommend reading Tony Banham's book *The Sinking of the Lisbon Maru: Britain's Forgotten Wartime Tragedy*.

The Lisbon Maru

Figure 3.2 The Lisbon Maru. Source: copy photo by kind permission of Tony Banham.

consisting primarily of rice and occasionally some vegetable soup. Sometimes, in an effort to enforce a sense of national sovereignty, their Japanese captors fed them a red salted plum on a bed of white rice. Maynard recounted that, although the Red Cross visited the prisoners, they only received two parcels during his entire stay. Maynard recalled how, even when the war was nearing its end, his prison guards maintained their cold authority: 'It was all this business where you could not go past them without bowing otherwise you'd get beaten up, that kind of thing; of course that was almost routine. The prison guards' dominance and "order" was preserved until the very end, but then, all of a sudden, it seemed to me that we were left on our own.' As quickly as Maynard had been forced to make the transition from soldier to prisoner of war, he was now suddenly free once more.

Clearly, the realisation that the war was over was hard for Maynard to comprehend. In a dreamlike interlude, he took it into his head to visit a POW friend in another camp round the bay. He boarded a train to Kobe. He managed to meet up with two Royal Signal friends, 'Red' Harrington and 'Badgie' Price. On the train he travelled with Japanese civilians, and perhaps his sheer brazenness prevented him being thrown off the train, or worse still happening to him. He was, after all, still in a hostile country and had not been formally released from captivity; his freedom was simply inferred from the lack of an authoritative presence. I didn't spend enough time talking to Maynard on what happened in the next few weeks but with a smile he said he and his mate, Reg Biggs, and checked into a hotel in Osaka. He said he felt they (the POWs) were in charge now! By now they were wearing American kit, which had been among the many items dropped by parachute. Among other things he went swimming at the coast! He concluded: 'It was like a dream', referring to their new-found freedom.

HOMEWARD BOUND

During the journey home from Yokohama, going by air to Okinawa and onwards to Manila, in the Philippines, the ex-captives were asked to identify their captors as war criminals and were debriefed about the events that had occurred in Europe. This process was bewildering for Maynard; he had been very politically aware prior to his period of service but was shocked to learn how Jewish persecution had developed into the Holocaust. He was also given the shocking news that a plane carrying ex-prisoners of war had crashed. Among those killed were his friends Red Harrington and Badgie Price.

From Manila they went on an American naval transporter called the *Admiral Hughes*, to Victoria and Vancouver, British Columbia, and then by the Trans-Canadian Railway to Halifax, where there were jubilant celebrations. There were many Canadian POWs returning home. Maynard described the euphoric atmosphere and the tactics involved to ensure all were involved: 'At "Medicine Hat" station they'd take all the trousers and things like that from where we were sleeping, and we'd find we didn't have any trousers, so well, it was "if you promise to come out and join the party, we'll give you your trousers back!". It was chaotic; it was of course a lovely time.'

A liner called the SS *Île de France* brought the POWs back to Southampton. Maynard Skinner completed his journey home to Taunton, England, on 4 November 1945.

CHAPTER 4

Harold Bates and Monty Truscott

This is the story of two members of the Royal Corps of Signals from World War II.

Early in 2013 I attended the funeral of Maynard Skinner down in Bournemouth. Maynard was a comrade of my father in Hong Kong (see Chapter 3).

At this funeral I met members of the family, but quite by chance afterwards I chatted to a brother and sister (Lizzie and John) who had come to pay their respects because their father, Harold Bates, had been a colleague of Maynard's. We got talking and Lizzie mentioned that she had various pieces of information about her father, who like my father had also been in the Royal Signals, served in Hong Kong and been taken prisoner. Sometime after the funeral, while I was carrying out other investigations jointly with Lizzie and her brother, Lizzie gave me a copy of a recording of a BBC programme in which her father speaks about his experiences in the Far East along with another Royal Signals serviceman, Monty Truscott.

Figure 4.1 Harold Bates aged 22 in 1942, pictured in his local paper after being reported missing in action.

This recording is especially interesting as both men talk about their experiences in Hong Kong, where my father served, and who were fellow servicemen in the Royal Signals. Also, Monty Truscott was a close colleague of my father's. They also go on to talk about their experiences as POWs. Here is my transcript of the recording, which was made in 1973 by the BBC in Hong Kong during a veterans' visit to the colony (as it was then) by Harold Bates and Monty Truscott.

The paragraphs in italics indicate the BBC interviewer speaking. Please note: in a rather old-fashioned way, she uses their military titles.

Figure 4.2 Monty Truscott in Royal Signals colonel's uniform in the post-WWII period. When he had been captured in 1941, he had been a corporal.

MONTY TALKS ABOUT JOINING THE ARMY AND HONG KONG BEFORE THE WAR

Let's hear your story first, Colonel Monty Truscott. It all goes back, really, to 1934, when you were 18 and decided that a career in the army was for you.

Monty: Yes, it was on my 18th birthday that I joined the army. I couldn't join before; my father wouldn't let me. I spent two years in Catterick Camp[20] and then I was posted to Bulford Camp.[21] From Bulford I got a posting to Hong Kong. I always wanted to come to the Far East. I arrived in 1937 and we went into Whitfield Barracks[22] and my job at the time was linesman[23] on the Kowloon side[24] in the New Territories in Hong Kong.

---

20 Catterick Camp is and was a major training centre for the Royal Signals. The British Army has had a camp there since 1914.
21 Bulford Camp is a military camp on Salisbury Plain in Wiltshire.
22 Whitfield Barracks was in Tsim Sha Tsui, Kowloon, Hong Kong. It was named after Henry Wase Whitfield, the commander of the British Army in Hong Kong in the 1860s. The area is now the site of Kowloon Park, where four reconverted barrack blocks and parts of the former Kowloon West II Battery remain.
23 Linesman is a 'trade' in the Royal Corps of Signals. A linesman is involved in constructing field communications. In the pre-war days this included underground cable laying and the erection of overhead telephone and telegraph routes.
24 Kowloon is part of the 'New Territories' on the mainland side of Hong Kong. It faces Hong Kong Island across a narrow stretch of water called Victoria Harbour.

In those days, in 1937, when you arrived, the area where the barracks were was almost in the countryside, wasn't it?

Monty: Yes, that is quite true. Kowloon, I wouldn't say it was sleepy, it was bustling but almost the only noise you heard in Kowloon was the clip clop of people's shoes, wooden shoes. I wouldn't say it was countryside, but it certainly is different today. It had a peacefulness about it. It was about the furthest point from the Star Ferry[25] [*from Wan Chai to Kowloon to Shamshuipo, also written Sham Shui Po*[26]] that I can remember that was built up.

---

25 The Star Ferry, or the 'Star' Ferry Company, is a passenger ferry service. Its principal route carries passengers across Victoria Harbour, between Hong Kong Island and Kowloon. It was founded in 1888 as the Kowloon Ferry Company, adopting its present name in 1898.
26 Sham Shui Po, or Shamshuipo, is an area of Sham Shui Po District, Hong Kong, situated in the north-western part of the Kowloon Peninsula.
  In my researches to find information about my father's fellow prisoners of war I seem to have skated over what the situation was like in Hong Kong in the lead-up to the actual battle. Early on in my research I missed this photograph, a copy of which was given to me by Harold Bates's daughter. I guess he must have taken it just before the battle for

Figure E.2 View of Hong Kong island and Chinese refugees, c.1942.
Source: from Harold Bates's memorabilia.

Hong Kong started. It shows a virtual flotilla of sampans, housing refugee families from mainland China, off Hong Kong island. As we see from the writing on the rear of the photograph, Harold notes that these are refugees that arrived overnight from the Chinese mainland. A reminder of how much war affects civilians as well as combatants.

You have actually been back to look around for some of the huts that you were in; did you find any of them?

Monty: I went back to Shamshuipo the other night as a guest of Major Muir. I didn't have time to go and have a look at the huts; however, I believe the commandant of Shamshuipo has asked us to go and look at the huts that we stayed in. I believe they are still there.

[Author's note: The colony of Hong Kong as it was then, and still is today, is primarily made up of Hong Kong Island, the New Territories and a number of other islands, the largest of which in Lantau. Kowloon was, and still is, the main town in the New Territories. Shamshuipo is in the west of Kowloon and at the time that Monty is talking about was at the edge of the built-up area of the settlement. When the Japanese Army took over Hong Kong they used Shamshuipo as the main prison camp.]

I'd imagine the life in Hong Kong for a regular soldier before the war was a pretty reasonable posting, wasn't it?

Monty: It was, it was very good. For example, we had a laddie who cleaned our shoes and boots and that sort of thing, and this was luxury for soldiering.

Yes. I suppose in those days too, the men outnumbered the girls, so I imagine you had a pretty enviable time.

Monty: Not really *[laughs]*. Not really, because we had very little chance to meet the girls. There were so few girls. Not like today, I mean today the colony is bustling with girls, very pretty girls, but in those days the girls, the English girls were very much protected, and one just didn't meet them at all. Probably one only saw them on the Star Ferry.

So, what did you do in your spare time because, you know, I suppose there wasn't much in Wan Chai[27] district then?

Monty: Wan Chai – Oh yes, it was there in full force, very much so. You asked me what we did in those days: it was sport, you worked hard and you played hard, and that was soldiering.

1938 – THE BUILD-UP TO WAR

Of course, you were here as part of our defence force, but I don't suppose for one moment you imagined there would come a time when you would in fact be defending

---

27 Wan Chai is a metropolitan area situated at the western part of the Wan Chai District on the northern shore of Hong Kong Island, in Hong Kong. One of the main ferries operates from here to Kowloon on the mainland.

the island or trying to defend the island against an enemy. Did that ever cross your mind?

Monty: Yes, it crossed my mind about… I would say about '38 when the Japanese came down and took a large strip of the China coastline, and instead of having Chinese soldiers there we then had Japanese forces. I think it was at Li Chi Coche and Shungchun. It then occurred to us that there may come a day when we would have to do something about it.

[*Author's note: Li Chi Coche and Shungchun – spelling and location are not known. Shungchun could be Zhanjiang.[28] Both the places that Monty mentions are thought to be to the south-west of Hong Kong – Zhanjiang is only about 400 kilometres, or 250 miles, away*]

But nobody really did do anything about it, did they, here? I mean from the impression one gets from people there was an attitude of, well, you know, it can't happen here.

Monty: No, not with the military, there wasn't this attitude with the military at all. We had limited forces, we had two British regiments and one Indian regiment, and you really can't do much with that in such a confined area. The problem, of course, was fixed defence. The old concept of fixed defence, where you locked yourself up in a fort and you could stay there for a long time, is now out in modern war, you've got to be fluid, as in the desert war in North Africa. I had misgivings at the time that if ever it started it wouldn't last long.

Yes, well, this is what happens always at the beginning of all wars: people never think it's going to last long, do they?

Monty: That's quite true.

Capture and Shamshuipo POW Camp
Very nostalgic all this going back, isn't it, for you? Were you both herded into the same camp?

Monty: No. I was caught at the Peak Tram, at the top. We were chased all along the hill, it was about a thirteen-day movement from Wong Mee Chun right the way back to the Peak, and we were cornered at the Peak. We then heard of the surrender and we were told to lay down our arms, which we did. We were quite dismayed about the whole thing, but it had to be; they'd cut the island's water supply, so no one could carry on. We were then marched down to Victoria Barracks, where we were interned for a week. But with Harold's

---

28 Zhanjiang is a city at the south-western end of Guangdong Province, facing Hainan to the south of Hong Kong.

case, he was taken off to hospital and spent quite a long time there because his shoulder was shattered.

Harold: I'm very pleased I never actually surrendered.

So, Harold, you didn't see the Japanese victory parade, which you did, didn't you, Colonel Truscott?

Monty: Yes, I saw the victory parade; we were made to watch it from Victoria Barracks, from A Block, and we saw thousands of Japanese troops marching past. Cavalry regiments, little light tanks, soldiers pulling small field guns. We were seven days in Victoria Barracks and after that we were marched to Shamshuipo [*in the New Territories*] via the Star Ferry.

[*The interviewer then asked Monty about the voyage on the* Lisbon Maru. *Before describing the trip, Monty spoke about the conditions in Shamshuipo Camp*]

One thing I must say about Shamshuipo, which probably hasn't come out before, is that the health of the camp so degenerated that they divided the camp up in half and then one-half again. Two-quarters of the camp held dysentery patients, about 500, and the other quarter were diphtheria patients, and you weren't allowed across. They put wire up. We had very few medical supplies. Health was so poor but a doctor in the camp managed to bribe a Japanese guard to get some yeast tablets. We had no bread as such, but we had sacks of flour for soup and that sort of thing, and sugar, and with this minimum amount of sugar and flour this doctor put the yeast in and made a yeast ferment. Every day we had to go to a certain sector with our tin mugs and we received a pint of this horrible floury liquid, but the health of the camp came up very, very quickly.

Probably saved some of your lives.

Monty: Exactly, yes. But to get back to your question, we left Shamshuipo on 27 September '42. We were taken out in lighters onto the *Lisbon Maru*. We were told that we were going to a very green country where we would work but conditions would be better.

HAROLD TELLS THE STORY OF CAPTAIN FORD OF THE ROYAL SCOTS AND FLIGHT LIEUTENANT WHITE OF THE RAF

But some of the POWs, I believe, were taken to Canton?

Monty: Well, this was connected with the incident associated with Captain Ford – probably Harold knows the story better than I do.

Harold: Well, Captain Ford and Flight Lieutenant White of the RAF were in touch with Chinese guerrillas and British intelligence outside the camp. This was done by a system of 'note passing'. The members of the ration party were the only people within the camp who were able to get out. They were approached by Chinese truck drivers and the notes were brought back into camp. Some notes were put in baskets of vegetables but there were all types of ways of passing the notes back and forth. I think Captain Ford thought that his main duty was to escape. The story goes that it was suggested to him that he should lead a mass escape from the camp, and this would be backed up by Chinese guerrillas. The complement of Japanese soldiers had decreased, and it looked as though there might have been a fair chance if this had occurred. They were going to make their way over the hills. Ford couldn't see his way to do this because it meant leaving half the camp, who were hospitalised. He had no idea what reprisals the Japanese might take against them, but it wasn't long after this that the Japanese became aware that something was going on. The consequence was that Ford and White were taken out of the camp and eventually executed. Both of them were posthumously awarded the George Cross. Other members were taken out of the camp, I think at first, they were taken to Stanley, but eventually to Canton where they remained till the end of the war. I believe that Major Boxer, now Professor Boxer, who was an interpreter, was one of the few people who refused to sign a declaration not to escape and possibly this was the reason that he found himself in Canton.

Monty: Everyone had to sign a declaration not to escape. At first, we refused. In the end we received a message from our officers, who were being held in Argyle Street, saying we should sign. They said every man's pay book would include a note saying it was signed under duress. So, we signed.

MONTY TALKS ABOUT THE BATTLE FOR HONG KONG

So, when the Japanese did come, where were you?

Monty: Strangely enough I was in Shamshuipo. I was part of what they called the 'Kowloon Construction Troop' [*Royal Signals*] and my job was to lay cables out in the New Territories, connecting up the various pillboxes and block houses to company headquarters and so on. On the morning of 8 December 1941 about 60 planes appeared over Hong Kong. We had been 'on alert' the night before, the sirens went off and I thought, 'Well, this is it.' They bombed Kai Tak [*the only airport*], they knocked out two RAF 'Vildebeest'[29] aircraft. This was the total sum of the RAF aircraft at the time, which shows how unprepared they were. I don't think it was the commander's fault as obviously the whole effort had to go towards Europe at the time. Then they came across Shamshuipo and dropped a stick of bombs [*I think Monty means a load of bombs thrown chaotically from an aircraft*] across the Jubilee Buildings. We lost one sergeant. At eight o'clock that morning, off we went to our various stations and started working again. We worked very hard for three days; then we had to fall back a bit. The Royal Scots Regiment were out at Tai Mo Shan [*centre of the New Territories*] trying to defend the area. It was on the fourth day following that that I was ordered back to Hong Kong and caught one of the last Yaumati[30] ferries over to the island with the vehicle I had.

Harold Talks about the Battle for Hong Kong and His Boots!
[*Turning to Harold Bates*] *Were you a regular soldier? And where were you on 8 December, Signalman Bates, as you were then, of course?*

Harold: I wasn't a 'regular' in the army; I was called up as a wartime soldier. I had a very short training period and by the time I'd got to the colony had spent more time at sea than I'd actually spent in the army! I hadn't had much training; in fact, by the regulars [*soldiers*] at the time I wasn't really looked upon as a 'soldier' [*Monty interjects here – 'that's nonsense', laughs*]. At the time, which was on 8 December, I'd just come back from a run to Mount Davis [*as a motorcycle dispatch rider*]. I was at Mount Davis when the actual message came through that the Japanese had bombed Pearl Harbor. By the time I got back to barracks, the sirens were going off. We then stood on the veranda and watched the Japanese planes come down and bomb the British RAF out of the colony, as it were. These were the two planes we were talking about.

I continued to do all my normal runs though the colony. By this time the Japanese were shelling and bombing every road within sight, so it was quite a hazardous occupation. When the Japanese landed, I had set off from HQ at six o'clock in the morning, but at HQ they were unaware that the Japanese had landed.

---

29 The Vickers Vildebeest were large single-engined British biplanes designed and built by Vickers and used as a light bomber, torpedo bomber. First flown in 1928, they remained in service at the start of World War II.
30 The 'Hong Kong and Yaumati Ferry' included the vehicular ferry which served to transport motor vehicles across Victoria Harbour.

The first thing I heard about it was from a local fireman. Actually, I had set off that morning towards Lai Moon [*actual spelling: Lei Yue Mun*], going to D'Aguilar [*Cape D'Aguilar is on the south-eastern side of the island*], attempting to cross the island via Wan Chai Gap. I had heard machine-gun fire and then saw figures running across the road. Then I was stopped by a captain in the Middlesex Regiment. They had machine guns and they were obviously on a recce [*reconnaissance*]. They asked me where I was going and quite promptly put me right [*laughs*]! So I then attempted to go across via the Wong Nai Chung Gap. Two or three hundred yards in front of the gap I stopped a Bren gun carrier [*a small armoured vehicle*] with a captain in it and asked whether they had seen any Japanese, and they said no. I went on another hundred yards and heard machine-gun fire, which raked across my motorbike, and I saw that I had two bullet holes in the tank and my tyres had gone down, so I had to leave it. I hid behind a lorry parked on the side of the road. Its tyres had gone down, so I jumped into a ditch by a bank at the side of Wong Nai Chung Gap. There were about a dozen Canadians there with their captain. They'd obviously been ambushed in the lorry. Some of them were quite badly wounded. Eventually I was hit by a sniper. Along with a Canadian I hid under a covered water nullah [*water channel or ditch*], where we stayed throughout the day. We could see the legs of the Japanese moving around us. We came out that night to escape but we left our boots there.

Monty interjects: This is the reason why he's come back to Hong Kong – he wants his boots!

Harold: This is true. I've been searching for my boots! It took us another two nights before we eventually cleared ourselves of the Japanese lines. We were able to get to some sort of first-aid station. Actually, on this visit to Hong Kong I have identified the spot where my boots should be but they're no longer there! Also, I've identified the position of the cave in which we hid one night along Wong Nai Chung Gap.

MONTY – THE TERRIBLE VOYAGE ON THE *LISBON MARU*

So, going back to your voyage on the Lisbon Maru. *Where were you at the moment it was torpedoed? Presumably you were battened down in the holds with everybody else?*

Monty: When the torpedo hit us we were on deck, but quickly they sent us all down below and put hatch covers on. We lay like that for the whole day, no food, no water, no toiletry, nothing, and it was pitch black dark, no air and it was foul. Throughout the night we heard some banging against the side of the boat, it was listing badly, and we learnt later that they'd taken the Japanese off the boat. There were about 1,800 prisoners in three holds.[31] Holds 1 and 2 forward of the bridge and the artillery were in the hold behind the engine room. The next morning the boat had got quite a list on it. Colonel Stewart of the Middlesex Regiment organised an escape. Major Hamilton, who was a volunteer from the colony, and his party cut their way through the canvas between the hatch boards and managed to prise a couple of hatch boards open and the first two out were shot and killed by a sentry who was standing there. The others rushed him and took his weapon from him. There were five sentries on the boat altogether and they threw about two of them into the water. Those that could get out on top were ordered to take the hatch covers off and help everyone out. We stayed for about 30 minutes to an hour, getting people out. Then I heard an ominous creaking of the vessel and I thought, 'Well, this is no place for you, Truscott, you've done all you can, get off.' And I went into the water. It was easy to get into the water as it had come up to the bridge area. I'd got about a hundred yards away from the vessel when she went down. And then we were machine-gunned from a destroyer that was laying off nearby and again I thought, 'This is no place for you, Truscott', and I reversed and saw an island in the distance and I swam for this island with one or two other people. I got off the boat about ten o'clock and about six o'clock that night we made it to the island.

Were there any left behind in the hold or did you all get out?

Monty: No, not all got out, quite a few went down. But I have a reunion each year, from 1968 onwards, I arrange to get my [*military*] company together each year. We haven't succeeded in getting them all together yet but that is the reason for holding reunions – to find one's comrades. One thing that was amusing at last year's reunion was that I met a William McCormack. I said, 'Well, how did you get on, McCormack, because you couldn't swim at the time?' and he said that during the rather tense moments when he thought the ship was going down he thought he'd best go and say his prayers in the *benjo*. Now, the *benjo* was a toilet slung over the side of the ship; they were rather large wooden things. He went into the *benjo* and the ship went down while he

---

31 The ship's hold is a space for carrying cargo. Access to holds is by a large hatch at the top. Today most cargo ships carry containers, which may be loaded into appropriate holds or carried on deck.

was in it and the next thing he knew was that he was riding high on the waves in this *benjo* [*laughs*]!

And he got away to the island too, presumably?

Monty: He said he stayed with the *benjo*. So, I don't know [*laughs*].

How long were you on the island?

Monty: We were taken to another little island by a fisherman, to a village. There we were fed and watered – wonderful. We thought we were going to be free because the elders of the village were planning to get us away to the China mainland.

They were very brave those Chinese, weren't they?

Monty: Oh, they were marvellous. And they gave us food, clothing, and so on. But next morning we woke up and saw Japanese marines swarming ashore from a patrol boat and we thought, 'Well, this is it.' The Chinese asked us to give ourselves up because if we'd hidden ourselves we could have only stayed in their houses.

And they'd have been shot.

Monty: They would have been shot without a doubt. And so, we were rounded up and put on this small boat. But I must tell you one thing here, that when we were put on this boat we were addressed by the captain, a naval captain, and he said, 'I've got milk coming round for you and biscuits, and I've got some cigarettes and we are going off to Shanghai.' We were amazed at his kindness and someone asked, 'Why are you doing this? Because yesterday our people were shot in the water.' This may seem amazing to you, he said the Japanese Navy would never do such a thing, and we said it was a naval boat. He said the reason for this was that the army had been taken aboard the destroyer from the *Lisbon Maru*. The army had seen us escaping from the *Lisbon Maru* and they took it that since we had signed the declaration not to escape, they should shoot us. The captain further explained that the destroyer captain had overpowered the army lieutenant, despite the army being the 'senior service' in Japan, and stopped further shooting. The Japanese captain concluded by saying, 'I can assure you that I would do no such thing, I was educated in the Naval College at Dartmouth, and we still have naval traditions.' And he then took us to Shanghai.

Reason to be thankful to him, then?

Monty: He was one of the kindest Japanese I've met, and there were one or two kind ones.

[*See Terence Kelly's and Maynard Skinner's accounts of the terrible voyage on the Lisbon Maru in other chapters in this book*]

MONTY – ON THE JOURNEY TO JAPAN AND POW CAMP AT OSAKA

Monty: We were to change ships at Shanghai. We got off the boat and were stripped of our clothes and left naked all day. That wasn't funny. It was most embarrassing with Chinese girls walking by. It was 1st or 2nd October and cold. That evening we were given Mongolian troop clothing, which is a corduroy type of clothing, which was not clean at all, and put on another boat called the *Shinsai Maru* [*spelling uncertain*], which sailed for Japan.

And presumably you spent the rest of the war in Japan. Whereabouts did you go to, which camp?

Monty: Osaka, and they sorted the weak out from the strong. We lost about another 200 in that camp from the exposure in the water and that sort of thing. They were taken away and put in what they called a 'hospital' but what was in fact the concrete roof of a stadium where a Dr Jackson, a naval doctor, had to look after them with very few medical supplies. He did wonders with a razor blade and a knife.

Did you have a pretty rough time in Japan, in your camp? I mean, I know the camps varied quite considerably.

Monty: I wouldn't say rough. We worked hard, we started at seven in the morning and we finished at six at night. You worked in foundries and cement works or you worked on the docks. If you did something wrong, you were punished. When I say 'something wrong': something very minor. You were punished as the Japanese punish themselves.

Did you hear or receive news of what was going on in the outside world?

Monty: Yes, I had learnt *hiragana* and *katakana*.[32] I think it is the 52 Romanised versions of the language. All the nouns are in *katakana* and you could read words like the Solomon Islands and then the Philippines and so on. So, the names were getting nearer. So, I knew how things were progressing in general. This was from the Japanese newspapers.

HAROLD – ON THE JOURNEY FROM HONG KONG, VIA FORMOSA, TO POW CAMP IN NAGOYA AND TOYAMA

So, Harold Bates, back to you. We left you languishing in hospital, then you went to the Shamshuipo Camp, and then what happened to you?

---

32 *Hiragana* and *katakana* are both *kana* systems; they have corresponding character sets in which each kana, or character, represents one *mora* (one sound in the Japanese language).

Harold: From Shamshuipo I went to Japan a month after Monty had gone on the *Lisbon Maru*. We had a very slow journey. It was said that the Chinese had sabotaged the ship. Anyway, it lasted as far as Formosa [*now Taiwan*]. We were in Formosa on Christmas Day 1943, where we stayed until they found us another boat. I was in a camp near Nagoya and then another one across the other side of the island, Toyama.[33]

What work did they give you to do?

Harold: Well, as Monty said, the work was extremely hard, although it wasn't hard for everybody. They picked out from our camp 30 of the fittest and I happened to be one of those, and they called us the 'strong arm gang'. We had to do all the really heavy work. The diet that we were receiving was inadequate for this type of work, and so consequently, those of us who were on really heavy work very quickly began to fail. In fact, I don't think that within our camp many of us would have survived another winter. Certainly, in a place like Toyama, which is very cold in the winter.

MORALE

What was morale like in your particular group?

Harold: Well, it was within the individual. Towards the end of the war many people who might have been considered weak or ill-fitted for this sort of treatment had already died, and so you were left with quite a strong collection of men. The tendency was to look after oneself. The spirit was there but it was not a community spirit as such; it was just a question of keeping going individually.

In response to questions regarding these factors in his camp, Monty replied:

It was not really the same for us. Our camp comprised of the remnants of two well-disciplined regiments – Royal Scots and the Middlesex Regiment. The discipline of the British part of the camp was very much admired by the Japanese, I suppose because they were a greatly disciplined army. A third of the camp was American.

---

33 Nagoya is north of Osaka and south of Tokyo. Located on the Pacific coast on central Honshu, it is the capital of Aichi Prefecture and is one of Japan's major ports. Toyama is about 200 km away on the north coast of Honshu. It is the capital city of Toyama Prefecture, Japan, located on the coast of the Sea of Japan in the Chubu region on central Honshu Island.

STEALING THE SALMON AND LOOT BAGS!

There must have been occasions when not every day was grim?

Monty: One always remembers the humorous side. One very rarely thinks of tragedy; it would be wrong to do so. I can remember one day, for instance, when we were working on a boat and we had a very good navy man with us, Monty Banks his name was, and no lock was safe with Monty Banks. The fridge sat amidships of this little boat. Within a few moments on the boat Monty was into that fridge. It was a cold store, and they had, in Japan, some wonderful great long salmon, beautiful salmon, and out came the salmon and we hid it. At about 12 o'clock that day, along came the cook, he looked into the fridge and couldn't find the salmon, so back he went to the captain and the captain came down, spoke to our guard, and we were asked if we knew where the salmon was, and of course we knew nothing about this. So, the cook scratched his head, and that evening we were searched, and they couldn't find the salmon at all. But on the way back to the camp this salmon appeared down someone's leg, it was falling out on the way back [*laughs*]!

Were you able to keep it?

Monty: Oh, yes, yes, we managed to get it into the camp. We were great rogues in those days; you had to be to survive! We had all sorts of loop bags! Arm loop bags [*see the description in Bill Butler's story*], head loop bags, bags stitched such that you could put them round your body. If you were lucky you could get past the guards. If you were unlucky you might have to kneel outside the guard room all night with, say, a brick being held above your head.

POW Life, Japanese Newspapers, the End of the War and a European Toilet!
[*In response to further questions, Monty said:*]

We were in that camp for three and a half to four years, but never received any mail from home. We did, however, get Red Cross parcels, one each Christmas Day, and so we had about three Red Cross parcels, which then had to be split between five or six people.

Were there any plans to escape? I mean, under those circumstances, when people got very fed up, there must have been some idea of 'How can we get away from here?'

Monty: Escape was impossible. You had the sea all round you; it was impossible. Although we were bombed out of three camps, because from March '45 onward there was incessant bombing of Japan. We suffered from fire-bombing every day. About two weeks before the surrender, two American officers were brought in. Apparently, they'd escaped their camp and were making their way to the coast, where they were going to get into a little boat if they could find one. But it was a foolhardy thing: they were caught, and they were tied to this log outside the guardroom for days.

One reason why we knew the war was over was because we were brought home from a working party earlier than usual that day and the Japanese had to stand to listen to a voice on the radio, which turned out to be the emperor, and he then told them that the war had finished and that Japan was negotiating for peace. We got back to the camp that night and the camp commandant released the two American officers and said that they were no longer under sentence of court martial. We then knew it was over. They were very lucky. One of these American officers took charge of the camp from then onwards, and after about three days of no food in the camp he ordered the commandant to find the best hotel in Osaka – and, incidentally, there was one hotel that was still standing. We went in there, but the camp commandant was worried about who was going to pay, and the American officer said, 'Don't worry, Uncle Sam will pay.' [*laughs*]

Turning to Harold, the BBC interviewer said: And what happened to you? Had you any idea that the war was ending in your camp?

Harold: Yes, we'd always had very good communication. We had a professor from Hong Kong University who could read Chinese. We were able to steal newspapers every day. He translated them in the evening and so we followed the course of the war. We knew that the war in Europe was over; we knew about Hiroshima, we knew about Nagasaki and we knew that something was happening. Then, at the end we were kept in the camp away from the dockyard for two or three days. On the final day, all the Japanese were assembled around the radio. We also listened to the emperor's speech. We didn't know what he was saying and then they told us that the war was over. There was no elation in the camp at all: everyone was very quiet, and there was great emotion, but no great elation. Everyone was just very, very stunned.

Monty interjected: I can tell you when I was elated: when I first met a European toilet again in this hotel. It was marvellous [*laughs*]!

Harold continued: We then had three weeks or more in the camp where we had been POWs. We got good food: the Americans had dropped tons and tons of food. We were also given new uniforms by the Japanese, but our actual situation had not improved; we were still in the camp.

Monty: Where we were we had American uniforms, which had been dropped by aircraft. So, we dressed up in those. We had a guard and a Union

Jack and Stars and Stripes flag outside the hotel, which remained our temporary billet. In the same way as we were made to bow to the Japanese flag every time we passed it when we were in camp, we made the camp commandant bow when he came to see us, which he was made to do every day.

After the War and the Return Visit to Hong Kong
So that was the end of the war for both of you, and presumably you were demobbed and then had to think about what you were going to do after the war. So, what did you do, Harold Bates, after the war?

Harold: Before the war I'd been working with a finance company and like so many soldiers I didn't want to go back to my old job; we all seemed to want a change, I don't know why. So, I was talked to by my old headmaster about going to teacher training college, which I did, and since then I've been teaching. At the moment I run a department in a large comprehensive school.

You tried to go back to Hong Kong, didn't you?

Harold: Yes, I enjoyed my stay in Hong Kong before the war and immediately after the war I tried to go back there but it was difficult to get work there in 1946.

You stayed on in the army though, didn't you, Colonel Truscott?

Monty: Oh, yes. I was, shall I say, born to be a soldier, and I signed on again for 22 years and have been in the army ever since. I retired two years ago. But I started the war as a corporal; I finished as a corporal; you don't get promoted as a prisoner. From 1945 up until two years ago I went through every rank and finished up as a colonel.

What brought you both out here? I mean, how did you arrange this trip and how did you decide to do it together?

Monty: Well, we both had different objectives. As I told you, I hold these reunions of the Hong Kong Signal Company every year, which are wonderful affairs where people all get together again. Our chief signal officer [*from the Hong Kong Signals Company*], Colonel Levett, attended the last reunion. A grand old man, he was a prisoner of war of the First World War and a prisoner of war of the Second, poor fellow, but he was a wonderful man and we had great admiration for him. He died two months after our reunion last year and left me his war diary of the Hong Kong battle. This was a communication diary. I thought the rightful place for this was with the Hong Kong Signals, so I had it printed and bound and contacted Colonel Benbow, who's the present Commander of Royal Signals Hong Kong. He said by all means he'd be delighted to receive it on behalf of all ranks, Royal Signals, and so that was my objective.

And, Harold Bates, how did you come to be out here then?

Harold: This is purely nostalgia on my part.

Monty: Looking for his boots [*laughter*]!

Harold: I'd reached the stage in life where the children were just off my hands, and for the first time I felt that I could possibly afford to come.

But how did you fix up the trip?

Harold: My son had visited Hong Kong twice. On each occasion he brought back a newspaper, and one of the newspapers had an article in it about the war. I wrote to the newspaper to ask them if there was still some interest in the war: if they were interested, if I got back to Hong Kong, could they possibly advise me about accommodation? They published my letter and luckily enough Colonel Benbow got to know about the article and wrote and offered me accommodation.

And your wife came with you?

Harold: Well, I told my wife that I would take her, but of course I couldn't ask the army to put my wife up as well – but the army have absolutely fallen over backwards to help us in every possible way.

[*Monty agreed with this sentiment, and with the interviewer saying that there is still a wonderful comradeship in the British Army.*]

Monty: It's always been there. One thing I would like to say is that Colonel Benbow and his officers have been absolutely wonderful to us and we're very, very grateful to them.

Well, your story is all part of the tapestry of Hong Kong and I'm glad that you have had this opportunity to come back and relive old memories. So, the very best of luck to you both when you get home.

Both men: Thank you very much.

CHAPTER 5

William (Bill) Alfred Butler

This is the story of a member of the Royal Corps of Signals from World War II, Bill (William Alfred) Butler – Far East prisoner of war, WWII, born 29 December 1916, died 4 January 2014 aged 97.

When I met Lizzie and John at Maynard Skinner's funeral in early 2013 (see Chapter 4, where I record the story of their father, Harold Bates), Lizzie mentioned that she had found another POW from the Royal Signals who also had served in Hong Kong and who was still alive. His name was Bill Butler and he lived in Mablethorpe. After meeting Lizzie at Maynard's funeral in Bournemouth, she made arrangements for us to visit Bill at his home in Mablethorpe on the Lincolnshire coast. Without that initial contact we would never have met Bill and discovered his wonderful story.

We arrived at the seaside town of Mablethorpe in July 2013 and found Bill's bungalow a couple of streets back from the seafront. It was a small place in need of some care but Bill, at the age of 96, seemed to be quite comfortable. He welcomed us in, and we gathered in the sitting room. On the walls were photos and memorabilia from the war years.

Although Bill lives on his own, he has friends who look out for him and one friend in particular comes to see him every day. As Bill says, without him and his other friends, he would not know what to do. The British Legion have looked after Bill and have provided him with his electric wheelchair, which enables him to get out to the shops and see people and, especially, go to the pub, where he meets his friends. He is clearly very happy in his little bungalow. He says he won't go into a home unless he has to.

(Left to Right)
Figure 5.1 Bill Butler – from a photo dated 1937.
Figure 5.2 Bill and me when I visited him at his bungalow in Mablethorpe on 2 May 2013.

(Left to Right)
Figure 5.3 Bill's bungalow.
Figure 5.4 Bill's wife, Vera.

We began to talk about his life since the war ended. He talked about the many happy years he spent with his wife, often taking holidays in their small caravan around the country. They hadn't had children, but it was clear that they had had a happy and loving marriage for many years until his wife had died some years before. Looking at his photographs on the wall it was clear that his time in the Royal Signals, and as a member of the Royal Signals Association after the war, featured highly in his memories. One photograph caught my eye and that was of a Royal Signals Hong Kong Signals Company Association reunion group photograph with all the members present. That got us talking about the Association reunions held every year for many years, often at Blandford in Dorset. Bill's eyes lit up when he began to talk about the reunions. He loves them and recounted many of the happy memories he had at the reunion weekends. We got the big photograph of the group down from the wall and the first thing he mentioned was my mother, who was seated next to my father in the middle of the photographs. 'Oh,' he said, 'Toby was wonderful!' My mum, Toby, and my dad were usually the hosts of these events as Dad was, for many years, the president of the Hong Kong Signal Company Association.

Bill recounted how they used to enjoy remembering the happier times they had had as prisoners when they used to smuggle food into their prison hutments by slinging a bag between their legs which might contain rice or some other food they'd stolen. This same method of smuggling is recounted in Chick Henderson's biography in Chapter 7.

This then got us onto Bill's account of his wartime experiences. I began by asking him if he knew some of the other Royal Signals servicemen who had been captured in Hong Kong. He said, 'Oh, yeah, Jimmy Dignan and I were big pals.' Lizzie asked about her dad and Monty Truscott. Bill continued, 'Monty Truscott… Oh, yeah, Monty, yeah… he was a lance corporal in Bulford with me. He was a long-distance runner.' Bill remembered Harold Bates and said he had kept in touch with Jean Bates after Harold had died. All these discussions reminded Bill of the Royal Signals Hong Kong Regiment reunions. Bill said, 'These reunions were something out of this world – from Friday lunchtime to Sunday lunchtime it was out of this world, it was.'

After a while Lizzie reminded Bill of the telephone conservation they had had. 'When we spoke on the phone you said you had written a book.'

'Oh, yeah, pass me that bag,' he replied. Getting an A4 booklet out, he said, 'That is my 13 years in the Signals.' Bill went on, 'Well, it all started with my wife watching a programme on TV. As a result, I wrote about the *Lisbon Maru* and a lady read it. She said, "Ooh, I bet you've had an interesting life," and I said, well, yeah. And so I sat down and just started to write that, with the help of a lady who sorted it out and typed it up.' Bill showed us his biography. It had been printed by the British Legion.

Bill has given me permission to use his biography, and the text below is taken directly from his book.

LEAVING SCHOOL

Bill left school at 14½. His first job was at a butcher's shop, where he learned how to make sausages. He remembers, 'But sausages were my downfall'. Next door to where he worked was a shop called Davy's. There was a blonde-haired teenage girl who worked there. So, one day, in an attempt to impress her, Bill came out into the back yard with about six feet of sausage, and seeing she was there, he started skipping with them, not realising the boss had returned from the bank and seen him. His first job was over.

His next job was at a wholesale grocer where he learnt how to drive a lorry. He remained there until the age of 16, when he was made redundant. This was 1933 and work was not plentiful, so he decided to join the army.

CATTERICK CAMP

Sitting in his armchair, Bill recounted his time in the Royal Signals: 'When I joined up I was in the Signals and I was a wireless operator, and I'd gone through all my training, but after all it was operating signals, you had to know "line work".[34] I volunteered to go with an infantry brigade section which was working with the artillery. It was 1933 when I joined up, there weren't motorised vehicles, the only vehicles were old Douglas motorcycles and Austin 7s or horses! Horses pulling the cable wagons. Yeah. We were laying cables; it was about autumn. I had a horse and I used to fantasise that I was a cowboy on a cattle drive! Yeah, an 18-year-old riding a horse. It was great!'

---

34   By referring to 'line work' Bill Butler was referring to the skills needed to install overhead and battleground telecommunications cables including terminating them so as to provide communications between forward military positions and Army HQ.

He went on, 'I trained at Catterick. I remember me first meal in the army. We went up there, booked in, and went into this room and they came and give us a mug, a pint mug each, they then said, "chow time". There were 6 of us at a table, your mugs for tea at the end. This chap came up and put a tin on the table – it had a newly baked loaf in it. He then put a big lump of cheese, a big lump of margarine and an onion on the table. Three of those on our table said, I'm not eating that, and they went. We three that were left had a real good meal with it, we enjoyed it.'

On 3 October 1933 Butler left for Catterick Camp in North Yorkshire and one week later had been accepted as a member of the Royal Corps of Signals. For three months he learned to drill, how to handle a rifle and how to clean and polish his 'wearing brasses' [*in those days, soldiers wore a number of brass fitments to their uniform such as buttons, belt clips and insignia – these were called 'wearing brasses'*]. When he 'passed out' [*a military term for successfully completing a stage of training*], qualifying as a soldier, he commenced technical training as a wireless operator, eventually qualifying as Operator Signals Class BIII.

In 1935 Butler was posted to 5th Division Signals at Burniston Barracks, Scarborough. After three months' training he applied for a position in an Artillery Brigade Signals Section where he learnt how to ride a horse on an 'equitation course'.

Bill described being posted to G Section. 'I was posted to G Section – every horse's name began with G. My horse was called Garcon. She had ears like a donkey; she had not one hair on her tail, just a stump. But she could fly – no other horse in the section could touch her and she could jump over almost anything. I loved that horse.'

Butler remembered this as the most exciting time of his life. His section left Catterick Camp for Newcastle. They rode and arrived at the station at Newcastle in the afternoon to collect the cable wagons, limbers etc., which had come by rail. They were to take them to Fenham Barracks, the headquarters of the artillery brigade, where they were to spend the night. As the wagons were being unloaded, the sky became very overcast and it went quite dark. Then suddenly there was a flash and an explosion in the goods yard and the heavens opened. Butler was mounted on Garcon and she reared and came down hard on her forelegs. As the horse went forward, the reins eased, and she grabbed the bit in her teeth and set off. She sped around people and trams and shot off up the cobbled road. Butler was 'frightened to death', trying to get control –

but to no avail. Bill said, 'I was expecting her to slip any moment, but she kept her feet. I saw Fenham Barracks on my right as we passed at 30mph. A short while later I saw some grass on my left and gradually eased her over until I had her shoes on grass. Once I got her on the grass my fears were over. I let her run herself out. Then, once I had regained control, I turned her round and eventually arrived at Fenham Barracks in time for tea!'

After a night in Fenham Barracks, the section headed north for Redesdale in Northumberland where they were to take part in manoeuvres with the 9th Brigade Royal Artillery. The ride up to Redesdale was uneventful until their arrival, when it was discovered they were ten days too early. Apparently, the typist had omitted to put the '1' in the date on the orders: they had arrived on 6 July and the correct date was the 16th. Their section officer decided he was not staying there for ten days and immediately wrote out a cheque for two weeks' pay for the section, giving it to the section sergeant, saying, 'I will see you on the 16th.' The next day 'Chalky' White, the section sergeant, came into the stables and instructed Butler and two others to saddle up the horses, change into uniform and report to the company office, where they were issued with revolvers, holsters and six rounds of ammunition each. Chalky appeared and told them that they were going to draw the pay for the section, which they did at a bank in a village situated about six miles away.

Butler commented: 'This was a fantastic time for me. I had the world at my feet, everything an eighteen-year-old could wish for. I was being well fed, well clothed, in good accommodation and had twenty-five shillings a week to spend – this was 1935! An engineer's wage was thirty shillings a week; I had almost that amount to spend. We had to exercise the horses every day. What did I do? I fantasised! I played Cowboys and Indians. I had a good horse to ride; the Yorkshire Moors was the wagon trail to California. It was a young boy's dream and I was able to satisfy that dream.'

Bill explained that the most exciting part of the manoeuvres, when they started, was riding the cable wagon. It was very dangerous because there were four horses pulling the wagon – big strong draught horses, one driver to each pair. The object was to lay the cable from the drums on the wagon as fast as possible (each drum carrying four miles of cable). The drivers would be told where the telephone exchange was, and they would then go in as straight a line as possible at full gallop. The two layers were each sat in a bucket seat at the back of the cable wagon. When the wagon began to roll one layer would pay off cable from his drum; the other would wait until that drum was exhausted, a joint would be quickly made, and he would take over and pay out from his drum. The danger lay in the terrain. Whilst the lead driver would try to choose the best route, he could not always see small gullies and ditches. The horses would leap these – the wagon had to follow – and consequently the ride was very rough. Bill said, 'I loved this life! It was very hard work, but I was young and very fit.'

Manoeuvres having been completed at Redesdale, the section returned to Catterick, the whole exercise having been a huge success. The next two weeks were spent grooming and exercising the horses, cleaning and repairing the limbers and cable wagons and equipment.

The next few months were full of activity – grooming and exercising the horses, lectures, doing guard duty or night picket [*guarding the perimeter of the camp*] in the stables. Every evening was free, so Butler went dancing at the Olympian Golden Slipper or the Territorial Drill Hall. They were allowed civilian clothes and with the money they were drawing could afford to dress well. Having qualified as a Class III Operator Signals and obtained his 1st Class Certificate of Education, Butler's pay was now 30 shillings a week.

One morning the section sergeant asked if anyone would like to volunteer for a cook's course, saying they were classified as a small unit and should have a qualified cook. Butler accepted the offer: 'I thought I might as well learn all I could – it cost nothing.' On the following Monday Butler reported to the cookhouse and was introduced to Jim 'Dutchy' Holland.[35] Bill said: 'He taught me how to cook. He was a wonderful pastry cook. When off duty he used to go to the Grand Hotel in Scarborough and make pastries for them. He taught me well, telling me what to do, but letting me do the work, and I learned quickly. After several months I went to York for three days where I cooked meals for 30 men of the Royal Engineers. I was successful, and I qualified as a cook!'

OFF TO NORTH AFRICA!

One Monday in July 1935, whilst on parade, names were called out – Butler's among them. The selected men were marched to the lecture room where Colonel Levett, the Commanding Officer, addressed them. He informed them

---

35 'Dutchy' Holland was one of my father's (Albert Ient's) great friends from his army days.

that Italy had invaded Ethiopia, and Britain had interests in the region. A unit was to be formed of the King's Shropshire Light Infantry and Butler's section was to provide the communications.

[*Author's note: Colonel Levett mentioned above was probably the Colonel Levett who eventually became the chief signal officer in Hong Kong during WWII*]

The rest of the week was very busy. A section was formed, equipped with three 3-ton lorries, an Austin Seven, two motorbikes and two 15-cwt. trucks. The wireless operators checked their equipment and Butler went with one of the 3-ton lorries to the depot at York to fetch tents and equipment to house the wireless sets. The following day they were given typhoid and cholera injections and issued with tropical kit. The paymaster gave them 28 days' pay plus ration allowance and railway warrant, and they were sent on their way for a month's embarkation leave.

Having enjoyed a month's leave, Butler returned to Scarborough. Two days later he was bound for Southampton. On arrival he boarded *HM Troopship Nevassa* and sailed on the evening tide. This was a whole new experience for Butler. 'The only boat I had been on before was the ferry from Liverpool to New Brighton.' The voyage was pleasant. The sea was calm. The first stop was Gibraltar, where the men were allowed ashore for eight hours, then it was on to Malta for a six-hour stay. On the tenth day they arrived at Alexandria and the order came to disembark.

ALEXANDRIA

Butler soon settled in. 'It was,' he said, 'a good camp, the food was good, and we had lots of free time. The lovely Mediterranean Sea was only across the road, so we indulged in plenty of swimming, but our holiday was soon at an end. After three weeks of luxurious holidaying, we were assembled and marched off to the naval dockyard in Alexandria, Ras-el-Tin.'

It was now November, and the nights were cold. They were moved out to a place called Borg-el-Arab, about 25 miles from Alexandria. They made camp inside an old fort, erecting bell tents in a square in the centre. 'We erected our wireless tent and aerial for the transmitter, then set up the receiver and began to establish contact with our station at Ras-el-Tin.' The following day they were joined by a company from the King's Shropshire Light Infantry (KSLI) Regiment, who were to guard the area.

The Signals were split up into four groups – HQ and three outposts, X, Y and Z. Z post was a disused lighthouse, X post was in some caves and Y post was about 10 miles out from HQ.

Butler's unit had to continuously monitor the radio. The three outposts sent in daily reports between the hours of 8 a.m. and 8 p.m. as well as orders for supplies from the canteen – cigarettes, chocolate, sweets, razor blades, soap etc.

There was excitement on one occasion when a message was received from El Dabha (where the Air Force were stationed) that a man had deserted. He had stolen the commanding officer's car, was armed and had a good supply of water and petrol and was last seen heading in the direction of Butler's camp.

Butler said, 'We assembled in three vehicles, three men to each, one of whom was a signalman equipped with a heliograph (a tripod with a mirror to send messages using the sun). We set off, with each vehicle being instructed to cover a certain area on the map. In our area was some high ground so we made for this. I set up the heliograph and we decided to stay at this place because we could see a wide area and could follow the other groups and contact them at intervals. Two hours later the deserter was seen and recaptured shortly after.'

This incident over, normal routine was resumed. After eight months at Bur-el-Arab, Butler returned to Alexandria and after spending an enjoyable weekend in Cairo, where he was able to visit the pyramids at nearby Giza, Butler finally boarded the *HMT Devonshire*, returning home in August 1936 to a well-earned month's leave. [*'HMT' was the abbreviation for 'His Majesty's Troopship', not to be confused with 'HMS', which was the prefix for British warships.*]

SCARBOROUGH AND BULFORD

Butler returned from leave and after two months at Burniston Barracks, Scarborough, he was posted to 3rd Divisional Signals at Bulford, who were under-strength, having had to provide units of communication for the troubles in Palestine. The army was now beginning to become mechanised, and instead of horses pulling cable wagons, lorries were now used for cable laying. One man would sit behind the cable drum with a machine, to which was attached a steering wheel. One quick turn of this wheel and the cable would spew out in a big arc, allowing it to be thrown up into trees by the roadside. This was a completely new technique.

After a short spell at Dalditch Camp near Exmouth for manoeuvres with a brigade of mobile 9.2 guns, Butler was back in Bulford, arriving late one afternoon in June 1937: 'I unpacked my kit then made my bed. It was now time for the evening meal and I was ready for it. Lo and behold, my favourite meal, steak and kidney pie, followed by jam roll and custard, washed down with a pint of sweet tea – lovely! Next morning, I reported to the company office only to be marched off to the quartermaster's store and issued with tropical kit. "Where to this time?" I enquired. "Where did you go last time?" was the reply. "Egypt," I said. "Oh dear, much further than that – China I think," said the quartermaster. I stuffed everything into my kit bag and marched off to the medical room where I was duly injected against typhoid and cholera.'

With sore arms and loaded down with kit, Butler received one month's pay plus ration allowance, a total of £12 for him to enjoy on his 28 days' embarkation leave. He arrived home in Sheffield in time for tea, his mother very happy to have him home for a month. Butler was engaged to a girl called Bessie. Butler said, 'She started pushing me to get married. No way! One had to be 26 in the army to qualify for marriage allowance and I was only pushing up 20.' Nevertheless, Butler had a good time on leave, enjoying himself with Bessie. One day they went to Blackpool for the day with his cousin Vera and her young man, Jack Brown. Vera was the daughter of Butler's stepfather's brother. Butler said, 'We were only related by my mother's marriage; however, we four spent a lot of time together during my leave. Vera was to play a big part in my life later.'

1937 – THE JOURNEY TO HONG KONG

Butler's leave over, he returned to Bulford and not long after, set off for Southampton to board *HM Troopship Dunera*, bound for Hong Kong on her maiden voyage. Butler was equipped with full kit: two bags, one large, which went into the hold, and a smaller white one containing tropical clothing, which was to be retained during the voyage. Butler considered the *Dunera* to be a big improvement on previous troopships he had travelled on, the main 'luxury' being the air conditioning that was installed on each deck.

They sailed on the evening tide on 28 July 1937. After a rough passage through the English Channel, with the wind blowing at gale force, conditions became calmer once they reached the Atlantic.

Butler recalled the voyage:

'It was lovely and peaceful seeing different countries and people through the Mediterranean Sea to Port Said, then on through the Arabian Sea to Colombo, where we stayed for two days taking on supplies. The journey to Singapore was interesting but we were beginning to feel the heat. The hosepipes were frequently in use, set at an angle so the water was descending onto the deck like a giant shower – it was lovely to walk under it and cool off.'

After a two-day stay at Singapore, the *Dunera* left for Hong Kong. Having been on the high seas for 22 days, the troops wanted to get ashore. As they left Singapore, Butler remembered the breath-taking view, with Sumatra to the west and Borneo to the east. He told of his sighting of a swordfish: 'I remember one day sailing through the South China Sea. I was looking out to sea, and then looked down to see the bows ploughing through the water, and there, swimming very close alongside the ship was a swordfish. It must have been all of 10ft long and it carried on in this manner for quite some time.'

HONG KONG – 1937

Five days later Butler arrived in Hong Kong and after disembarking marched to Whitfield Barracks in Kowloon. There were three sections in the Hong Kong Signal Company: Headquarters Section, which encompassed administration and mainly clerical staff; Wireless Transmission Section (WT Section), comprising wireless telegraphy and switchboard operators; and Line Section, consisting of linesmen, who laid and maintained underground and overhead cables.

Butler belonged to the WT Section. His first job was in the school, brushing up on sending and receiving speeds, before doing duties in the signal office, communicating with the stations in Tientsin, Shanghai and Aldershot. He soon settled into the routine duties and found Hong Kong to be a fantastic place. He said, 'We were paid a flat rate of 1s 3d [*one shilling and three pence, which is about six pence in today's money*] to the Hong Kong dollar. That meant I drew 25 dollars per week, so I lived well. The food was good in Hong Kong and we had Chinese boys working in the barracks, who cleaned our shoes, took our washing to the laundry and made our beds. It was a good life for almost four years. Dreamland, China Emporium and The Lido were all dime-a-dance halls and I danced my way to heaven in all of them.'

When Butler arrived in Hong Kong, the Chinese had been at war with Japan for some time. The 1st Battalion Middlesex Regiment was stationed at Lo Wu on the border between Kowloon and the Chinese Mainland. Butler went out to Lo Wu several times; there was a wireless truck there providing communications.

In 1938 came the first war scare. An infantry brigade signal section was formed in which Butler was included. The section consisted of approximately 30 men, along with cable-laying trucks, wireless trucks, an Austin Seven for the section officer and a couple of dispatch riders. Their first big job was to lay 30 miles of cable in the 'New Territories' from Kowloon to the border. The job took two days, after which the men had to go back, lift the cable off the ground and tie it up in the trees by the side of the road.

'It was good fun climbing trees and tying up, but when we went back the next day, monkeys, who live in abundance in the woods in the New Territories, had been swinging on our cable, which was now hanging down to the ground. So, we had to start again, taking in the slack and making the spans shorter,' Bill said.

The war scare turned out to be a false alarm and normal routine was resumed. When the war in Europe did start, Butler's section was put on a war footing in Hong Kong but was not affected much. There was rationing, but otherwise life carried on as normal, except that when they went on guard duty they had live ammunition. In November 1941, two Canadian battalions arrived – the Winnipeg Grenadiers and the Royal Rifles of Canada.

THE BATTLE AND FALL OF HONG KONG – 1941

The battle of Hong Kong started on 7 December. Butler recalled:

'We were on the mainland at the start but retreated with the main battalions to the island of Hong Kong, providing communications for the Raj Rifles Indian units. The phone went early one morning. Corporal Scully answered it and I could tell by the conversation a W/T [*wireless telegraphy*] set was required on the mainland as nothing had been heard from the one we knew to be there, which was providing communications for the Indian battalion still there. I volunteered with Bill Bevan. We were driven down to the dockyard with our equipment and were to travel across to the mainland by launch. This was loaded up with bales of hay for the mules of the Hong

Kong Singapore Royal Artillery. It was fortunate for us that the hay was there because we were caught in crossfire and could hear the bullets thudding into the bales as we lay on the deck. We arrived intact, only to be dive-bombed as we unloaded our equipment. I well remember Bill Bevan's words: "Why didn't you keep your big mouth shut?"'

After reporting to Colonel Stewart, who asked them to set up their W/T radio set and contact HQ, they discovered that the W/T set they had gone to replace was in fact ok and in communication again. It had been off the air because the batteries had been overworked and needed to be recharged. Being surplus to requirements, Butler and Bevan got a lift back to the island, only to arrive to a huge shelling bombardment at Lai Moon [*actual spelling Lei Yue Mun*], both men fortunately managing to escape death or injury.

Butler arrived back at Victoria Barracks, and was told to proceed to Stanley Point, where the Royal Artillery were being heavily shelled, to provide secondary wireless communication in case the landlines were put out of action. This they did, making calls every 30 minutes [*to maintain contact in a rapidly changing battle situation*] until a message was received from GHQ to lay down their arms and surrender.

THE FALL OF HONG KONG

The day after the surrender the Japanese entered Stanley Fort, instructing the British to lay down their rifles and ammunition in lines on the parade ground. Butler remembers nothing eventful happening for several days, before one of the Japanese officers, who could speak English, came up to his group during morning roll call and asked each of them in turn whether they could drive. They all could, so they were marched away to where the vehicles had been parked on one side of the parade ground. They were each allotted a truck or lorry and told to follow the vehicle that contained the Japanese officer. Butler continued:

'We went down to the dockyard and drove on to a barge that had been adapted as a vehicular ferry. We were taken across the harbour to Kowloon, from where we drove through the New Territories to La Wu and across into China. I do not know how far we actually went into China, but we drove all day, stopping once for a meal of rice and vegetables. We arrived at our destination and were loaded up with cases and packages, which we were told were medical supplies. We slept in a hut that night and next day returned to Kowloon by the same route. We were taken to a hotel where we stayed, along with the Japanese soldiers, for about a week. We were then taken to Shamshuipo Camp, where a large number of British troops were prisoners of war. Every morning we would march down the parade ground for '*tenko*' (roll call), and the same in the evening to the strains of military music played by the band of the Middlesex Regiment. If we had a fag issue, or meat was in the stew for tea [*an English term for dinnertime*], everyone would step lively to the tune of "Happy Days are Here Again!"

Every unit had their own cookhouse; oil drums were cut in half to make cooking vessels. Butler was put in the cookhouse along with Eddie Lander. Using bricks from broken down buildings together with some clay, they built an oven. If there was a flour issue they would make some bread cakes. Someone managed to obtain two cakes of yeast. These were put into a bathtub, flour and sugar added, which fermented overnight and from then on, they had a constant supply of yeast. 'I used to go and drink a mug full of yeast every day,' Butler recollected. 'This was full of vitamin B and I am sure this helped prevent me suffering from beriberi.'

Butler's worst experience at Shamshuipo Camp was when he caught dysentery, spending all night in the toilet with a blanket around him. In the morning when he reported sick to Dr Rodrigues, he was told: 'We have nothing, only this,' whereupon the doctor pointed to a couple of large tins, one of which was cut open. It was Kieselguhr (kee-sel-gar), a German product, a white sand, used for filtering reservoir beds.[36] 'That is the only hope you have got!' he said, so Butler started shoving handfuls into his mouth and washing it down with boiled water.

Butler started a routine of two tablespoons of Kieselguhr every hour, washed down with water – and survived. He was out of the hospital in five days but in a very weakened condition, down from 10 stone 8 lb to 9 stone. Within a few months his weight was back up to 9 stone 10 lb, attributable in part, no doubt, to Butler's resourcefulness. He recounted:

'One day when I was stood at the cookhouse door, I saw this hand barrow being pulled by four POWs, loaded with sacks of flour, with a Japanese sentry marching in front. I knew it would pass where I was stood and that one of the sacks was unsafe and I knew it would fall off. I shouted to Topper (Signalman

---

36 Kieselguhr is actually 'diatomaceous earth', a soft, fine, naturally occurring white powder. It is often used as a filtration aid, amongst other things.

Toppliff) to stand behind me to catch something. As the end of the barrow drew level I reached out, grabbed the sack and threw it into the waiting arms of Topper. That night for tea, everyone in the Signals Mess had a whacking great dumpling with his bowl of rice.'

THE *LISBON MARU*

The *Lisbon Maru*, a Japanese transport ship, left Hong Kong on 27 September 1942 with 1,816 prisoners of war and some Japanese troops aboard. The prisoners, Butler among them, were accommodated in three holds. No. 1 hold forward consisted of Royal Navy men and a few troops; No. 2 hold amidships consisted of 1,150 officers and men of the 2nd Battalion Royal Scots, 1st Battalion Middlesex Regiment, the Royal Corps of Signals (to which Butler belonged), Royal Engineers and a few Artillery (under the command of Lieutenant Colonel H.W.M. Stewart); and No. 3 hold, adjoining No. 2, consisted of Royal Artillery personnel. The ship was armed with guns fore and aft and had a small armed force for custody of the prisoners.

Butler remembered the first few days as uneventful. The weather was good, although there were complaints about the lack of exercise and time on deck, difficulties over drawing water and a lack of sufficient latrine accommodation. The food was good, and cigarettes were issued.

Shortly after 7am on 1 October an explosion shook the ship, coming from the stern. Butler recalled the Japanese troops in pandemonium and both guns came into action. The prisoners were ordered to remain below.

In No. 2 hold the men were uncertain about exactly what had happened; the engines had stopped but there was no apparent list. The men remained calm at their places and joked about rescue at sea. After a short time, the firing ceased and the noise on deck quietened. The men began to think about breakfast, which, however, was not forthcoming and in fact no further food was issued on the *Lisbon Maru*. The day dragged on and a Japanese plane circled overhead, but that provided the only relief. There was much difficulty over the calls of nature, as the latrines were on deck and at first no receptacles of any sort were available in the holds. As many men were suffering from diarrhoea, conditions became rapidly unbearable. Finally, after repeated requests, the Japanese passed down two old petrol cans for 1,150 men, but no one was permitted to go on deck. It was impossible to empty them, and they were soon overflowing. There was also an acute shortage of water. The Japanese finally passed down two buckets of soiled water, but it was almost undrinkable.

At 7.30pm a ship came alongside. It seemed to Butler and the other prisoners that she tried to take the *Lisbon Maru* in tow but failed. Immediately afterwards the Japanese troops were seen to embark on the rescue ship and at this point the holds were closed and battened down. Tarpaulins were secured over the hatches, leaving the men in pitch darkness and with no ventilation. Soon afterwards the rescue ship was heard to cast off and leave the Lisbon Maru. It became obvious that all was not well. No. 3 hold got in touch with Colonel Stewart by tapping Morse code on the bulkhead to say that they were manning pumps but without much success. No. 1 hold reported that they were battened down, and the heat was bad.

As time went on conditions grew worse. An ominous creaking was heard, as if the ship's ribs were being squeezed, and there was a continuous banging, which seemed to come from loose objects floating in the flooded compartments. The heat in Butler's hold was stifling and everyone was having great difficulty with the latrine situation. No. 1 hold reported that one man had died, and several men had collapsed at the pumps in No. 3 hold for want of air.

Colonel Stewart attempted repeatedly to get in touch with the Japanese, and Lieutenant Potter of the St. John's Ambulance, a Japanese interpreter, spoke to the armed sentries mounted at the companionway, but they refused to pass on any messages. The ship was now listing considerably, and it seemed as if she would sink with the prisoners battened down in her holds. 'Like rats,' said Butler.

At about 8.30 am the following morning the ship gave a perceptible lurch. Blankets and personal belongings slid to the side of the ship and water poured into the hold. Colonel Stewart continued to ask the guards to uncover the hatches but was told that they could not be removed until midday. At 9.00 am the Colonel realised that it was only a matter of minutes before the ship sank and gave the order for the hold to be broken. Lieutenant Howell, of the Signals Corps, armed with a butcher's knife, cut open the covers and followed by a few men, got onto the deck. In spite of being shot at and one or two men being hit, including Lieutenant Potter, who was killed, Howell opened up an exit sufficient for the remainder of the men to leave the hold.

The sea began to pour into the holds as the men climbed out and many of them were washed back into the bottom of the hold. Butler described the escape:

'Although our first feeling on reaching deck was one of relief at the fresh air and daylight, and at the presence of ships and land within sight, our troubles were by no means over. Many of the men did not immediately leave the ship when the order was given, some having no lifebelts, and others appeared utterly unconcerned at the danger – the ship had come to rest on a sandbank with its bows in the air. Many of the men went down with the ship when it made its final plunge.

'I saw John Scully walking about with his life belt unfastened. He was very weak, having had a bad dose of dysentery. I went to him and fastened his life belt properly, then went to help put some of the battens over the side so we would have something to hold on to when we left the ship. I turned round to help John and he was nowhere to be seen. I never saw him again. Vernon Talks was very reluctant to go over the side because he could not swim. I took off my lifebelt and put it on him, and helped him over the side, then followed him.' [*The name 'Talks' seems very unusual but on checking with recorded lists of dead & survivors I have found this to be correct. His rank was private and his army number was 4626315. He died in 1943.*]

The order was given to abandon ship. The sea was soon dotted with heads. Some men were swimming, some holding onto driftwood, the wooden latrines, ladders or anything that would float, making for a group of small patrol vessels that were lying a few miles off or to some islands about eight miles away.

Most of those who could swim made for the Japanese ships, expecting to be taken aboard at once. They were however shot at in the water and knocked off ropes as they tried to clamber aboard. The Japanese drove the ships to wherever there were groups of men in the water, upsetting men on rafts and threatening them with the propellers. Butler, when he saw what was happening, swam for the islands, finally being picked up by a Chinese sampan about half a mile from land.

It was not until after midday that the Japanese appeared to alter their approach and allow those who had the strength to do so to climb up the ropes hanging from the ships. By this time however, many had started for the islands or been drowned. On seeing that men were being taken aboard the ships, several turned back and were eventually successful in reaching the boats and in dragging themselves aboard. Those swimming for the islands made steady progress. But as they approached, two dangers became apparent. The first was a very strong cross-current, which swept the weaker swimmers past the shore and out to sea, and the second an exceptionally steep and rocky coastline, which made landing very difficult. Though many reached the islands, comparatively few managed to land. The majority of those who did, Butler among them, owe their lives to the Chinese fishermen who picked them up out of the water.

An officer who was swept out to sea and not rescued until nearly midnight stated that hundreds of bodies floated past him. Those who succeeded in landing on the island received a warm welcome from the Chinese, who fed and clothed them as best they could, and did all that their limited means would allow to make those rescued feel comfortable. They even offered to assist would-be escapees and in fact, succeeded in getting at least one prisoner to freedom. The large numbers and the weakened condition of the majority precluded any large-scale attempt at escape.

On 3–4 October survivors were collected and transferred from the islands to the two Japanese patrol ships that remained in the vicinity. Conditions became more and more crowded as additional men were taken aboard until, eventually, there was scarcely room on deck to sit down, let alone stretch their legs. Nearly all of them, moreover, were scantily clad and the nights were bitterly cold. Under these conditions sleep was impossible and the nights that followed the rescue were a nightmare. More than one man died of exposure and was buried at sea.

The ships were not equipped for these large numbers and the only food provided was an issue, twice daily, of two biscuits and a cigarette tin of warm powdered milk. After two days during which they had no other food at all, their hunger became overpowering. On 5 October the survivors were landed at Woosung.[37] Of the 1,816 that had embarked on the *Lisbon Maru*, only 900 remained.

TO JAPAN AND THE POW CAMP

After landing at Woosung, Butler was unwell for a week, suffering from diarrhoea brought on by the long period swimming in the China Sea. He was to recover on board a Japanese cargo vessel as they left, bound for he knew not where.

Butler arrived in Osaka, Japan, six days later. As he walked down the gangway two men in white overalls were at the bottom with disinfectant

---

37   Woosung is Wusong, an area of Shanghai.

sprays. As each man stepped off the gangway he was sprayed from neck to toe. 'I looked around as they sprayed me and thought, how very considerate of them – they do not wish me to catch any disease from this dirty hole, because not twenty yards from me, was a Japanese workman urinating in the gutter!'

Butler was then taken to what was to be his home for the next two years. It was a two-storey wooden building. The ground floor consisted of the guard room, stores, two rooms for accommodation and toilets; upstairs was one big room. The sleeping accommodation comprised two tiers of bunks in a hut, accommodating about 80 men on the top and 80 men on the bottom.

Butler soon settled into his new quarters, wondering what was to come. It was not long before he discovered they were to be employed in various jobs. Some went to work in the shipyards, some on the docks unloading ships, others into the foundries. Butler, along with approximately 30 other prisoners, went to work for Nagatani, a subsidiary of Mitsubishi, located on the other side of the harbour.

Butler fared better than some POWs in as much as he was working on the docks, loading and unloading ships and barges, so was able to steal tins of salmon, crab and other tinned food, plus rice and sugar. Some of his fellow prisoners were employed in the foundries. Butler explained: 'We would supply them with food and they would make us keys to open warehouses with. This is how we managed it – one of the dockyard policemen had had a restaurant in Kobe before the war and spoke a fair amount of English. He had keys to the warehouses and would unlock the one in which we were going to work and open the doors. He would then stand against the door until we had finished. One thing in our favour was that he always left the key in the lock, so one of our men would engage him in conversation whilst the other took an impression of the key on a tablet of soap behind his back. This would be passed on to one of the foundry workers who would make us the key, so we no longer had to pick the locks!'

Butler remembered one occasion where he picked a lock and entered a warehouse, looking for some cloth to make bags for stealing sugar and rice with. All that was in the warehouse was pre-war bales of silk stockings and underclothes, but Butler was determined not to return empty-handed, so he took about 10 pairs of stockings and six pairs of French knickers. As prisoners were usually searched before being allowed back in the camp, Butler thought the best way to get these in would be to wear them. 'I put them on. I also put a small bag of sugar on my arm. This I covered by hanging my raincoat over my arm. I also filled my hat lining with sugar. I had got in with this many times before.'

Butler and his party were marched back to camp and brought to a halt outside. The NCO in charge of the guard came down the steps with the Japanese interpreter and the usual search commenced. Butler got the sugar through without discovery – he had made it! But then to his dismay a shout went up: something had been discovered. He explained, 'I had to do something, so the brain went into overdrive. If we had to strip, I was going to look a right clown peeling off the stockings and knickers. I decided to surrender my bag of sugar and handed it to the NCO, who immediately belted me on the back of the neck with it. I staggered forward with the blow – two and a half pounds of sugar make a good cosh! Then I was marched inside to the guardroom. Everyone outside had to strip, except me and the twit who had spoilt it all! When they found nothing more, everyone was dismissed and went into camp.

'The buildings in Osaka are mostly wood. I believe it is in the earthquake zone. The rooms are partitioned off by sliding doors that run on a steel rail let into the floor about a quarter inch in diameter. The two of us had to kneel on this rail near the front of the guardroom. Every officer who carried a sword, knowing we were there for punishment, would unclip the sword in the scabbard and belt us with the flat of the blade, across the back shoulders and sometimes the head. I did not mind the head so much because my hat was packed with sugar between the outer cover and the lining!

'After four hours we were allowed to crawl back to our rooms. I say crawl because after kneeling for four hours on a quarter inch rail, it is not possible to straighten your knees for quite a while. We had also missed our evening meal. The main thing to me was I had beaten them – I had still got one and a half pounds of sugar in my hat and 10 pairs of stockings and six pairs of French knickers into the camp.'

On one occasion, Butler had a 'near miss' – he caught bronchial pneumonia and was so ill that he went into a coma. He remembers being carried on a stretcher by Joe Hogan and Arnold Swaine, his two roommates, but a little after that, he came round in the hospital with the doctor in attendance, an American Air Force surgeon. He was informed that he had been in a coma for three days and would not have seen the light of day again, but fortune smiled on him. A Japanese sergeant major had developed appendicitis. Whilst the Japanese had a small medical unit in the camp, they had no one capable of performing an operation, so they appealed to the British surgeon who said he had no equipment. The Japanese said that they had plenty and opened a store opposite the hospital that was full to the roof with British, American and Canadian Red Cross supplies, taken from the Philippines, Hong Kong and Singapore. The surgeon said, 'Let me have half an hour and three of my men in this store, then I will operate on your man.' To which they agreed. So, after dealing with the removal of the Japanese sergeant major's appendix, the surgeon turned to his patients and began administering drugs that were not available before. Butler was a beneficiary, survived and returned to work a few days later.

One day Butler was unloading sugar captured from the Philippines, using a barrow and wheeling bags from the barge on the jetty to the warehouse where other POWs were stacking it. After many trips it was approaching lunchtime, so Butler parked his barrow and went into the shack where they took their meals. Jimmy McCann, who was the tea boy for the day, had just finished putting the 'bentos' (Japanese term for packed lunches) on the table and was starting to pour out the tea into the bowls. He had poured out about 10 or 12 bowlfuls as Butler entered and stood about two feet away from the end of the table. Then all the tea in the bowls began to slop over. Jimmy shouted to Butler to stop knocking the table. 'I am not near the bloody table!' replied Butler and then both realised something was wrong. They went outside, and the Japanese were running from the offices and the warehouses, making straight for the railway lines and sitting on them. It was Butler's first experience of an earthquake. 'It is very frightening because you don't know where it will come from next. It is everywhere underneath you.'

Butler recalled an incident at the camp involving two Naval ratings POWs. One was a Cockney called Alexander. His mate was a Liverpudlian[38] called Levi. At this time the Americans were getting closer to Japan. Now they had airfields near enough to raid mainland Japan:

'One day we had a raid by B29 bombers, which did substantial damage. On the evening roll call the Japanese duty officer came in and gave the order to "number",[39] which we did. On arriving at number 29 he called a halt, then told the sentry who accompanied him to escort No. 29 outside, who happened to be Alexander. The duty officer followed them, failing to carry on with the roll call. We all wondered what had happened. We found out later that this

---

38 A Liverpudlian is a person from Liverpool in the UK.
39 To 'number' was the common way the Japanese checked all the POWs were still in camp. Each person called out his number in Japanese.

was the case in each room (hut) – number 29 was marched out. We all settled down to sleep. At about midnight we were woken by a commotion. There was Alexander straddled across Levi giving him a belting. When we asked what all the noise was about, Alexander calmly said, "We are mates, and we share everything, I am just giving him half of what I have just had!" That was the spirit that kept a lot of us alive.' The reason why the Japanese were punishing prisoners with the number 29 was because the US bombers were the Boeing B29.

He continued: 'The Japanese were losing the war. "Jimmy Doolittle"[40] (a US bombing raid) paid us a visit and using incendiaries burnt out one third of Osaka, including the POW camp.' Fortunately, the prisoners were all at work. Following the raid, the POWs were moved to a disused concrete warehouse where they remained until the end of the war. The harbour had been badly hit during the raid, so they could not go across the bay to Nakatani's to work. The Japanese paraded the prisoners outside and told them they were going to clean up the areas the Americans had bombed. Butler was in a party of about 40 who were marched off to a bombed area. They were set to work and soon discovered sacks of Demerara sugar and drums of 100 per cent proof alcohol. Butler comments, 'It did not take long for "Scrooge" McElroy and Mick Murphy to "acquire" these "ingredients" before they were producing very potent rum! By 3 am the six Japanese guards were trying to assemble a very rum-sodden mob into two lines to march back to camp. That night news came that Saipan (about 1,500 miles from Japan in the Western Pacific) had fallen and that Iwo Jima and Okinawa were in Allied hands.' This news must have reached Butler and his fellow POWs in about June 1945.

END OF THE WAR IN JAPAN

When the bomb was dropped on Hiroshima (on Monday, 6 August 1945, at 8:15 am) Butler 'knew something had happened but did not know what.' When the second bomb was dropped on Nagasaki, news of what had happened was broadcast on the camp radio the same night and it became clear that the

---

40 'Jimmy Doolittle' was the name given to the American Air Force bombing raids over Japan in the earlier part of the war – at the time they were not designed as part of an invasion but simply to boost morale at home in the USA, and also to prove to the Japanese that their homeland was vulnerable to attack. Lieutenant Colonel Doolittle planned these first retaliatory air raids.

war was coming to an end. 'We heard the distant rumbling of gunfire, this we found out afterwards was the battleship *HMS King George V*, plus other British and Allied heavy ships, laying down barrages on the Japanese mainland prior to assault and landing.'

Butler's most vivid memory of that time is when American and British planes flew over at tree-top height, firing at trains moving freight from the shipyards and the docks:

'Bobby Phillips of the Middlesex Regiment, who was one of our work party, climbed on top of a huge stack of cork, took off his white vest and waved it at the planes, one of which turned and swooped down low over Nakatani. We could clearly see the pilot and his mate sat behind him, the cowling was pushed back, and they waved to us – it was a wonderful feeling. The planes continued throughout the day. We could see them attacking different areas of Osaka and Kobe without any retaliation. The icing on the cake came at about 3 pm when an aircraft with the two men who had waved at us flew over again. The man in the rear held a white bag over his head. They circled round, came down low and threw this bag into the clear area near the jetty. We ran and picked it up. It was a naval pillow case – inside it was a loaf of bread, a tin of butter, a tin of jam, a tin of luncheon meat, two bars of chocolate, a tin of Nestle's milk and a packet of tea. But best of all, written on the back of an envelope it said, "With the compliments of the crew of the *HMS Indefatigable* – it won't be long now boys." I cannot describe my feelings; really it was mixed elation and a feeling of foreboding because we were [*still*] on Japanese soil.'

Butler and the work party returned to camp and were told the next day would be a holiday; in fact, they had done their last day's work in Japan as POWs. That night news was received on the radio that the war was over. Japan had surrendered.

When the POWs had to parade for *tenko*, the men had to call their number in Japanese. The morning after the surrender the Scottish sergeant major in charge (Butler refers to him as 'Mac') called the men to attention, then without any hesitation said, 'The war is over, you are now back in the British Army, so you will number in English.' The Japanese camp commandant came out of the guardroom and called a halt. Through the interpreter he asked why the men were numbering in English, to which Mac replied, 'The war is over, and we have won. Japan has surrendered, we have heard it on the radio.' In fact, the camp commandant was under the impression that it was a truce but was later instructed, after the second bomb had been dropped on Nagasaki, that Japan had surrendered. The commandant then asked to see the radio and on seeing it he was furious and kicked it all around the compound.

Mac told the interpreter that now the war was over, European food was wanted, not rice and beans, and would he convey his request to the camp commandant. The next day two lorries entered the compound, one loaded up with sacks of rice, the other with courgettes. Mac saw these and went looking for the interpreter. After giving the order to unload the lorries Mac told 'Tiny' Wilson – a big man who was a gunner in the Royal Artillery – to get behind the wheel of the first vehicle, which he did, chucking the Japanese driver out without ceremony. Mac instructed about six or eight other POWs to climb in the back, then turned round and asked Butler if he could drive. Since he could, he jumped behind the wheel of the other lorry (the Japanese driver had not waited and was on his way out of the gates!). After taking some guns and ammunition from the guardroom (the guards had all disappeared) and putting a sergeant in charge with instructions to keep the remainder of the POWs within the compound, Mac climbed into the first vehicle with Tiny and instructed Butler to follow.

Butler recalled, 'We left the compound, turning right to go over the bridge to make our way to the docks where we knew that there were stores taken from the Philippines, Singapore, Hong Kong and Java … We came back a few hours later – we had tinned sausages, tinned oranges, powdered milk, several sacks of potatoes, a 280-lb. barrel of lard, cigarettes, chocolate, ground coffee, tomatoes and fresh fruit. Immediately everyone set to, opening tins, peeling potatoes – within an hour we were all settling down to a meal consisting of sausage and chips, followed by oranges in a thick cream made up with the powdered milk. When we were half way through the dessert, we heard a noise in the roadway. On investigating, lo and behold, Scrooge McElroy, Pat Murphy and another POW were each rolling a barrel of beer down the road. Needless to say, the meal was rounded off beautifully. Not without its consequences the following morning – the toilets were in constant use! However, we all survived.'

The following day Butler, accompanied by McElroy and Pat Murphy, took the lorry and went to the brewery McElroy had found. Before they left they loaded up about ten sacks of rice that had been brought in by the Japanese. On arrival at the brewery they found the gates open and drove straight in. They tried to tell the Japanese at the brewery that bottled beer was wanted but were not very successful until they showed them the sacks of rice and said they would trade rice for beer. This clinched the deal, and they traded five sacks (half a ton) of rice for 20 cases of beer.

ALLIED RELIEF FROM THE AIR

That afternoon, back at the warehouse that was their home, B29 planes were spotted flying around. After a while it was surmised that they were looking for POW camps. Butler recalled trying to get the pilots' attention:

'We took the mirror from the door of an old wardrobe we found and went on to the roof. Some of the men laid out strips of cloth on the flat roof to make "POW". We tried to catch the sun on the mirror to reflect onto the plane's cockpit. After about ten minutes we managed to attract the attention of one plane, which circled round and flew over our home at about 1,000 ft. – he had found us. The plane made one circuit and flew low over the wood yard, dropping a sheaf of leaflets. We dashed around picking up the leaflets, which had a message stating that an airdrop would take place the following day into the wood yard area, consisting of clothing, boots, food and medical aid.'

The next day the POWs were on the roof of the warehouse once more, eagerly awaiting the planes. Butler's feelings were mixed: 'I knew that I was going to make it back home but was apprehensive because I was still on Japanese soil, even though the Japanese had surrendered.' The roar of the engines of a B29 bomber, accompanied by an escort of two fighter planes, brought Butler and his comrades down from the roof. They went down into the compound to be greeted by a sight that still lives in his memory: 'Blue, red and white parachutes were raining down, drifting over the wood yard; suspended under the 'chutes were drums, boxes and sacks. When they had landed we ran and collected these goodies from heaven – courtesy of the US Air Force.'

These 'goodies' turned out to be clothing (US army shirts, socks, trousers, underclothes, towels, waterproof jackets, and jungle boots) as well as food (K. Rations plus bully beef, spam, powdered milk, chocolate, coffee and biscuits). In addition, there were medical goods – field dressings, sulpha powder, bandages, and a lot of vitamin tablets with instructions on how to medicate.

Things settled down in the camp, with the men having pretty much all they needed and feeling reassured that the Allies now knew where their camp was. The next day in the wood yard, someone sighted a water buffalo. With visions of roast beef, some of the men, armed with sticks and ropes made into lassos, chased it round the alleys until finally it was cornered. Then it turned, took a good look at them, and charged! Everybody scattered, trying to get away from the formidable horns. It made its way to the road and escaped. Afterwards

McElroy wondered why no one had shot it. 'No one thought about the guns we had from the guard room,' said Butler.

RELIEF OF OTHER POW CAMPS

Sometime later Butler and the other men from the camp all moved to the New Osaka Hotel. They obtained a radio transmitter and receiver, contacted the *HMS King George V* in Tokyo Bay and sent them the names, regimental numbers and unit of everyone in the camp. They were told a recovery team was on its way and arrangements were made to accommodate the recovery team in the hotel. An office was set up and transport was commandeered from the police station. Butler remembers claiming a Scott Squirrel motorbike (English, made in Yorkshire) from a yard and bringing it back to the hotel. 'We were building up quite a transport section!' When the recovery team, led by Major Mitchell, arrived by train, they were met and brought back to the hotel. The following day volunteers were requested to remain behind and help find the other camps in the area. Butler readily volunteered, as did 39 others. The rest of the men were on their way home. Butler worked as a driver: if a car or lorry was needed by any of the recovery team they would go and say what they wanted, and one of the drivers would take them. Dressed in American khaki drill, with no insignias denoting a unit, they were accepted by everyone as US recovery members. Butler recalls one mission at this time:

'I was approached by an Australian officer of the team about a vehicle to go to the castle [*Osaka Castle was the summer holiday residence of the reigning Japanese emperor*]. He told me it was believed arms were at the castle and he had to corroborate if this was true or not. So off we went in a truck we had. The entrance to the castle was a long driveway with four arches at intervals. On the approach to the first archway I noticed a sentry. As we went through the arch I saw it was a Japanese soldier. I stopped the truck about 15 yards past the arch. I said to the officer with me, "I won't be long," and walked back to the sentry, calling him to attention. "Why did you not salute me?" I said. The formal salute is to bow. He began to stammer an excuse. I immediately slapped him hard across the face, which is normal practice in the Japanese Army. I knew because I had been belted a few times during my captivity. I then put my face up to about 3 inches from his face and said, "See this face, remember it well and every time you see it '*ichirei*'!" (pronounced "kerry!" this means "salute" or "bow"). At this point the Australian officer left the truck and walked towards us. He had been observing what was happening through the wing mirror. He said to me, "What was that all about?" I replied, "I have been bowing to these bastards for four years – now they bow to me!" He smiled and said, "Carry on, I am enjoying this." "So am I!" was my reply. This happened at all four arches. When we arrived at the castle entrance I felt like I had won the pools, a feeling of elation that takes a lot of explaining. From that moment on I knew that I was going to see my family again.'

After loading the pistols and ammunition that were found at the castle on to the truck, Butler returned to the Osaka Hotel. Later that evening all the transport section were swaggering about, each with a holstered gun at the waist, Butler also managing to get hold of about 40 rounds of ammunition.

Each day the 'recovery' staff were driven wherever they wanted to go; the objective was to find POW camps and get the men out of Japan:

'We worked our butts off during the day, but at night we relaxed. I achieved my ambition one night. We used to go to the brewery and fetch lorryloads of bottled beer back, so we had plenty to drink. I fetched a lorryload back one lunchtime and took about four cases up to the room I shared with George Kim, a Naval POW. George came into the room at about 4 pm and remarked about the smell. He said, "It smells like a bloody brewery in here!" I shouted from the bathroom, "You would think it was if you were in here!" On entering the bathroom George opened his eyes wide but remained silent. There was I, laid back in the bath full of beer doing what I had always dreamed of – bathing in beer!'

Butler and his mate Jimmy McCann wrote a poem, which 'explains a lot' about what they were doing at that time:

> The days are over of rice and stew,
> we're going to drive for the Yank's H.Q.
> Pack your bags, leave your gal,
> move to the New Osaka Hotel.
> Up to the Cop Shop we go hot foot,
> draw charcoal cars all covered in soot.
> Petrol cars are total wrecks.
> Here we come boys, clear the decks!
> To the station to meet the train,
> we wait and wait but wait in vain.

We wish the Yanks to bathe in gore,
to the hotel, sleep on the floor.
Out next morning go the cars,
all the drivers chew Mars bars.
At the station, single rank,
all eyes open for a Yank.

THE LONG JOURNEY HOME

On 15 September the work was completed and Butler and the other volunteers who had remained behind were told that they would be on their way home in two days. On 15 September they left Osaka by train, bound for Yokohama, arriving that evening. They saw for the first time in almost four years members of the US Women's Army Corps (WAC), who helped them with their luggage and escorted the men to dinner, one on either side. 'It was fabulous,' remembered Butler. 'It was about 1 am when we went to bed. The following day we marched on the parade ground, each man individually was introduced, and shook hands with Lt. Gen. Eichelberger, Commanding Officer of the American Eighth Army, who presented each man with a letter which was as follows:

> Headquarters Eighth Army
> United States Army
> Office of the Commanding General

20th September 1945

To Sig. Butler, William Alfred, R.C.S.

As Commander of the United States Eighth Army it is my privilege to extend to you the heartfelt thanks of your American Allies for the splendid spirit of generosity and unselfishness you have displayed these past two weeks.

In volunteering to remain in your prison camp to assist in the liberation of your comrades, you have proven again that the strength of the United Nations is built on that most solid of foundations - the fellowship of men.

We of the Eighth Army are proud to be your liberators. We congratulate you on your newly gained freedom and wish for you the best of good luck, good health and happiness in the years to come.

Most sincerely yours,
R. Eichelburger

Lt. General U.S.A Commanding

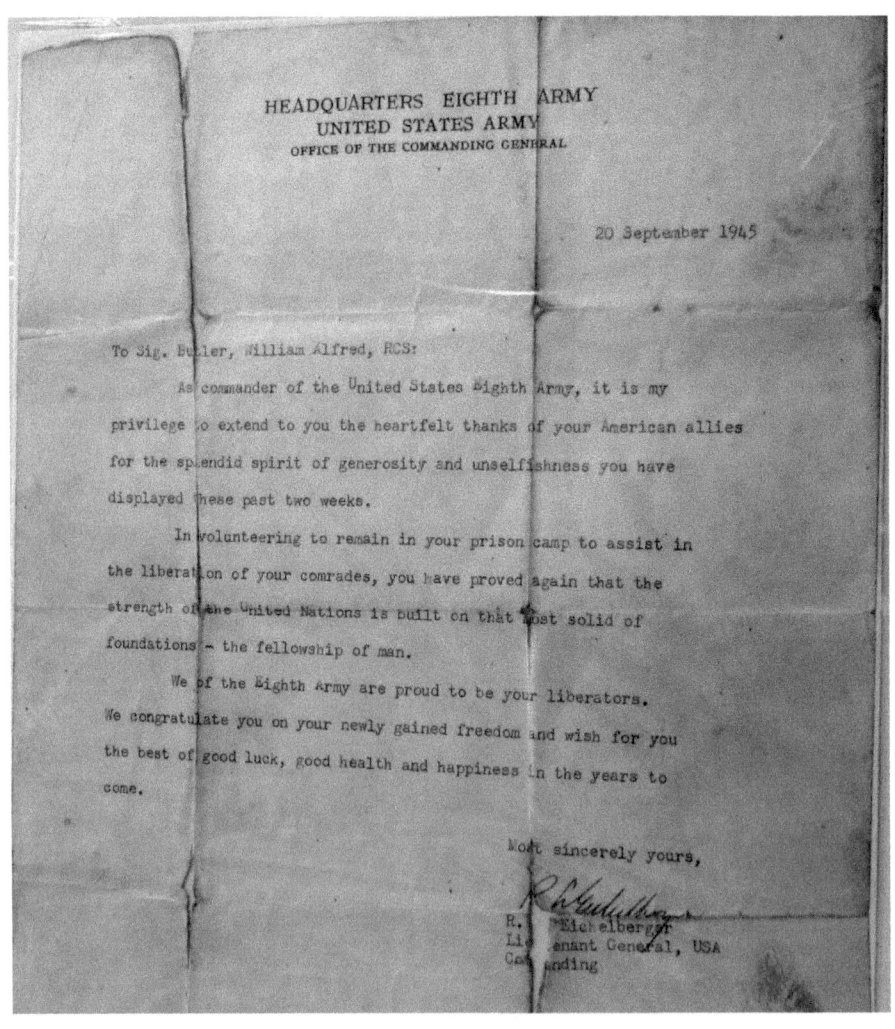

Figure 5.5 Letter from Lt. Gen. Eichelberger.

After the presentation they went to the dining room where there was beer to drink and time was spent talking to the WACs and nurses. After that Butler went by truck to the airfield where B29 and B25 bombers were waiting to take the men on the first stage of the journey home. It had been eight years since Butler had seen his home; 'I began to wonder what it would be like,' he said.

They travelled in the bomb bays of the planes, fitted out with wooden catwalks, each man clipped to a parachute harness. They could move about and look through the Perspex windows at the wide expanse of the Pacific Ocean below them.

After a few hours they landed at Okinawa and spent the night in the US Army Air Corps barracks. The weather turned bad, with heavy rain and strong winds, so the men were grounded. On 25 September they were woken early, dressed and given a breakfast of pancakes, bacon and eggs with plenty of coffee, then taken down to the airfield where they once more climbed into the planes. 'This was a thrilling moment for all of us, knowing we were going away from the area where so much fighting had taken place, and moving another step nearer to our homeland.'

FLIGHT FROM JAPAN TO THE PHILIPPINES

Butler remembered, 'We took off from Okinawa. The first plane heading up the runway could not take off. At the end of the runway was a 100ft drop, so he veered to the right and the plane ran into a bank. I found out later that two of the men of the Hong Kong Signal Company were killed in that crash, Red Harrington and Signalman Price. Red had been my roommate in the Old Central British School in Kowloon. To have survived the war, and as a POW, then to die in this manner on the way home was tragic.'

Butler was in the third plane to take off and saw the wrecked plane with the ambulances and rescue teams, so it was with both a sigh of relief and a heavy heart that he felt the plane lift off and soar away. That afternoon they landed at Clark Field, Manila in the Philippines and from there were taken to a transit camp where they were to spend the night.

The following morning after breakfast they were transferred to the 5th Replacement Camp, 14 miles from Manila Town, a large camp with plenty of recreational facilities.

After breakfast the next day, 28 September 1945, Butler was taken to a medical centre where he was to undergo a very rigorous medical examination by ten medical examiners, each one a specialist. 'We went to each one in turn, arriving at the end in a room where there was a team of American, British and Australian nurses waiting to inoculate and vaccinate each one of us. We were then issued with more clothing and other requisites and told we would have to relax and wait for the boat to take us on the next leg of our journey home.'

JOURNEY HOME

The rest of Butler's journey home is detailed in the diary he kept at the time:

Sept. 29th – I awoke this morning, washed, shaved and dressed, went to breakfast. The food was good and plentiful. I was putting on weight – when released I was 7 stone, 2 lb., now I was approaching 9 stone and felt good. This feeling no doubt was due to the fact I was on my way home after 8 years away. I sat down and wrote letters home.

Sept. 30th – The next day I went into Manila Town which had been heavily damaged but was beginning to recover. Lots of rebuilding was in progress. I came across a jeweller's shop and bought a jade brooch in the form of a V for Victory, but to my mind this meant Vera. I returned to camp that night and went to the cinema and saw *The Sullivans* (*The Fighting Sullivans*), a war film about a family of that name.

Oct. 1st – I awoke to the sound of heavy rain – it rained all day. We were paid 40 pesos (£5). Now I was beginning to become a bit frustrated, the waiting was affecting us all. We were wanting to begin the next leg of our journey home.

Oct. 2nd – The weather was beginning to deteriorate. Winds were getting stronger and we were all beginning to be apprehensive, wondering if a typhoon was on its way. That night I went to our local cinema and saw Judy Garland in *The Clock*.

Oct. 3rd – This morning when I awoke and saw the date, October 3rd. I realised that I had been a serving member of His Majesty's Forces for 12 years, and was still waiting for a boat to take me home. I had served my time, 8 years, and four years reserve, which was what I had signed on for.

Oct. 4th – The weather had improved this morning and the sun was beginning to show itself through the clouds. This was the only good thing about today because no boat had arrived to allow us to be on our way.

Oct. 5th – Alf had been informed that his wife was in Australia, so was moved to another camp to proceed to join her. We went to the PX [*the canteen*] where doughnuts and coffee were available all day. One just had to help yourself. I sat down after helping myself with one or two ex. POWs, naval ratings. After a few minutes a chap entered the PX; I noticed he was dressed in khaki drill shirt and shorts with the Air Force insignia of wings on his left breast, but a naval cap with gold braid on the peak. I thought, 'Who is he?' One of the naval ratings turned and immediately called us all to attention, saluting as he did so. He had previously served under Lord Louis Mountbatten – who put out both his arms and indicated that we sit down and relax. He then helped himself to coffee and doughnuts and joined us. Lord Louis wanted to know all about us, to what branch of the service we belonged, our unit where we served, and where we had been held as POWs. That evening we went to the local cinema to see *Back to Bataan*, but before the film started, Lord Louis Mountbatten and his wife Edwina, who was a ranking member of the Red Cross, came on to the stage. They asked us if we had any questions we would like to ask.

It was amazing, we were asking questions naturally about our homes, and had they been bombed. Lady Mountbatten knew every district in every town that had been bombed because she had visited them. I remember one question she was asked was, 'What is the beer like?' Her reply was, 'Great, and it is only a bob[41] a pint!' When the picture started, they both came down and joined us, drinking cans of beer with us. It was a great morale booster and eased the pressure of waiting for the boat.

Oct. 6th – No news of the boat yet, still lots of rumours. Went to the local cinema – saw Barbara Stanwyck in *My Reputation*.

---

41   A 'bob' was slang for a shilling in pre-decimalised currency. One shilling is equivalent to 5p

Oct. 7th – The same as yesterday but there was a strong feeling in the air that something was about to happen. Nothing one could explain, but like the lull before the storm. Went to the cinema – saw Edward G. Robinson in *Our Vines Have Tender Grapes*. Went to bed that night with a feeling of apprehension – something was going to happen.

Oct. 8th – Went for breakfast – rumours were rife. 'I know something is going to happen today.' At 9.30 a.m. the announcement came over the Tannoy – 'All ex-POWs to assemble at the cinema.' We were informed that a ship, the *Marine Shark*, was docked at the harbour and we were to be prepared to board her the following day. Went to the cinema that night – saw *Patrick the Great*.

ABOARD THE MARINE SHARK

Oct. 9th – Packed my kit, waited all day, then at 5.45 pm boarded the *Marine Shark*. The evening meal was great, it probably tasted better because we were another stage nearer home.

Oct. 10th – The boat left Manila and went to the outer harbour to fill with oil from a tanker. We left the outer harbour at 4.30 pm. The sea was very calm.

Oct. 11th – Today is Thursday and we are on our way home. The ship had a slight roll as we passed the southern tip of Luzon (the north main island in the Philippines).

Oct. 12th – Today we are 790 miles from Manila – 6,068 miles from San Francisco. It is raining slightly but who cares, this boat is pointing in the right direction and is moving nearer home.

Oct. 13th – Slight improvement with the weather now. We are 1,197 miles from Manila and 5,661 from San Francisco. This is going to be a pleasant trip.

Oct. 14th – The weather is the same, we are enjoying it, having good food, putting on weight. We are now 1,588 miles from Manila, 2,402 miles from Honolulu and 5,493 miles from San Francisco.

Oct. 15th – From this date the journey was very much the same routine, we were on our way home, but I was beginning to get a little impatient. It was 8 years since I had left England's shores and I was beginning to wonder how things were at home. I knew my parents were okay, but I had seen the devastation in Japan and was beginning to think, 'Is it the same at home?' We had so much time to spare and so little to do, one's thoughts began to wander, and when this happens one is always inclined to think the worst.

The weather varied between the 15th Oct to the 19th, from slight rain to glorious sunshine. On the 19th we passed the International Date Line, so we had two Fridays. We were now 4,000 miles from Manila and 3,074 miles from San Francisco.

Oct. 20th – We had a 12-hour delay owing to some engine trouble but were underway at 1 pm. The weather was quite good. Went to the pictures, saw *March of Time* and *A Royal Scandal*.

Oct. 23rd – Arrived at Pearl Harbor, Hawaii at noon. We were now 2,090 miles from Frisco. Went ashore – stayed in barracks overnight. Went to a show – saw Danny Kaye and Ella Logan, it was great. Back on board at 2 pm. Left Pearl Harbour at 5.15 pm. Should arrive Frisco by the 29th Oct.

Oct. 25th – We had boiler trouble and were stopped until 5 am whilst repairs were carried out. Once underway we carried on at a steady 15 knots.

Oct. 26th – We expect to be in Frisco in a week's time. The medical officer wanted to conduct a short arm inspection. This is a normal inspection, usually carried on in the barrack rooms under normal conditions, where one strips to the waist, stands at the foot of one's bed and drops one's trousers. As the officer approaches, he looks you up and down, then if satisfied, passes on to the next person. We were an unruly and undisciplined lot, so in order to carry out this inspection a notice was displayed, stating that all ex-POWs who paraded at the aft (rear) gun turret for a short arm inspection would receive a quart carton of buttermilk.

We strolled off aft to the rear gun turret, which had been stripped of the gun, but the turret was being used as a store for supplies instead of ammunition. There were two doors, one either side, so one was used for an entrance, the other for exit to speed up the proceedings. I entered the door behind a fellow from the Royal Scots who stepped in front of the medical officer, dropped his trousers and held out his arms sideways. The officer looked him up and down, nodded his head in satisfaction, and the orderly on his right then planted a quart carton of buttermilk into the Scot's hand – who immediately looked down, gave a cheer and said, 'Good Heavens, it's won me a prize!' Then pulling up his trousers, he ran out of the door amid roars of laughter.

Oct. 27th – Today we received a fag issue, a 200-carton of Lucky Strike. But the wind was getting up and it was turning colder. The ship was pitching and tossing. Many were seasick – I am, fortunately, a fairly good sailor.

Oct. 28th – Sea is still rough, but the wind is slightly warmer. We are informed that the destination is now Seattle. We have another 3-hour delay through engine trouble.

Oct. 31st – Wednesday, a chilly day, need to wear more clothes. Due to arrive Frisco by 10 pm tomorrow. I received my debarkation ticket, No. 3252. This boat I would not recommend for a round-the-world cruise. I shall be pleased to leave it, but it has brought me nearer home – for that I thank it and its crew.

Nov. 1st – Arrived Frisco. Passed under Golden Gate Bridge at 8.30 am. Docked at 2.15 pm in San Francisco. Disembarked at 2.30 p.m. Proceeded to Fort McDowell on Angel Island. We were issued with Canadian battledress and given Royal Signal insignia to sew on shoulders.

San Francisco
Nov. 2nd – We went into 'Frisco after a pay issue of 14 dollars. Went into a bar which was divided into cubicles seating four. Opposite us sat four females, we spoke to them. They answered, so I walked across to introduce myself. They immediately jumped up and all four of them ran outside. I wondered what was wrong. I looked towards the door where they had made their exit, and lo and behold, they were beckoning to all of us to follow them. We did so, they immediately linked arm in arm with us and marched back in. It appears that the law at that time in that particular area was such: 'A person could take a companion into a bar but was not allowed to attach oneself to another person whilst in there'. In other words, you could not pick up a 'broad' in a pub – funny lot! Each state had its own laws, so you had to check in every state what

you could do and not do. Anyway, we had a good night and got pretty well tanked up.

The Journey through Canada
Nov. 3rd – After breakfast, we were told we would be leaving Frisco by hospital train for Canada. We got our kit together and were taken to the station where there were 10 coaches, all with two-tier hospital beds. We climbed aboard at 1.30 pm into bed, then the train left at 2 pm. It was a treat; we had American and Canadian Red Cross nurses to look after us, meals in bed, books to read, daily papers, plenty of fruit to eat. The only time you were allowed out of bed was to answer the calls of nature. The scenery was fantastic, with massive Redwood trees – we were heading for the Rockies.

Nov. 5th – We arrived at Fort Lewis in Tacoma. We left the train and went into billets. There I met my mate George Kim. We went into town at night, had a few beers. The following afternoon we went into town, there we met two American girls, Lucerne and Delores. We went to the cinema. Everything went well until I lit a cigarette. I was pounced on by an usherette and a fella, they grabbed me and frog-marched me up the aisle to an auditorium at the back. Fire laws are very strict, and I agree with it, but I did not know about it until now. Smoking is only allowed in the auditorium where there is a big window where one can watch the screen, and speakers in each corner issue the dialogue and sound. After I finished my fag, I returned to my seat. After the show we took the girls to the bus station and arranged to see them the following morning at 11 am.

Nov. 7th – We were awakened at 7 am. Had breakfast and boarded a Canadian National Railway train which left at 9 am bound for New York. It was a beautiful train, plenty of room. I am afraid Lucerne and Delores are due for a let-down. Hope they forgive us. At 11 pm, we passed over US/Canadian border.

Nov. 8th – Thursday. We entered into the Rockies at 10 am. Stopped at Jasper for 30 minutes. Then carried on passing Alfreda Summit (2,870 ft) at 3.50 pm. There were nine coaches on the train. The centre one was the dining car, which could accommodate two coachloads at a time. The two outer coaches would go for breakfast, the two inner coaches for lunch, and the two centre coaches for dinner. The next day the order would be reversed.

Nov. 9th – Friday. We are out of the Rockies now and on the prairie. We stopped at Saskatoon for 30 minutes. The scenery has been breath-taking on this trip, I will never forget. There is 6 inches of snow and the temperature is below zero, but the coaches are lovely and warm.

Nov. 10th – Saturday. We arrived at Winnipeg at 5.30 am. The temperature is 16 degrees below and there is 1ft. of snow. We stayed here for over an hour because the heating on one coach was at fault, so the coach had to be changed, so we had to walk around. The exercise did us good. Our next stop was at 'Sioux Lookout' at 5 pm. We had a walk round, finishing up having a snowball fight with the local kids.

Nov. 11th – The journey was uneventful, but there was different scenery every day. We arrived at Capreal at 1.45 pm. It was amazing but every stop we had, where we had time for a walkabout, people seemed to know we were all ex-POWs. We were told the next stop would be Ottawa. This was so, and we arrived there at 10 pm. It was a wonderful reception we received. There on the platform were the pick of Ottawa's loveliest girls, each with a tray of goodies around their lovely necks. I remember very well one of them approached me with a tray of fruit, she held out a pair of bananas which were welded together like Siamese twins, saying, 'Would you care for twins?' I thought to myself, it's a good job you said it!

NEW YORK AND THE *QUEEN MARY*

Nov. 12th – New York. Arrived at 1.30 pm. after a 6,000-mile trip, taking 6 days. What a sight, there on the pier was the *Queen Mary* waiting to take us home. We boarded her at 2 pm. Bill Bevan and I were in a cabin together. It is a beautiful ship without any doubt. We were due to sail on the evening tide, but the port was fog-bound, so would have to wait until midday tomorrow. I was among a party of about 20 who went ashore. We had a great time. One thing that stands out in my mind was seeing at 5.30 am, as we were returning to the pier, hundreds of Bobby Soxers (pop music fans of the 1940s) queuing up to see Frank Sinatra who was singing at this theatre at 10 am.

Nov. 13th – Left New York at 12 noon. There was nearly a mutiny – whilst the ship was crewed by British sailors, the Yanks were running things on the decks. We got no lunch – they expected us to work. No way! We got supper at 4.30 pm. I met Alf Taylor on board, I thought he was on his way to Australia to join his wife and daughter, but he found out his wife and daughter were on their way to England, so he was sent home too.

Nov. 14th – The next four days were beautiful, travelling at a steady 29 knots. It seemed very fitting that the fastest ship in the world was taking me home to the country I had not seen for eight years.

Nov. 17th – We are due in Southampton tomorrow. I have received my disembarkation ticket, and 'K Rations'. It is hard to try to explain my feelings because I do not know what to expect. My hometown, Sheffield, was bombed, this I know, but what will it look like? On the other hand, what do my parents expect to see? I was a POW in Japan for almost four years. I was 7 stone 2 lb. when the war ended. I think we are both going to be surprised.

Nov. 18th – I have been up all night; I could not sleep. We entered the Channel at 4 am, passing plenty of ships. Arrived at Southampton at 11 am and I have been feasting my eyes on those White Cliffs of Dover for hours. We are going to Amersham to be processed before being sent on leave. We disembarked, climbed onto the lorries and were on our way, speeding to the final stage of our journey.

Nov. 19th – Today we had our medical. I was told by one of the staff that if I told the 'M.E.' I suffered from bad feet and they would swell up in the evenings, I would get a lovely pair of shoes like the RAF are issued with, so being at the top of the alphabet I was first in to the M.E. I spun him the yarn, knowing I have very good feet, and duly received a note from him – but on reading same, I discovered I was 'pregnant' and should receive extra rations of eggs and milk! What a laugh – away from home for eight years and come back pregnant! I received an issue of full kit of clothing plus overcoat and £150 pay!

Nov. 20th – Left Amersham, going to London by train. On the arrival, I must praise the Red Cross and the Salvation Army who were waiting at the station asking where we were bound for. Then they whisked us away to the appropriate station for our destination, finally leaving us with a box containing sandwiches, an apple and a bar of chocolate – but not before asking if we wanted to send a telegram home, which I did. This I still have in my possession. I arrived home at 5 pm. A round-the-world trip, taking eight years.

HOME AT LAST!

Butler arrived at Sheffield on 20 November, alighting from the train with his two kit bags, a big army backpack full of American cigars and cigarettes and a Japanese sword wrapped in a piece of blue parachute slung over his shoulder. He gave his ticket to the ticket collector and handed his small kit bag to a young lad, who dashed off to find him a taxi. On his right-hand side were three phone kiosks; Butler did not notice that his mother stood between two of these. Butler followed the lad out of the station and unloaded the kit he was carrying into the taxi, giving the boy five bob. He turned round…

As he recounted: 'And there was my mother walking towards me. I shall never forget her face – she was expecting to see something like the photos she had seen of survivors of Belsen. Instead, there was 13 st, 12 lb of overfed ex-POW who had been eating steaks big enough to milk, on his way back home.

'My Dad arrived home from work shortly after Mother and I got back. He grabbed hold of me, then turned to Mother and said, "We won't be long," and took me down to the pub, which was only two hundred yards away. He went to the bar, then stopped suddenly, turning around, and said to me, "What are you having?" There was a questioning look on his face. I realised he did not know whether I drank or not. I said, "A pint, the same as you." He grinned and passed the first pint to me. I drank half of it in one gulp. He turned round and saw my glass. His face lit up like a neon sign, and he did the same with his pint. That is the face I will always remember.'

CHAPTER 6

Terence (Flash) Kelly

TERENCE KELLY – FEPOW (FAR EAST PRISONER OF WAR, 1942–45)

Terence was a fellow WWII Far East prisoner of war with my father, Albert Ient, 1942–45 at Habu Camp (Hiroshima Camp 5), Hitachi dockyard, Innoshima, Japan.

Terence wrote a book about the POW camp in which he, my father and many others were imprisoned. Originally titled *Living with the Japanese* (in later editions it was titled *By Hellship to Hiroshima*), Terence covers the dreadful journey which he and other RAF POWs captured in the Dutch East Indies (now Indonesia) took but also details his experience of life in the POW camp at Habu. Although he and my father were in separate sections of the same POW camp, this book is a very interesting exposé on the details of what life was like and it has been very useful to me in corroborating my own father's story as well as those of the other POWs sent to Japan. *By Hellship to Hiroshima* is published under ISBN reference: 9781844154036.

ABOUT TERENCE

After flying Hurricanes against the Japanese in Singapore, Sumatra and Java (now part of the Dutch East Indies) in 1941, Terence was taken prisoner in early 1942. For seven months he was held in Boei Glodok, a squalid native prison in Batavia (now Jakarta) on the island of Java in what was the Dutch East Indies (now Indonesia), before being transported to Japan with more than 1,000 fellow POWs in the ancient freighter *Dainichi Maru*. When he arrived in Japan he was taken to Habu, the principal township on Innoshima Island, and the prisoner of war camp named Hiroshima 5.[42] From this camp he went daily to work in the Hitachi dockyard.

After the war, Terence became a quantity surveyor and set up offices in London and the Caribbean, handling many different projects. His experiences led him to write his first novel, *The Carib Sands*, and persuaded him to become a full-time author. His first play, *A Shake in the Sun*, went to the West End and many more novels and plays for stage, television and radio followed. In addition, Terence wrote a number of non-fiction books, including *By Hellship to Hiroshima*, which is the updated version of *Living with the Japanese*. Both of these books vividly describe his experiences as a Far East prisoner of war and, of particular interest to me, what life was like in Hiroshima Camp 5, his relationship with his captors and men from the Hong Kong Volunteer Defence Corps, and the nature of work in the large Hitachi shipyards.

Terence Kelly died in September 2013 aged around 94.

MEETING TERENCE KELLY

In March 2007, I was privileged to meet Terence, pictured overleaf with me, on the occasion of my visit to interview him at his home in Marlow. We talked about many things relating to his captivity and possible similar experiences to those of my father. For example, both men recalled the incident when a request to go swimming was agreed to and how they were marched into the freezing-cold sea, in the dark of night; and their mutual friendship with Geoffrey Coxhead, the English artist and diarist. The following notes are a record of our discussion.[43]

---

42 At the time of Terence's arrival, the camp was called Fukuoka 12. It was subsequently renamed Zentsuji 2 and later again renamed Hiroshima 5.

43 Terence Kelly has a copy of the diary Coxhead kept throughout this captivity in Hiroshima 5.

Figure 6.1 Terence Kelly (left) and me when I visited him at his home in Marlow, Buckinghamshire, March 2007.

CAPTURE

Terence started by talking about the capitulation of Java (part of modern-day Indonesia, what was the Dutch colony of the Dutch East Indies) by the Dutch administration (the Netherlands, thousands of miles away, had succumbed to the German invasion two and a half years before) and his subsequent capture. It was obvious that he still had some reservations about the necessity of this drastic action. He said:

> Well, what I mean is that the invasion force of Japanese was so modest, that any real effort to fight against them, in a country of 60 or 70 million people and 600 miles long, with hilly terrain and God knows what, should not have presented a problem; but it did because nobody fought them! ... Disgraceful.

He felt the fall of Hong Kong, on the other hand, was different. 'At least in Hong Kong, although it didn't last very long, they put up a jolly good show against the Japanese, more than they did in Singapore.'

INTERNMENT AND JOURNEY FROM JAVA TO JAPAN

After the seven-month internment at the hands of the Japanese in Java, Terence was transported aboard the *Dainichi Maru* to Japan.[44] Talking about the journey to Japan, which took four or five weeks, Terence said that the conditions were so dreadful, especially when it rained and snowed, that in effect it winnowed out the weaker people. 'Because, when we got there [*Japan*] we were all terribly ill, after four or five weeks… some just died, and others fought it off.' He explained that some of those who were strong enough took every opportunity, despite the bitter cold, to take what exercise they could. They determinedly marched up and down in the space available to them once or twice a day for half an hour or so, just to keep moving. However, Terence admitted that he was not sure whether this made any difference at all to their survival prospects:

> We were very lucky, because in the neighbouring camp of 100, 23 died as a result of the voyage. In another camp that I know of, of 150, 35 died. We were very lucky in that only eight of us died and one was shifted away somewhere for some reason that I never did discover. So, we ended up by being 86.

HIROSHIMA CAMP 5

Terence stayed in Hiroshima Camp 5 for the remainder of the war, from 1942 to August 1945. The prisoners held there were not transferred to another camp even after the Allied bombing of the dockyards and the camp itself in 1945.

The first 100 men to arrive, including five officers (with the exception of one naval officer) were RAF, then, two months later, 100 Hong Kong Volunteer Defence Force and army people arrived. In this Terence was able to be very specific because he could refer to his log book:

He was, he said, 'The only pilot who kept their log book through a Japanese prisoner of war camp, everyone else destroyed theirs, because we had been busy strafing the Japanese.' From this he confirmed that, on 23 January 1943, 100 POWs (mostly of the HKDVC plus some regular soldiers) arrived from

---

44   Batavia, now known as Jakarta, is the capital and largest city of Indonesia, located on the north-west coast of the island of Java.

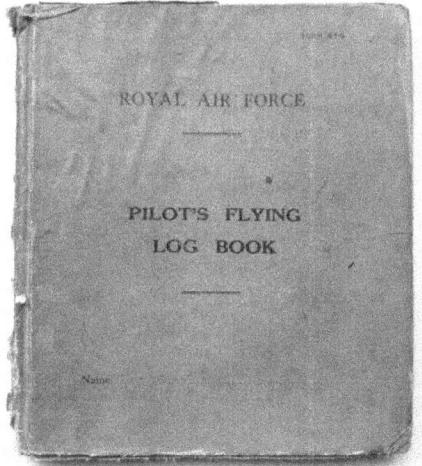 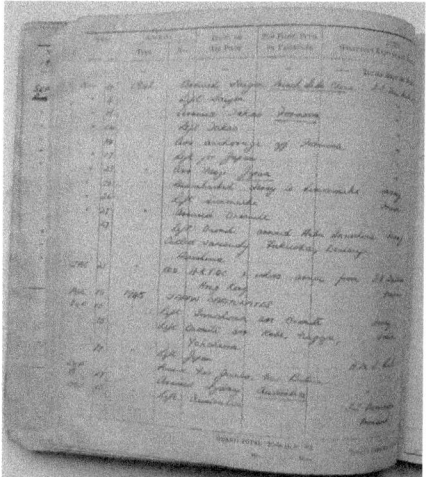

Figure 6.2 Terence Kelly's log book.

Hong Kong on the passenger liner *Tatsuta Maru*. Their journey, to the best of his knowledge, had been relatively uneventful. Albert Ient was one of the prisoners on this ship.

Asked if he knew Albert, Terence replied, 'We were in different working parties in different buildings. No, we didn't know each other. We didn't ever run across each other. The only Hong Kong people I ever came across were those I worked with and Coxhead, because I played chess with him and Freddie Clemo. Also, of course, I did organise one or two concerts and I got one or two Hong Kong people to take part in the concerts, so I knew Ginger Day.'

With the aid of photographs taken of different groups of POWs, Terence was able to definitely say that Albert had been in the same camp as him.[45] He showed me a group photograph and was able to confirm the names of the men in the picture – Smith, Reed, Kean, Blount, Ient and Hailstone (Figure 6.3).

The camp had just been built on a narrow wedged-shaped piece of land, next to the sea near the road which ran from Habu dockyard (which was on the western side of Innoshima Island) to another smaller dockyard called Mitsunosho on the eastern side of Innoshima Island. Huts for the prisoners had been built either side of an administration block: to the south, a single-

---

45   I felt that it could be possible that Albert was the only member of the HK Royal Signal Regiment in this camp. However, Levett's war diary claims that the third draft included six of his men.

Figure 6.3 My father is in the front row on the left.

storeyed wooden hut to accommodate 100 prisoners; to the north, two parallel rows of identical, wooden two-storeyed huts to accommodate 400. Beyond these huts at either end, under a projecting canopy, was a row of ablution troughs and, as separate buildings, lavatories. Terence was in the single-storeyed southern hut which consisted of a continuous corridor, with a small room at the end and seven rooms leading off the corridor, each large enough to take 16 prisoners. In the centre of each room was a wood-burning stove with a pipe. The dividing walls were made of plywood and the wall facing the sea had continuous sliding windows. Behind each bed space was a single shelf for clothes and personal possessions.[46]

THE CAMP'S WORKING LIFE

Asked what camp life had been like, Terence easily recalled their daily routine and meagre breakfasts: 'Well, you had to get up at a quarter to five and you had to do Taiso, as it was called, that's exercising, which took about a quarter of an hour or so, and then there was breakfast and then we marched to the dockyard. We left at six.'

Once at the Hitachi Zoyen-owned dockyard Terence found that Japanese people living on Innoshima Island worked alongside the prisoners. Terence

---

46 Kelly, T., *By Hellship to Hiroshima*, pp. 49–50.

recalled that his party had the job of looking after the railway lines on which the tractors went and that their ganger had been called Murakami:

> He was an old man, as bad-tempered as can be, but he was delightful, one of the Japanese I really liked, and he had been looking after these travelling cranes ever since he was a child. He was in charge of us and we had a Korean guard who was considerably unpleasant. We were a party of our own. Other people worked on ships or things.

Here Terence asked which working party Albert had been with, but unfortunately I did not have this information. I was able to say, however, that my father had been involved in building ships and working with metal. Terence confirmed that this was, of course, very possible and small working parties of about 17 or 18 people had undertaken riveting work on the ships.

When I mentioned that my father had told me that the winters were so cold that if you put your hand on the metal you were working on your skin would stick to it, Terence suggested that it was indeed cold, but it wasn't really bitterly cold – it was nothing like 30 or 40 degrees below freezing. Terence believes that it only felt that cold to the prisoners because they were so badly dressed and underfed. He said:

> It is a beautiful area... The summers are pretty hot, but on the whole it's good weather there. Even in the winter there are lots of sunny, cold, crisp days, but as far as we were concerned then, the winters were bitterly cold. There was icy wind blowing through the so-called clothes we were wearing.

When working the prisoners wore a dockyard uniform, rubber shoes called Tabis and their bamboo identification tag.[47] Terence's is shown in Figure 6.4 overleaf:

Albert Ient had a similar one with his name on it. Sadly, I have lost my father's name tag.

What amazed Terence was that the Japanese seemed to be more concerned with counting the prisoners than with their productivity within the dockyard. They were counted in and counted out of the yard. 'I mean, there were a few

---

47 I remember playing with my father's bamboo tag when as a boy. Unfortunately it is now lost.

"Stakhanovites"[48] who worked their heads off but, on the whole, if a Japanese could get out of work by scrounging, he would.' Terence went on to say that after the war when he heard about the kamikazes, he was astonished: 'I didn't believe it because of the way the Japanese had been in our dockyard.'

PUNISHMENT

There was absolutely no hope of escaping from Innoshima Island and, as with all camps, the enforcement of rules and punishments depended very much on the camp commandant. Terence compared methods of punishment used in his camp with those the Nazis used to get information out of their prisoners, saying, 'There wasn't anything like that, but you try kneeling on a thin piece of bamboo for a few hours, that's a pretty mean punishment. Not that I ever had that. Other people got beaten up for misbehaving, that sort of thing. The Japanese were very free and handy with their fists and hands.'

Figure 6.4
Terence Kelly's identification tag.

Terence felt that they had been quite fortunate with their camp commandant, who was regarded as quite a weak man, concerned only with himself and avoiding any trouble. Although well-educated, he did not hold a very high rank. Terence concluded that, on the whole, life could have been a whole lot worse than it was with Nimoto.

MALNUTRITION

All the prisoners suffered at different times from illness and disease, but in Hiroshima 5 they were lucky enough to have, according to Terence, 'a

---

48 A Stakhanovite is someone who works overly and excessively hard. The Stakhanovite movement took its name from Aleksei Grigorievich Stakhanov, who on 31 August 1935 mined 102 tons of coal (14 times his quota) in less than six hours.

marvellous man who became our camp doctor. A marvellous man named Mogford.' Nevertheless, beriberi was a real problem for them: 'As a prisoner of war, if you got beriberi then, as you sat down, your legs would swell up and you could stick your finger into the skin and it would take half an hour for the indentation to come out.' Even after the war had ended the effects of beriberi could still take effect and be clearly visible, especially when prisoners began to eat better food and they became bloated. Terence was best man at the wedding of his friend Bill May; a photograph taken on the day shows his face was, to use his words, 'very sort of fat – that was the effect it has but it gradually disappeared.'

PRISONER OF WAR LETTERS

Letters and a connection with home were naturally very important to the POWs. At Hiroshima 5 the prisoners did receive incoming post, handwritten letters and cards, but not until a year and a half or perhaps two years of imprisonment had passed. When post did eventually get through it came in batches and Terence received letters from his mother, stepfather and one or two girlfriends. Outgoing correspondence usually took the form of cards on which prisoners were allowed to fill in certain words.[49] Terence remembered:

> You just had to fill it [the space] in. It said something like 'Please see that [name] is taken care of', and I put 'Peggy and Josephine' and my stupid stepfather showed the card I'd sent to both girls! Well, one of them was married when I came back and the other was in South Africa. So, it was alright; it let me off the hook.

RED CROSS PARCELS

Terence could not remember representatives from the Red Cross visiting the camp. There were only ever four or five consignments of Red Cross parcels during the whole period of their imprisonment – three and a half years. Most of the Red Cross parcels were held back until towards the end of the war.

---

49 I have the cards Albert sent to Toby during his internment at Hiroshima 5.

Despite the rigours of prison life, humour in the camp was still very much alive. The menu below was made up by Terence after receiving a Red Cross parcel in October 1944, which was probably the first to arrive for over two and a half years!

AMERICAN BOMBING

Bombing of the camp by the Americans started early in 1945. Terence recalled that the first mission involved a dozen aircraft, just strafing the camp.[50] B-52s started to come over soon after that (see Chick Henderson's biography for more information about the waves of B-52 bombers that came over the camp).

Figure 6.5 Terence Kelly's menu.

> We had this one particularly fearsome raid. They killed a lot of Japanese. They didn't kill any POWs. We were not in the camp but at the dockyard at that time. They sunk a submarine though and damaged the area quite badly.
>
> Later, in May that year, things took a more portentous turn. We saw these huge formations coming over. We couldn't count them. I'll always remember; some day in May, there was lots of cumulus cloud. Out of it appeared the nose of a B-29 and then there was another one and another one and eventually you got a formation of 27 on each side. Then as that came out, another formation of 27, making it a formation of 81, and eventually there were three or four hundred B-29s and they just went straight overhead thankfully. We heard them bombing somewhere else. I don't know where it was. But we were fortunate because records show that the Americans had decided to carry out complete pattern bombing, with these huge forces, of our dockyard on the 18th August. That was three days AFTER the war ended!

---

50 Terence said that later he discovered that they came off the Indomitable, the British aircraft carrier which he had flown off.

The dropping of the atom bomb had saved us! If they hadn't dropped the atom bomb they would have had to invade Japan. The first thing the Japanese would have done would have been to kill all the prisoners. They just wouldn't have been able to put up with us. The death toll for fighting the Japanese, on both sides, would have been absolutely horrendous. We were really lucky.

ATOMIC BOMB – HIROSHIMA

Hiroshima, where the first atomic bomb was dropped, on 6 August 1945, was only about 24 miles from the POW camp where Terence and Albert Ient were interned. Asked if he knew that the bomb had been dropped, Terence said:

No, we didn't. We would have heard it but then we heard the noise from bombs dropped by the big formations of American aircraft. They made horrendous sounds. A formation of 200 to 300 B-29s dropped all their bombs on an area, and even if it was 30 miles away, we continually heard rattling. But we didn't know about the atom bomb. What was strange was that we obviously saw the aircraft which dropped it, because, curiously, on that very day when they dropped it, we were working in the dockyard and a single B-29 came over.

Yes, just one, most unusually, and if you draw a line from the airport where it took off, over Innoshima, it goes straight to Hiroshima. There's no doubt. We just looked up and saw it. It was eight in the morning, or something like that, and we just saw it come over and we thought, 'That's very odd!' and carried on working. We no doubt heard the thing, but we just thought it was another formation bombing from another direction. We didn't know about it until about ten days later.

CONDITIONS GET WORSE

Leading up to the end of the war, things in the camp got a lot worse. The prisoners were very close to starvation and the Japanese themselves were not well fed. Terence felt that if the war had gone on the death toll would have suddenly become enormous because there was just not any food. Rations had been severely cut, to the extent that they were minuscule.

THE END OF THE WAR

Neither the prisoners nor guards realised that the end of the war was going to come as quickly as it did. The prisoners continued to think that one day the Americans would invade. Terence recalled what actually happened:

> A few days after the atom bomb we were working as usual in the dockyard and we, that is, the prisoners, were suddenly ordered to stop work. Along with all the other dockyard workers, the Japanese were summoned to listen to a broadcast from [Emperor] Hirohito, which, of course, was extraordinary because he was wasn't known to the public, he had never spoken to them, and he told them the war was over. Well, we were then told to go back to work. We had no idea what this broadcast was about and although I knew a bit of Japanese it wasn't good enough to translate it. While we were working on something or other, a Korean came up to me and said, 'The war's over', and we thought it was all very odd, so we went on working. When lunchtime came, if you could call it lunchtime, we went to the canteen and I saw Freddie Clemo, this man who was marvellous at producing news and I said to him, 'The war's over,' and he said, 'Nonsense!' So, we went back to work and at about half past four in the afternoon or four o'clock, we were told to pack up work and return to the camp. So, we returned to the camp to find it temporarily empty of Japanese. It was all very odd and weird and then the Japanese came back, and things went on more or less as normal. The usual thing in the evening was that Freddie Clemo used to come along the passage behind the windows on those photographs to give the news. He was marvellous at getting the news. He stuck his head into my room, he looked at me, grinned, and said, 'You're quite right, the war is over, but I wasn't going to be scooped!'

Freddie Clemo was in a small working party of electricians, four of them, which had a Japanese foreman who was pro-European, who kept them informed, and he had told them what the broadcast said. On hearing the news Terence sat down and wrote his reactions; he had just finished when the camp commandant, Mori, who had replaced Nimoto a month before, came into the hut and saw him. Mori took the paper: 'I thought, "Oh, Lord!" and with that we got an air raid warning. I hadn't written anything terribly nasty about the Japanese as it happened. I had written about what I felt like. My reactions, as it were. I thought as it [*the war*] was resolved it was safe to write. Then the all-clear went and the commandant came back in and handed me the piece of paper back. That was how we knew the war was really over. It was all very strange. It was very depressing, actually, because although there was a sense of glee, we thought, what is the difference, in this ghastly place, what are we going to do, what's going to happen? It took a lot of time to adjust to the war being over. We did, gradually, because we sort of took over the island. We didn't take it over in the sense of running everything, but we had our own way. The Japanese, once the war was over, didn't seem bothered at losing it [*the war*].'

In fact, there were not many Japanese troops on the island. The camp had a permanent staff guard and a small batch of between six and ten soldiers who came for one month and were then replaced by another batch; there were sailors who came off ships, or if a troop ship came in then there would be a lot of army in the dockyard, but, by and large, the prisoners did not see large numbers of Japanese Army personnel. When the war ended the guards who had looked after the prisoners stayed in the camp, but, as Terence says, 'They made themselves as invisible and as small as possible.'

During this gap of almost a month the prisoners gradually organised themselves; a bomber plane came over and dropped Red Cross parcels and they were able to blackball the Japanese into giving them more food. Asked how they negotiated with the Japanese, Terence remembered with pride that this was something he felt he personally had to do:

> I decided something had to be done. Why me, I don't know, because I was only a youngster. Anyway, I did. I said to the commandant, 'Look, we've got to have a meeting for food,' so he said, 'Well, who do you want at the meeting?' I said, 'Well, we want you and we want the bank manager and we want the man in charge of food on the island and we want an interpreter.' Anyway, we had this meeting in the boardroom of Hitachi dockyard! I wasn't the only POW. There was a sergeant from the Hong Kong group as well. He didn't say very much I remember, but he was there. And we sat at this table and I started to lay down the law as to what we should have.

Well, first of all it was about food, and I asked for the most monstrous amount of rice. 'The men want it,' I said, 'and if you don't give them what they want, they'll be over the wall looking for it and there will be trouble.' And this was true, actually, they would have been. People were getting very restless in the camp. We'd won the war, for God's sake! So, they agreed to these utterly ridiculous demands. I was enjoying myself. So, then they said, 'Is there anything else?' and I said, 'Well, yes, we want some money!' They said, 'What do you want money for?' You see, you couldn't buy anything in Japan, there was nothing for sale. There was a shop we used to go by, but all it had in its window for sale was a hat! Anyway, I said, 'They want money, if they haven't got money, well then, they'll be over the wall, breaking into shops and things.' So, then he said, 'Well, all right, so how much do you want?' So, I said, '200 yen a man.' Well, as we got paid 15 yen a day for working, that's 1,200 days' work. They said, 'So what are you going to do with 200 yen?' I said, 'That doesn't matter, that's what the men want and if they don't get it they'll be over the wall causing trouble.' So, the commandant said to me, 'Where do we get this money?' I said, 'Well, the bank manager has got plenty of money.' The bank manager resisted. He said, 'I'm not giving you any money!' So, we were at an impasse. Then the most astonishing thing happened. This commandant said to me, 'If I advance the money, how will I know I'll get it back?' I said, 'Well, it's quite simple. You sign a short document saying in good faith that you have lent 30,000 yen and I will sign it that you have done so and when the first of the occupying troops arrive, you can present them with this and they will repay you.' He said, 'Will they?' and I said, 'Oh, yes!' So, this commandant wrote a cheque out for this very large sum of money, handed it to the bank manager, and the bank manager went off and we went on talking, and he came back with all this yen in a shoe box and I went back to the camp and I distributed 200 yen per man.

THE BRITISH NAVY ARRIVE IN THE INNOSHIMA SEA

Terence's log, which he secretly kept in his pilot's log book, notes that the war officially ended on 15 August, but it was sometime in September that the first Allied officer arrived.[51] As Terence related to me and also as noted in his book,

---

51 The date given in *By Hellship to Hiroshima*, p. 224, is 11 September 1945.

on Tuesday 11 September, a small pinnace[52] came round the headland flying the White Ensign and shortly afterwards a British officer stepped ashore to tell the men that they were all going home. He went on to give details of departure information and dates. With some amusement Terence remembered that the officer said he couldn't stay long and boarded his boat, disappearing again round the headland!

RETURNING HOME – FIRST THROUGH JAPAN

Terence recalled:

> We got rid of most of the money when we got on the train to Yokohama - you've never seen a country like it, as we went through towns it looked like allotments, there was nothing left. It had been bombed and they had been wooden houses. There were children begging at the railside as we went past. They were very interested in the train and holding their hands out and we threw out all the money.

With a month to kill, people came up with all sorts of ideas to pass the time. One such idea was to collect the signatures of everybody in the camp as a sort of souvenir and Terence was able to show me a copy of this, with his and Albert's signatures clearly visible (Figure 6.6).

Albert Ient's signature is in the top right-hand corner – the 'Albert Victor' is quite distinct.

JOURNEY FROM JAPAN TO AUSTRALIA

On the day of actual departure, 15 September according to Terence's log, a boat came and took the prisoners from the island to Onomichi railway station, where they boarded a train to Osaka and HMS *Ruler* (Figure 6.7), a British aircraft carrier, which took them directly to Sydney, Australia.

---

52 A light boat used as a tender for merchant and war vessels.

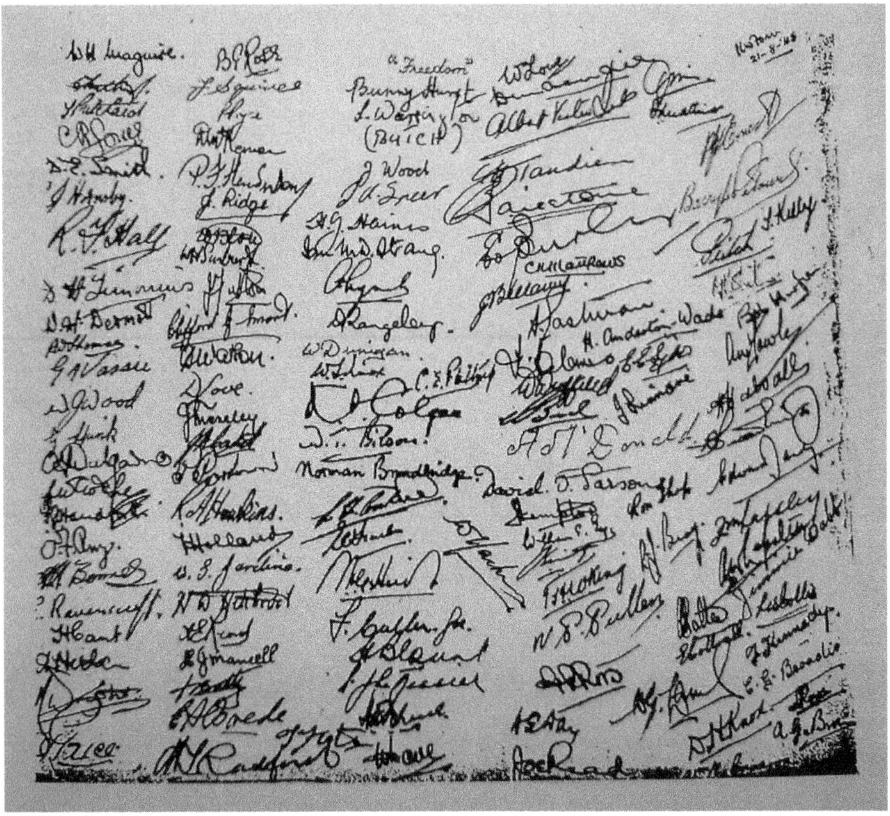

Figure 6.6 The signatures of the men held in the POW camp.

Figure 6.7 HMS *Ruler* (from my father's collection of photos).

CHAPTER 7

Philip (Chick) Henderson

PHILIP F HENDERSON (30 MARCH 1920–5 SEPTEMBER 2013)

Philip Filou Henderson is an RAF veteran and was a POW during World War II in the Far East. 'Chick' Henderson (as he was known to his RAF colleagues) was captured in Java in the Dutch East Indies (Indonesia, as it is now) and transported to Habu POW camp in Japan, the same camp where my father was imprisoned.

A friend, Adrian Batty, whom I met while tracing my father's prisoner of war history in the Far East, recommended that I attend a POW reunion in Stratford-upon-Avon, England, in August 2013. I wondered: what is the point? I can't imagine that there will be many POWs left for me to talk to. World War II ended 67 years ago! Further still, this particular POW club was concerned with those who were captured in Java (modern-day Indonesia). I really couldn't see this being much help with my project relating to my father's wartime experiences in Hong Kong and as a POW in Japan. However,

Figure 7.1 Philip (Chick) Henderson.

Adrian Batty, whose father was captured in Java and transported to the same prisoner of war camp that my father was in, convinced me that there would be some purpose in attending the reunion. So, I went along. I met up with Adrian and it was a thoroughly interesting and enjoyable reunion conference. But, more especially, I met some very interesting veterans. In particular, I spent a long time talking to Chick Henderson (Philip Henderson), who was an RAF POW captured in Java.

It was fascinating meeting him – he was a great guy! One afternoon, we sat together for over three hours and the whole time he was telling jokes and humorous anecdotes about his WWII experiences. He made light of his hardship as a POW. I came away thinking what a wonderful man he was and what an enjoyable experience it was to meet him. As the conference finished on the Sunday I said to him that I would like to visit him and chat some more. Chick and I agreed that I would publish his story on my website, along with the stories of other POW veterans.

A few weeks later after my further travels I came home to find I had had a small parcel delivered. Chick had sent me a video disc and two tapes. The note attached said:

> Victor, hope you will enjoy the disc. If you can make use of it, I shall be delighted. Many thanks for an interesting weekend!
> Kindest regards,
> Chick (in haste)

The video was a copy of a talk he had given to the South Shields Probus Club in 2004. The tapes were copies of recordings from BBC radio interviews he had given in about 1998. These recordings were about his experiences as a POW. The video recording was a detailed talk about his journey from England to Singapore, escape to Java, capture and transportation and, finally, imprisonment as a POW in Japan. It is a wonderful first-hand record of the wartime experiences of a POW in the Far East.

I was on the verge of calling Chick to thank him and to make arrangements to visit him when I had an email from my friend Adrian informing me that Chick had died. I was shocked, but also felt privileged to have met him and to be in possession of his wartime record.

I duly copied and transcribed the recordings (the originals being returned to his family). My transcriptions have helped me write this biography and epitaph to Chick Henderson and his fellow POWs.

The funeral of Philip Filou Henderson took place on Monday, 23 September 2013 at All Saints Church, Headley, Hampshire, and I was privileged to meet his lovely family and hear their tributes to Philip, especially those from his son and his grandsons.

Figure 7.2 Chick and me at the Java Club FEPOW reunion in August 2013.

PHILIP (CHICK) HENDERSON TELLS HIS STORY

This is the transcript of a talk given by Philip Filou Henderson, better known to his RAF colleagues as 'Chick' Henderson, given to South Shields Probus Club. Chick had a broad Geordie[53] accent and I have tried to use the words and phrases he used in his talk.

There is welcoming applause as he rises to speak and smiles:

Thank you to Mr Chairman, nice warm welcome, very appreciative. I'm a member of North Shields Probus Club, and they send kind regards to you all.

Figure 7.3 Chick Henderson in his RAF uniform.

---

53 Note on Chick's recordings. A Geordie accent is both a regional nickname for a person from the larger Tyneside region of north-east England and the name of the English-language dialect spoken by its inhabitants. The Geordie dialect and identity date back to the settlers in the north-east area as far back as the post-Roman period in Britain.

I was Founder Chairman over there about 20 years ago. They're still going strong. We have about 46 or 47 members, but they are better looking over there than what they are over here!

[*The audience laugh and some joke, saying, 'get him off!'*]

Anyway... I was talking to a friend of mine, because I'm not very good at this public speaking bit, and I said, can you give me some advice on how to approach a talk of this nature? He said, 'Well it's perfectly simple, all you have to do is remember the alphabet.' Well, I can manage that I thought. He says, 'It's A, B, C, can you remember that?' Oh yes, I say. He says, 'A, B, C, which stands for "Always Be Cheerful".' I said, I can manage that. He says, 'Or, Always Be Concise'. Thanks, I said, anything else? He says, 'Yes, X, Y, Z, most important, X, Y, Z, particularly if you're addressing a ladies' meeting.' I said, what's so special about X, Y, Z? He said, 'Remember X, Y, Z, before you start, it means, Examine Your Zip!'

[*Again laughter!*]

Now that's the only time you're going to laugh this morning, so put your miserable faces on because that's the only time you are going to laugh today.

In England, in the RAF

First of all, like a lot of young men in me time, I was in the services. I joined the RAF during 1940 at the age of 20, at the time of the Battle of Britain. I did my training and all the rest of it. One day I was sitting in an aerodrome down in Lincolnshire. It was freezing, perishing cold, and the word came across that they wanted six riggers for the Middle East. I says, put me name down! So, they put me name down for the Middle East and they gave us a week's leave. I came back and went across to Liverpool, but the draft had gone, so I was sent to the Far East instead!

Singapore

I boarded the boat in about August 1941, which, as you recall, was just prior to 7 December 1941, when war broke out in the Far East. So, in effect we got to Singapore during peacetime, which was great! Whisky was ten bob [*ten shillings, is now 50p*] a bottle, fags were cheap, everything was dirt cheap, you were able to save money. It was too hot to work, you finished work at 12 o'clock and the rest of the day was your own. What we found was there were no aircraft, so nothing for us to do. There were hundreds of us by that point. So, they had spent all these thousands of pounds on us in training to be riggers and fitters and wireless mechanics and all the rest of them. So, what did they do? They gave us rifles and bayonets and marched us up and down! We were doing drills. Then war was declared in the Far East. To release the army, we were put on guard duty. RAF tradesmen doing this guard duty business! Well, the Japs came down (through Malaya) to Singapore. I'll tell you about the fall of Singapore another time.

It was an absolute shambles. For instance, you could have any choice of car you wanted, if it was a Rolls Royce you could go down to the dock and pick yourself a Rolls Royce, or a Daimler, or whatever you wanted; the civvies had gone and left all that gear behind them. We were told, 'No more people to leave Singapore'. There was nothing we could do; all the ships had gone. Anyway, this squadron leader who was in charge of us, he came along, and he said, I've just received word, he said, every man for himself. Well, you won't recall, but Singapore fell over Saturday/Sunday, over the weekend.

The Japs had got into Singapore, infiltrated, got the MacRitchie reservoir and turned the water off. So that was that! This was Thursday morning – Japs all over the place!

Escape from Singapore!

So, the squadron leader comes in and says we're going to get off this island. He said, 'I've got a boat,' which we thought was ridiculous. He said, 'We will march down to a place where I know there is a ship.' He said, 'We will get off this island.' So, we get down to a ship breakers' yard, and there's this hulk right by the side of the dock, everything had been stripped off it and all that was left was just the hull. There was some coal in the boiler and the propellers would turn. So, we all piled on board. We took a few Chinese women and kids and Malayans and whatever on board this 'ship'. We started stoking it up and we sailed out of Singapore Harbour. We said, where are we going, sir? He said, 'Well, there's a sergeant navigator on board and he's got this school atlas and apparently if you come out of Singapore and turn right you come to Java.'

[*At this the audience laughed.*]

This is true, I'm telling you! Turn right and you come to Java! Well, the coal ran out so in went kit bags and anything we could lay our hands on. The Japs came over and bombed us, missed us of course, 27 bombers, a waste of bombs really on a little ship like that, but never mind. Anyway, we had run out of fuel and we finished up bobbing about in the South China Sea.

[*Referring to the map, Chick went on:*] This little island is Singapore and as you can see, you come out of there, and it's perfectly right, you come out of Singapore, turn right, and you come to Java! We got to Java – eventually. We were bobbing about on this little ship. There was plenty to eat, mind – we'd got plenty of food on board. Anyway, after a while there was a smudge of smoke on the horizon. We didn't know if it were a Jap or whatever; luckily for us it was a tug coming out of Batavia. I call it 'Batavia', which is the old-fashioned name for Jakarta. [*Batavia was the Dutch colonial name for the modern-day city of Jakarta.*]

So, this tug dragged us into Batavia. When we got there they said, who are you? We said RAF. They said, we can't feed you, we can do nothing for you, there's 50 quid, come back every day and report at 12 o'clock, which we did. We were staying in a school actually, so we reported every day at 12 o'clock and nothing happened. Three of us had met these Dutch girls who were living there with their parents in Java. We had a fine time. I was single, so it was great. They had a swimming pool and we had a smashing time! It got to quarter to 12 and we said we'll not bother to report in, so we didn't go. We did go eventually, the next day at 12 o'clock, but everybody had gone! There were just three of us left. So three of us, out of the whole 205 squadron, were still in Java. So, what happened? Again, shambles.

In Java
So, we attached ourselves to the City of Birmingham Squadron, 605, who were still in the area. They said that a third of the Australian Navy was in Southern Java, down here [*pointing to the map*]. So, we got on board these wagons [*I presume they commandeered them*], just as we were, no kit, just as we stood… khaki shorts, khaki shirt, straw hat, gum boots – that's a crazy thing to have in the tropics! – knife, fork and spoon and your gas mask and your tin hat. So, we got on board these wagons and we went across Java, across a range of mountains over there [*pointing to the map*]. We got to Southern Java – nothing! We had one of these big wireless wagons with us, you know, a whacking big thing, the type they had before transistor radios. As you know, Java used to belong to the Dutch. Well, word came over this wireless that the Dutch had capitulated, and all Allied prisoners of war were to wear a white arm band and report to the nearest Jap and we were to hand in our weapons. Well, we'd never seen a Jap until up to this point. So, there we were waiting to be taken prisoner, as I said, we had nowhere else to go. We were living on… I remember, it was a ten-pound tin of tomatoes and ten-pound tins of apples between 12 of us [*the three men of 205 squadron and*

some of the men from 605 Squadron] and that was our rations for the day. Well even these rations were running a bit short by now.

Becoming a POW

Anyway, we eventually found a Jap to report to. The first Jap I saw was this little fella who was directing us into this compound [*on the island of Java*]. A whacking great place, barbed wire compound, all the way round, no electricity. There were thousands and thousands of us. There were Dutch, Malayans, Brits, Yanks, New Zealanders, Aussies and Chinese but no Japanese. We were all milling about in this compound, and this is where we started to live on rice. Rice was our diet from then on. We got fed three times a day with rice. The Japs didn't know what to do with us, because Japanese don't take prisoners. The Geneva Convention, which no doubt you've heard of, indicates, among other things, that you treat prisoners in a certain way. You've got to give them the same rations as your 'enforcers', you've got to pay them for any work they do, you can't put them in any areas of danger. The Red Cross would have been party to it. But Japan didn't sign the Convention; she wouldn't sign it at all, because at the time it was introduced, in the 30s, Japan was at war with China. Japan didn't want to take prisoners in China; I mean, Japan would be outnumbered! They didn't bother with prisoners. Anyway, I'll come to that a little bit later on. So, there we were in this whacking great big compound, they didn't know what the devil to do with us. So, they said, you've got to march back where you came from, back to Batavia. So, by this time things were getting a bit bad in the tropics, your shoes were going, you know what it's like, perspiration and all.

Which reminds me – just diverting slightly – you know the Scots came down marauding in England, they got down as far as York and their shoes were wearing out, so word was sent back for some shoes and some stockings. They could neither read nor write in those days, so it was word of mouth. So, in Scotland, you know, shoes are called brogues, and the socks are called hose. So instead of saying brogues and hose, they sent down rogues and hoes and that's why Yorkshire is full of them! [*Laughter*]

[*Turning back to his talk, Chick went on:*] We were badly shod, and we were in a bit of a bad way, so we had to march back over the hills, occasionally getting some transport by trucks and train. It was difficult because they'd blown up the bridges. It was an absolute shambles. We finally got back to Batavia. Up till this time it had been a bit of a joke, I mean we were 20, 21, 22 and… and we saw it as a bit of an adventure. When we got back to Batavia I knew I was a prisoner of war because the monsters had put us in this great big civilian prison, a massive place. It was terrible! We were marched through these whacking great big doors and in front of you there was a whole semi-circle of cells. Now these cells might take 40, 50, 60 or even 200 men. So, they marched us up and pressed us into these cells, different sized cells, and crammed us in. Well it's in the tropics, humidity about 90, 95, certainly it's up to 85 or 90°F [*29 to 32°C*]. Not much water; there was a barrel of water in the corner and a little hole. So, everything had to be done in that corner, that's where you got a drink, or you did your toilet. They had crammed us in there and we were there for three days. Horrendous! Well, this is where the trouble started. There wasn't sufficient room for us all to lie down on the bed boards. The place was full of bugs, not the bugs that we see in England, ours are nothing; these things were so big that if you had a saddle you could have thrown one over and rode them back to England, they were that big! If you killed them the stink was horrendous, and of course they went for all the warm parts of your body, inside your leg, inside your arm and on your neck, all the warm parts; biting and all. This is how the lads got 'tropicalosis' [*probably Chick's name for various medical conditions*]. There was no medicine of any description. As I said, they kept us there for three days, eventually letting out about 50 of us at a time to have a bath. Marvellous!

Then they formed us into working parties. There were a thousand of us, but it wasn't too bad, I mean the sun was shining, we're getting three meals a day, rice and soup or whatever. We were out of the cells by going to these working parties. We were buying or bartering stuff from the Japanese, cigarettes or whatever. It wasn't pleasant exactly, but nobody was getting knocked around, not yet! Well, the first thing we had to do was learn some of their language, because these Japanese thought that the louder they shouted at us the more we'd understand.

Learning to Count and Speak in Japanese

So, the first Japanese we learnt was the words of command – fall in, left turn, right turn, how to count, that was the important thing. You may have heard, or you've seen the programme *Tenko* about life in a POW camp in Singapore,[54]

---

54 *Tenko* is a television drama, co-produced by the BBC and the ABC. The series dealt with the experiences of British, Australian and Dutch women who were captured after the fall of Singapore in February 1942, after the Japanese invasion, and held in a Japanese

but *tenko* in Japanese means 'roll call'. So, they called *tenko* two or three times a day. Well, there were no British Army numbers or English names or anything. When they shouted *tenko*, you had to call out a Japanese number. Men formed a line around the cell and '*tenko* numbered off' [*the men sequentially shouting out their number*]. Well, of course we didn't know the numbers, so what you did, you learnt one number and you stood in that place every time. I was number 29, so when it came to me to shout my number, I shouted '*ni – ju – kyu*' (29 in Japanese). To count in Japanese, it's perfectly simple, one to ten is [*Chick counts off with his fingers*]:

      1 *ichi*
      2 *ni*
      3 *san*
      4 *shi*
      5 *go*
      6 *roku*
      7 *shichi*
      8 *hachi*
      9 *kyu*
      10 *ju*

Now, if you remember that *ju* is ten and *ichi* is one, well, 11 – automatic – is *ju ichi*, isn't it? Quite simple. If you remember *ju* is ten and *ni* is two, 12 is *ju ni*, ten and two. Now if you say 21 – two is *ni*, *ju* is ten and *ichi* is one, *ni ju ichi*. Perfectly simple – have you got that?

[*laughter*]

So, it's no good shouting '*tenko*' here, is it?

[*laughter*]

When you got to 20 (which is two tens), you shouted *ni ju*. *Ju* is ten, *ni* is two, so 20 is *ni ju* (two tens). Twenty-one is *ni ju ichi*, 22 is *ni ju ni* and so on… *ni ju san*, *ni ju shi*, *ni ju go*, that's 25. So, I had to learn how to count in Japanese.

You must remember, this was the very first time that 'Asiatics' had ever beaten Europeans in battle. For the most part the Japanese soldiers we were

---

      internment camp on a Japanese-occupied island between Singapore and Australia. Having been separated from their husbands, herded into makeshift holding camps and largely forgotten by the British War Office, the women have to learn to cope with appalling living conditions, malnutrition, disease, violence and death.

guarded by were ordinary working-class folk, peasants in their society. Some of them weren't very bright – they had a good fighter's mind but they weren't very bright – and, of course, here are the Europeans who had dominated the Far East for decades and decades. As far as these Japanese soldiers were concerned, this was payback time. Every one of those Japanese soldiers was representing the emperor, in the Japanese Army culture, so virtually anything that we did or said, we were insulting that emperor. So, the first thing they did, we had to learn how to bow. They don't salute the way we do; they're doing the bowing bit. Now, bowing doesn't come easy to an Englishman, I don't know why, but we never bow, do we? Well, if we get the OBE maybe but this bowing took us a while to learn and we couldn't do it correctly.

The Japanese word for attention is: *Chusti* [*Chui!* is the correct dictionary translation] and *keirei* which means salute, and of course if you didn't do it right, as we never did, then they made you go down on your knees… which made us about the same size as what they were, and then they'd proceed to knock hell's bells out of us because we'd insulted the emperor by not bowing correctly. So, this was our first culture shock. For example, one time I was standing in the corner, minding my own business, and this Japanese guard came over and shouted *Chusti!* (attention) and got me on my knees and kicked hell out of me. In the camp we had a Japanese chap who was a bit of an interpreter as he had worked as a cook for a lumberjack company in Canada. I said to him, what was that for? He said, you are a naughty man. I said, why? I was just standing in the corner doing nothing. He said, well, yes, but how were you standing? I said, like this. He said, you can't stand with your arms folded in Japan: you are adopting a superior attitude. If you stand like that in Japan, you are making out you are superior to the Japanese. You are a prisoner of war; you've got nothing to be superior about. So, this is the culture shock that you get for just folding your arms!

[*laughter*]

The Culture

Of course, I've got to talk to you, finally, about the Japanese. I'm not making excuses for them but it's this culture bit. In Japan, there's a culture known as *bushido*.[55] Now, *bushido*, literally translated, it means the spirit of the warrior. *Bushido* indicates that under no circumstances do you capitulate; you fight to

---

55 *Bushido* literally means 'the way of the warrior'. It is a Japanese word for the way of the samurai life, loosely analogous to the concept of chivalry.

the death. You fight to the death and you go to your Valhalla[56] – you fought for the emperor and off you go to your heaven. Now, when it came down to the prisoners of war, by virtue of being prisoners in their eyes we were less than the dust on the ground. In their view if they gave us a cup of water they were doing us a favour. Here you have 300,000 prisoners of war; they were rubbish, less than dust. In their eyes we should have fought until we died. In their view, if we had fought in the proper way we wouldn't have been in the position we were in. Therefore, when they gave you a bowl of rice or a cup of water, we should think ourselves lucky. Whether we liked it or not, this was the Japanese attitude towards the prisoners of war, and this is basically why we were so badly treated. The Japanese weren't signatories to the Geneva Convention. Their concept was *bushido* and we were less than the dust, so if we died it didn't make the slightest difference.

The Terrible Journey to Japan
After about six months in Java they said pack your kit, which was a bit of a laugh! I mean, all I had was my fork and spoon, chopsticks, my gum boots and a few things. They marched us down to the docks and onto a boat bound for Singapore. We got to Singapore, we were on the docks, and we thought, well, they're going to take care of us here. Well, they put us under a hosepipe, a thousand of us blokes on the docks being hosed down to get us clean. Then they came round and dusted us all with this powder, whatever it was. I said (to those around me), Well, they're looking after us, at least. Now lined up on the quay were ships – 'ships' in inverted commas; they were all tramp steamers really. In 1930, when things were bad, particularly in this part of the world [*the north-east of England*], we were selling old ships to Japan as scrap. Well, the Japs didn't scrap them at all because many of them became part of their merchant navy. Now, every ship I ever worked on, whilst a POW in Japan, was either built on the Clyde or the Tyne or the Wear.[57]

Anyway, back to our situation in Singapore, we were told to get on board these ships. They were horrendous! If you talk to any of the WWII prisoners (POWs) you will get different views. The Jews, for example, they'll tell you about the gas chambers; that was their war in Germany. If you talk to the

---
56 In Norse mythology, Valhalla means 'hall of the slain'.
57 The north-east of England was a major shipbuilding area, mainly based on the Tyne and Wear rivers.

Yanks they'll talk to you about the death march in Bataan,[58] where they were marched up and down by the Japanese soldiers till they all died. If you talk to the Dutch, they'll tell you about the atrocities that were carried out in Sumatra [*the northernmost island of modern-day Indonesia*]. If you talk to the majority of the British servicemen they'll tell you about the railway in Thailand [*The Burma Railway*]. If you talk to people like us we'll tell you about the journey from Singapore to Japan proper: it was horrendous!

It was one of the worst episodes that I ever experienced. They jammed us down into the hold of the ship along with everything they could take to Japan, including cars and coal and oil. The ship we got on was loading down to the Plimsoll line[59] before we got on, and with bauxite (aluminium ore), which was wet and damp. The ship was loaded down to the gunwales[60] more or less before we got on. They piled us onto these ships down one ladder into this hold. In our ship there were three holds and the hold we were in measured 60 ft × 80 ft (approx. 18m × 24m). There was 286 of us down there! Two hundred and eighty-six in this small hold, crammed in tight and we were in the tropics! This journey was horrendous, no two ways about that! The *Dainichi Maru* was only about 3,000 tonnes. It took us 28 days to go from Singapore up to Japan proper.

To give you an idea of what it was like, I will read a piece from a book written by a chap in the same POW camp I was in. It is called *The Emperor's Guest*:[61]

> Throughout the voyage the food had been of very poor quality and quite insufficient. After Formosa the portions of rice got smaller and smaller. What was far worse was the diminishing of the quantity of water provided, for men

---

58 The Bataan Death March began on 9 April 1942 and was the forcible transfer by the Imperial Japanese Army of 60,000–80,000 Filipino and American prisoners of war after the three-month Battle of Bataan in the Philippines during World War II.
59 The Plimsoll line, also called the international load line or water line (positioned amidships), indicates the draft of the ship and the legal limit to which a ship may be loaded for specific water types and temperatures in order to safely maintain buoyancy. The purpose of a load line is to ensure that a ship has sufficient freeboard (the height from the water line to the main deck) and thus sufficient reserve buoyancy.
60 In simple terms, the gunwale (pronounced 'gunnel') is the edge at the top of the side of the ship. Originally the gunwale was the 'gun ridge' on a sailing warship. This represented the strengthening wale or structural band added to the design of the ship, at and above the level of a gun deck.
61 *The Emperor's Guest* is Donald Robert Peacock's diary of 1,276 days as a British prisoner of war of the Japanese in Indonesia during World War II.

wracked with fever this was unendurable deprivation. It was then that dying men drank each other's urine, it was then also alleged that shrouded in the shadows of darkness, men would open each other's veins with razor blades and suck each other's blood. Many knew they'd got hours to live, many knew they'd never see the light of day again. Despite the ministrations of comrades there was nothing that the latter could do to alleviate the agony.

This was the start of all our troubles. We sailed out of Singapore and we were battened down in the hold. The hatches went down and that was it! We could feel the ship's motion, but we could not feel the wind. The ship's sides were hot. Imagine you were down there with these 280/300 men in this hold with rats and God knows what flying all over the place. There was no water, nothing at all to start with and obviously there were no toilet facilities; you just did it wherever you could. You found a place and you laid down. They kept us down there for three days, then they opened up the hatches; the place was stinking to high heaven! Obviously… but we weren't allowed on deck.

They gave us two meals a day: we had a bowl of rice at about ten in the morning and to start with we had sweet potato soup. Well, it was rotten before we got it, so I didn't have any of that sweet potato soup. I had managed to accumulate rather a lot of sugar. I have a sweet tooth! There is rather a lot of sugar in Java and I was living on rice and sugar. Water was two or three cups a day and that went down to one cup a day. This was when the men started going down [*becoming sick*]. They were bitten by the bugs; they got tropical ulcers. We were now going from Java at 90–95°F, gradually north, and when we got to Japan it was November. When we got there it was snowing, freezing perishing cold, and there we were in khaki shorts, with khaki shirt and straw hat and gum boots and knife, fork and spoon. This was all I had.

So, this was the horrendous journey we suffered. By virtue of the changing climate you got pneumonia, then with a lack of vitamin B you got beriberi.[62] This is where your body just swells up: it gets full of water like phlebitis.[63] When you press on your leg the indentation stays in. Your neck swells and you'll waddle like the 'Michelin Man'.[64] Vitamin B cures that in no time at all if you can get it. We only got 'polished rice'. Rice in its original state has got

---
62   Beriberi is a disease brought on by a vitamin B1 (thiamine) deficiency.
63   Phlebitis is the inflammation of a vein, usually in the legs.
64   The Michelin Man, the cartoon living tyre man, is the trademark of Michelin Tyres.

a little husk which contains the vitamin B, but we only got the polished rice – hence no vitamin B! Later on, we asked for these husks to be given to us, but they said no, you can't, it's for the pigs! Then a lack of vitamin C and you get pellagra.[65] You get ulcers – a mouthful of ulcers, you can't drink, you can't swallow. The men got pneumonia and so on. We were getting all these diseases on the way to Japan proper. We had no deaths at all until we got to Taiwan. It's Taiwan now – in those days it was Formosa. And strangely enough the first death was on 11 November, Armistice Day, that's how I remember. The body was taken up the top; they'd found a Union Jack from somewhere; this lad was buried with full military honours. The Jap officer turned up with white gloves and in full dress uniform, saluting and bowing and all the rest of it. As the body went over the side they were throwing rice bowls, cigarettes and sweets into the sea. I mean, if they'd given the bloke that in the first place he wouldn't have died! But he's being celebrated now that he's dead – he's a warrior, and he's going to his Valhalla so now he gets buried with full military honours.

After this first death things got desperate with more and more deaths. Firstly, we had six Jap officers turning up, then there were five, then there were four, then there were three. Eventually there was no ceremony, the bodies were just dumped over the side and that was the end of it.

Arrival in Japan
As I said, it took 28/29 days to go from Singapore up to Japan proper. Now, Singapore to Nagasaki is about 2,500 miles.

This [*pointing to the map*] is the route we took up here, we called in there to Hong Kong, and went across into Taiwan and to Japan. Japan is made up of three large islands: Hokkaido, Honshu and Kyushu. Down here where these islands meet in here, that's called the Inland Sea, just in there [*pointing to the map again*].

We, 100 RAF personnel, finished up on a small island on the Inland Sea called Innoshima. We arrived at the entrance to the Inland Sea and we landed at a place called Shimonoseki[66] and from there we were then taken by train

---

65 Pellagra is a vitamin deficiency disease most commonly caused by a chronic lack of niacin (vitamin B3) in the diet.
66 Shimonoseki is a port at the north-western entrance to the Inland Sea of Japan in the straits which separate Kyushu (capital Nagasaki, which was bombed in WWII by an atomic bomb, as was Hiroshima) and Honshu. From here it is a short train ride to Hiroshima and on to Onomichi, which is probably where the prisoners were put on ferries to take them to Habu POW camp on the island of Innoshima.

and ferry to Innoshima. I will read you a little paragraph about our arrival at Shimonoseki from a book written by a fellow POW:

> By this time, as you can well imagine, we were in a pretty bad state. Our first stop was Shimonoseki. We left the ferry, we were herded like cattle through specially constructed wooden passageways with waist-high wooden bars on either side. We didn't march, we struggled through this place the best way we could. And beyond these there were hundreds of Japanese civilians, row upon row, bidden no doubt to see some of the spoils of war. We were on display! The crowd didn't jeer, they didn't roar, it was absolutely silent and inscrutable. The sound was punctuated by the gasps and groans of those riddled by dysentery and malnutrition, who were collapsing. The brutish guards reasserted themselves. Men were beaten and clouted unmercifully. If that didn't serve to get them on their feet, they prodded and jabbed them with their bayonets. Some of them, unconscious, would never move again, the cortege was not allowed to stop or even pause. If a man failed to walk towards the head of the column passing fellas might, with luck, haul him back to his knees and drag him along. If he was in the rear he had to be abandoned for there was no turning back, not even looking back. The whispers ran up the files that those who had fallen well behind were being bayoneted to death where they lay.

So, this is our introduction to the Japanese people and Japan proper, and as you can imagine we were in a bad way and, as I've explained to you, if you talk to us, we talk about that journey from there to there [*pointing to the map, Singapore to Japan*]. I've glossed over quite a bit of it, but it was bad, no two ways about it. Our poor state on the journey formed the basis of the sickness: the dysentery, diarrhoea, beriberi, and all the rest of it.

Innoshima

This little ferry took us to this little island called Innoshima on the Inland Sea. There were 100 of us, 40 of us on our feet and 60 on their back with all the diseases I just mentioned. There were no doctors, no pills, no powders, no nothing, so, I mean, what can you do? The cure for dysentery, as far as the Japs was concerned, was to go to the cook house and grind up the wood and make charcoal out of it. Grind up the charcoal and swallow that! The charcoal was supposed to 'bind' us, to stop the dysentery! That's their cure!

As I say, 40 of us on our feet, 60 on our backs. We did the best we could but started to lose a few blokes. Now, as I say, we're only kids, 20, 21, 22. We had read that you can sit in a corner and give up hope and die. Now, I never believed this. But it happened. If you think about it, it's the first time we've been away from home, there was no newspapers, there was no letters, no Red Cross, we didn't know where we were, no concept of how the war was going, how long it was going to last, when do we get out of this, how long is it going to be and so forth. So, they just gave up hope. They sat in the corner and they died! Not all of them died that way, but three or four, they gave up the ghost and they just faded away. They just stopped eating, got dysentery and died. I don't know why it is, but if you've got dysentery and you've started to hiccup, hiccupping was the first sign that you were going to die.

We learnt that very quickly! If a man with dysentery got hiccups, he was finished. There's only one man I ever knew out there who, with dysentery, with hiccups, lived, but when the rest of them got hiccups, we knew that nothing more could be done. This went on and after about three or four weeks they started forming working parties. They marched us from the camp about three or four miles to the docks, the shipyard. They lined us up and they picked out the six biggest blokes – I was one of them – and they gave us shovels and from then on, for the next three and a half years, we got all the dirty, stinking, filthy jobs there were to do in the dockyard. Cleared out engine rooms, boiler rooms, dry docks, coal havens.[67] Because it was an island, there was nothing there at all: everything had to be imported. Coal was very precious as far as the Japs were concerned: we couldn't use coal in the camp; we had to use wood. For the first year the Jap guards stood over us with rifles and bayonets fixed; prodding us with bayonets and knocking us about generally. Morale was very low. Up at five o'clock every morning, did your physical jerks from five till quarter past, then a cold-water shave, if you had a razor blade. My razor blade lasted three years. We sharpened it by firstly putting the razor blade in a drop of water and then ran it round the inside of a glass tumbler. That is the way you sharpened your blade [*demonstrating*]. It lasted three and a half years, saved a fortune!

[*laughter*]

On top of that all our hair had to be shaven off; everybody was bald, which was a good thing really, we didn't like it to start with. I mean, the lads with curly hair were crying. It doesn't matter about being a prisoner of war, they get

---

67 A 'coal haven' is a place for storing large quantities of coal. These were very common in the late nineteenth and early twentieth centuries, when most ships were powered by coal-fired steam engines.

that curly hair cut off, they were in tears. Anyway, it was explained to me later on that if you've got curly hair to start with, when it regrows it will grow curly, because if you've got curly hair you've got a fault in the skull. Apparently, as far as I understand, inside the skull there's follicles, and the hair comes from these follicles, and if the holes don't line up you get a kink in the hair like that and that's how you get a curly hair.

[*laughter*]

Working in the Dockyard

Anyway, moving on, after a year or so things were going a little bit badly for the Japanese and the Japanese guards were taken away from us and we had civilian guards put over the prisoners. We still had the Jap soldiers at the camp; there were three, four, about five of them, including the commandant. The soldiers marched us down to the dockyard every day and then they passed us over to the Japanese civilians. After a year things were getting a bit easier. We weren't getting knocked about quite as much because the Jap guards had gone. The civilian guards had done their time in the army, so they had a militaristic approach to everything, but it was better.

The six of us became known as the 'genki boys'.[68] Well, the word *genki* in Japanese means if somebody meets you in the street, says hello, how are you, you might reply I'm great, I'm fit, I'm top of the bill, I'm champion. *Genki* means you're good, you're fit and you're well, you're healthy. So, we became known as the 'genki boys'. We were relatively healthy because we were the only ones who were getting on board these oceangoing ships, and of course the first place we made for was the galley. In the camp, hunger overtakes you. All of us were starving, hungry day in, day out. We got a bowl of rice at six o'clock in the morning, just an ordinary bowl, chopped off at the top, you couldn't get any more no matter what. There was a pinch of salt on the top. We used to get a day off every three weeks, and that was to clean up the camp! So, on our day off they gave us long bamboo rakes and we waded out into the sea, up to our chests and then raked in the seaweed, got it on shore. We chopped it up very fine, and that was our breakfast for the next three weeks! So, it was seaweed soup and rice for your breakfast. Sometimes we got it for lunch. But the big treat was when we got carrot tops or turnip tops or whatever from rubbish was going; but no meat, no eggs, no fish, no sugar, nothing like that at all, just

---

68 'Genki boys' are extensively referred to in Terence Kelly's book *By Hellship to Hiroshima*.

the rice and very, very weak soup, whatever they might give us. Consequently, we were permanently hungry. I mean, rice, as you know, is a top carbohydrate, with some salt it gives you energy, quick energy. You can work like a slave for about two or three hours until you've worked it off. By the time ten o'clock in the morning comes you're starving of hunger with pains in the stomach. To alleviate this, we drank gallons and gallons of water, just to fill the stomach.

So, we had a bloke working in the machine shop, and, for a consideration, which was X number of bowls of rice, we asked him to make us three skeleton keys each: small, medium and large. So, he made these 18 skeleton keys for us, three each. By the way, everything was under a padlock in Japan. Now, you give me a padlock, don't put it in front of me – I couldn't open it – but you give it me behind my back, I can do it! So, with these skeleton keys we were able to open the padlocks. They used to spring open! So, we were able to get into the stores.

Now prior to this if you saw some food, you ate it. It didn't matter; if it looked like food you ate it.

I remember we were going down to the dockyard one morning from the camp; there were about 50 or 60 in the working party. It got passed back that there were onions by the side of the road. So, as you marched by you grabbed these onions, ate them and got rid of what was left. The next morning, they couldn't get a working party out except one man, only one man on his feet! The guard couldn't understand this at all, and couldn't decide what we'd eaten: everybody had eaten the same but only one man was fit. Anyway, it turned out he hadn't eaten his onion. He still had it – it wasn't an onion; it was a bloody daffodil bulb, and we'd scoffed the lot!

[*laughter*]

So, we got these skeleton keys and we were doing rather well by virtue of stealth. Mind you, we took chances, make no bones about it, and when I think back now I get horrified at the risks we took. Well, of course, you couldn't carry the stuff or put it in your pocket. So here is what we did… we were on board this ship one day and there were some life jackets there. The life jackets were filled with kapok, which I think is Dutch cotton. We threw the cotton away and we kept the material, got it back to the camp. Then we took the wool thread from the blanket we had, and we made a bag.

[*Chick then shows an example he had made*] This is not the original, by the way, I made this specially for this morning! The straps of a bag like this went over the head. The bag part hung down below the waist inside your trousers [*demonstrating*]. It had a flap lid. We were all skinny by this time so if you walked, like, in a stooped way [*demonstrating*] the bag would not be noticed by the guard. This is of course how we got the stuff back to the camp. We were searched time and time again, but the Japs never touched the front of us; they went down the sides. I bet they'd have been a bit embarrassed if they'd gone round the front way to see what they didn't have!

[*laughter*]

The Side of Pork Incident!

There was one famous, well, I should say, infamous morning, when we got on board this oceangoing liner, the *Île-de-France*. The Japanese had picked it up, probably, in Indochina.

By the way, as you know, my nickname is 'Chick' Henderson, which I got in the war. I was called this after the wartime singer Chick Henderson. I was sort of unofficial interpreter: the Japs would say 'Chick, bla bla bla' – saying what they wanted done. Well, with a few words and a few gestures here and there, we would find out what they wanted. So, we got to work. In the *Île-de-France* there was a great big fridge. We opened the door. You wouldn't believe it; there's half a pig hanging there. How the hell do you get half a pig back to the camp?

[*laughter*]

Well, we had had no meat in the camp. So, I said, I'm going to nick this pig. We got it into a basket and took it down to the toilets. Not toilets like what we have. These are Japanese toilets. You squat, you know.

So, I got this pig and I tore it, cut it into four pieces and got mine strapped on. I said to the big lad with me – he was about 6'2" – you take the knuckle end as you are a big lad and to another, I said, you take the end bits. Then the fourth lad went in to get his – you'll never believe it, but someone had gone in there and stolen it! We never found the fourth portion from that day to this. Thieves! Unbelievable!

[*laughter*]

This happened at about seven o'clock in the morning. However, the actual task that day was to move great piles of coal from there to here [*demonstrating*]. So, we had to carry these lumps of raw meat around all day whilst we were working at shovelling the coal. The funniest sight I saw was Chris with the knuckle of pig hanging round his neck while he was shovelling coal. Every time he shovelled the coal over, the knuckle end of pig came out of his bag and hit him in the face! This went on from seven o'clock in the morning till six o'clock at night! Of course, the pig had been frozen and by God it was cold. I thought I'd done myself a mischief, because by getting so hot it had all started to melt and all the liquid and water was running down my front. Dear God, it was uncomfortable. Anyway, we did get back to camp. We thought, what do you do with this? If you started to cook it the smell was going to permeate the whole building and we would be found out.

We had received a Red Cross parcel. This rarely happened. In Japan I got three and a half parcels in three and a half years. I got one a year, and even that I had to share. The Japs held onto them and would not release the parcels and the letters and the clothing that people were sending to us. Tokyo was full of foodstuffs which were going rotten; the Japs just wouldn't deliver them to us.

We had three different Red Cross parcels – there was the American Red Cross parcel, the Canadian and the Brits'. The Canadian one was very good, and in the American one there was a tin of dried milk. It was called 'klim', which is milk spelt backwards. So, with an empty klim tin we had to boil down half a pig. In a tin this size [*demonstrating*]! You can think how long it took us to render the fat down to get this to the point where we can eat it.

And, of course, all the lads were sitting there with their tongues hanging out; the smell of bacon was all the way through the camp. It must have been a bit disconcerting. By this time, there were 100 extra prisoners arrived from Hong Kong,[69] so now there were 200. But to share with them we would have had to take the meat to the cook house. If we did this the Japs would find out and they would say, where's the pork come from? So, we couldn't do that. So, we had to go through all this pork and eat it ourselves as long as it lasted, and it lasted a long, long time! That was the pork incident.

Getting Caught and Punishment!
The other big incident was when I was caught. We were on board a ship, two of us, and we got to the store and opened it, and dragged out this great big crate. It was full of cigarettes! If we could have got this back to the camp life would have

---

69   I think Chick is referring to the Hong Kong Volunteer Defence Corps (HKVDC). Established in 1854, the 'Hong Kong Volunteers' were also known as the 'Hong Kong Volunteer Defence Corps' and the 'Royal Hong Kong Regiment'. In the early days, the force recruited members from an elite group. As times went by, different classes of society and different ethnic groups also joined the force. Despite being volunteers, they received professional training. Their missions were to make contributions to society and protect their home. They fought bravely against the Japanese during the WWII invasion.

been a lot easier for everybody: cigarettes were the barter. You get what you like with fags. We pulled this crate out, then we heard a noise. Chris, the lad I was with, took a dive straight over the side. So, I'm stuck there. So, I sat in the corner and a Jap came down. He said, what are you doing here, and went on… yakkety yak, yakkety yak: he was full of hell. I said I fell down those stairs and I've hurt me head. He didn't believe me, so he took me upstairs. This was an army ship so there were soldiers on board. They knocked me about a bit, then they stood me in front of a brazier about from here to there [*demonstrating*]. I'm standing to attention in front of this brazier, at first a bit uncomfortable. Then I start to burn, singe and smoke. Then the Japs started kicking me, hitting me and all the rest of it. Then this lad (a POW from Hong Kong) had a word with these chaps. Now, I've always had my suspicions – well, not suspicions, that's the wrong word – but he spoke more or less in fluent Japanese. He was making the point that how could one man steal a whole crate of cigarettes? It was ridiculous. Anyway, this went on and on. I'm still standing there. Anyway, when they finished talking the soldiers kicked me about a bit more, cuffed me about the ears and gave me '25' and told me to go, which I did. [*'25' could have meant 25 cigarettes or it could have meant something else, like a punishment.*]

But by this time a report had gone to the commandant so when I got back to the camp I was punished a second time, well, given two punishments. The first one was where they sit you right down on your haunches like that [*demonstrating*], and they put a bamboo rod behind your knees. At one time it used to be barbed wire, but this was a bamboo rod. Then you have to crouch in a sitting position. And, of course, after two or three minutes it would stop the circulation going to your legs and you start to keel over. They then kick your back. This went on for about an hour and a half or two hours. Then, secondly, you get kicked about. I was never caught stealing again!

The other punishment we had was when we retaliated against some kids throwing things at us. We were digging coal and some Japanese kids, about 16 or 17 years of age, started throwing lumps of coal at us, which was a bit off-putting. So, one of our lads, a bit of a firebrand, he went up the hill and he got hold of one of these kids and thumped him. The worst thing, of course, was the Jap kid just stood there – he didn't expect to be hit by a prisoner of war – so our lad hit him and hit him hard.

Of course, our lad was dragged back to the camp to a little cell, only about as wide as this [*measuring about 3' with his arms out*] and about 5'5" high and with a grill here [*demonstrating*]. The punishment was that the prisoner had to stand crouched like this [*demonstrating*] with his face on this grid all day! You weren't allowed to lie down. Well, it got to night time, about nine o'clock, and he had to crouch down in this little square and sleep the best way he could. You were allowed out every three hours, to walk around, and you got three bowls of rice – three handfuls of rice – which was as much as the commandant could put in his hand. Well, the Japanese, their hands aren't very big, so that was what you got! That was your breakfast, that was your dinner, and that was your supper. No soup, no nothing, not even a cup of water. So that was the punishment. He was there for a week. He was in a bad way when he got out.

Nothing to Read
Anyway, life went on. With the best will in the world, this is like trying to describe the sunset to a blind man, not that you're blind, but trying to explain to you what the sheer boredom of the thing was… I mean, you got up, as I say, at five o'clock every morning, you went to work, and you came back, you went to work, and you went to bed by nine o'clock. There were two books in the camp and one pack of cards and by the time we'd finished with the cards they were circular, not square; they had been worn that much! Nothing to read. But we used to pinch a newspaper from time to time. For example, there was this old Jap civilian guard, he had three men under him, three prisoners, and he used to always leave his newspaper at lunchtime, and when he came back it had gone. And he knew fine well where it had gone. We brought the paper back to the camp.

Now some of these lads from Hong Kong spoke Japanese. There was one little lad from Hong Kong who I spoke to one day, saying, 'what the hell are you doing here?' His mother was Japanese, and his father was a German and he was fighting for the Brits in Hong Kong! He used to do the interpretation. There was the Japanese 'newspaper' they gave us to start with. It was in English. Of course, when the war was going well it was full of the Japanese victories and all the rest of it. But they stopped those newspapers after 1942. Anyway, we had our stolen Japanese newspaper and translator. It had a lot of propaganda in it, but we could get some sense out of it.

American Bombers
By this stage of the war we hear American bombers coming over, bombing and machine-gunning and all the rest of it. After the war was over I got a postcard from a colleague. It was of a photograph that he'd taken of the camp from a distance [*Chick then describes the scene on the postcard*].

There's a mark down the middle, that's where it got creased, so don't take any notice of that. There's the camp up and down there, there's the Inland Sea down there, there's a gantry, we were in these huts, and you can see PW, meaning prisoner of war, on top of our buildings. This was the cook house, and you can see round there in the bottom right: this is where the Yanks came and bombed and machine-gunned us. Oh, we had a great war, we're fighting everybody!

[*laughter*]

Figure 7.4 Cartoon by the camp artist. Source: these were shown in Chick Henderson's video. This copy, however, is by kind permission of Adrian Batty from his father's collection.

For the Japanese it was pretty pointless taking our names and addresses. So, what they did, they took group photographs of us, no names of course, took us in groups of four or eight [*showing a photograph*].

In this photograph they took of us we are shown with Japanese uniforms on. I'm in there somewhere.

[*Turning to another item, Chick says:*] This over here is a leaflet that was dropped by air to tell you that the war was over. This here is a photograph, an aerial photograph from possibly 25,000 feet, of the camp and dockyard before they came over and bombed us. Here is my work card, which got stamped every day. If you worked, you got tuppence a day [*2 old pence, less than one penny in today's money*] and you got two cigarettes a day. If you didn't work you got nothing and half rations.

Yes, they came over and they bombed the shipyard. This was the most glorious sight you'd ever seen! Sounds stupid, but here are the Japanese scurrying about all over the place getting ready for the bombers coming over, and there's 100 prisoners of war with our shirts off and cheering them on! Bloody bombs dropping all over the place. And, of course, a lot of the Japanese blamed us for the bombing. They said it was our fault, as we directed the bombs over there.

Here's a bit of a cartoon drawn by the camp artist, and this is it: I'll pass this around (see previous page).

That's me [*at left-hand side*]; it's supposed to be me: there's the key I was telling you about, there's the padlocks, that's the lookout there, this is the fella filling the bag, and if you turn it over [*he turns the cartoon card over*] you walk back to the camp with your bag sticking out of your belly like that, out there!

[*laughter*]

POW Pay

As far as the tuppence a day to work was concerned, we started accumulating Japanese money, which was absolutely useless to us; I mean, there's no shops, nowhere to spend it at all. So, we spoke to the interpreter, said, look, we've got this money, what are we supposed to do with this? At this point we had an accumulation of two or three years' money. So these questions went on for a while and one day we were told 'Japanese commandant good man, we will let you buy things in the canteen'. Great! We were to get ten 'sen' [*Chick explained – sen is a 1/100 of a yen, like a cent to a dollar*]. In other words, ten sen a day, which was worth about tuppence. One hundred sen makes one yen. At the end of the month we were able to accumulate three yen. So, we were led into this little hut that they'd built, called the 'canteen'. There was a barrel of apples – we had never seen apples for years – a barrel of oranges and tooth powder and toothbrushes. We said, how much are the apples? Answer: three yen! We said, how many do you get? Answer, one. What about the oranges, we said? Answer: three yen. The toothpaste was the same. So, in effect the Japanese commandant was buying this stuff at whatever price and selling it to us. In other words, we were working for a month for an apple or an orange! The month after that, the same thing: one apple or orange, and so on.

Wakamoto Tablets

Then Wakamoto tablets appeared. Now, these Wakamoto tablets were vitamin B. We were told they were three yen. I said, I'll have a bottle of those. So, I took one Wakamoto tablet every day because I had beriberi, and after two or three of those the beriberi went. The trouble is getting beriberi and dysentery at the same time. The lavatories, which were just a hole in the ground with a bit of wood over the top, were quite a way away. If you tried to run while you had beriberi, it wasn't the dysentery that killed you; you'd have a heart attack because you were carrying all this extra weight! Then they brought out what they called cod liver oil. Well, it had never been near a cod [*laughter*]! It was a bit greasy, so you just poured that over your rice and just ate it, and that helped me, I think.

Life in the Camp

Red Cross parcels came from time to time and we had a bit of a 'divvy up' of the contents. This is how we kept sort of body and soul together, plus with the stuff that we were stealing down at the dockyard, barley or rice or whatever was worth stealing. We also stole tools: hammers, scissors and saws and all sorts of things, like razors. As I've tried to explain, it was sheer boredom we were suffering from. If you commit a crime [*in this country*] for the most part the judge says, right, three years. As our friend from Yorkshire knows, you get time off for good behaviour, don't you [*laughs*]? But here in a prisoner of war camp you don't know what's going on in the outside world: there's no communication except for the bits of information you're getting from a Japanese newspaper, which was full of propaganda. I had only two letters in all the time I was in Japan. We were allowed to send a card when we were first caught in Java, a postcard, and it had five sentences on it and you had to cross out two which weren't applicable – 'I am happy', 'I am working for pay', 'The Japanese are very kind to me'. So, you just crossed out a load. It took exactly a year for my mother to get that card from the end of 1941, for it to get back to England via India and so on, via Switzerland.

It was sheer boredom and monotony. I mean you're working, you're working hard, especially the six of us [*here he is referring to the 'big lads'*]. Of course, some had easy jobs.

Oil from an Oil Tanker!

One job we had was in the summer when this great big oil tanker came in. So, typical Japanese, they just bore a hole in the bottom of the ship and caught the oil coming out! As you may know, the bottom of the tanker was full of residue from the oil; it sinks down to the bottom. So, the Japs, being short of oil, were not going to waste anything. This all ran into four-gallon tins and we were underneath this ship with a four-gallon tin, passing it from hand to hand and tipping the oil into an iron bucket. The crane was to come along and pick up the bucket. The top of the jib of the crane would reach the area where we were under the hull of the ship in the dry dock. So, typical Japanese, they get a telegraph pole [*laughs*], and they lash it onto the end of the jib with wire rope. Then they put a block and tackle on the end of the telegraph pole. We're down here at the bottom of the dry dock. They let down the hook and we put it on the great bucket. As it is not a clear vertical drop from the jib it bumps its way up. The crane swings around and the bucket is tipped into a lighter [*like a barge*]. This went on and on; it was a backbreaking job, filthy dirty, we had no soap. Anyway, then the winter comes. By this time the oil has solidified, so it didn't run, obviously. So, they lit fires down there in the hold at the bottom of an oil tanker, lit fires [*gasps*]! You had to put your shovel into the fire to get it warm. Then you cut a cube out of the oil, like that [*indicating the size*], and put it in a basket. The basket was hauled up by three or four blokes pulling on a rope from down in the hold, up to a bloke sitting astride a girder above. The basket was then tipped into the great iron bucket and off it went. This went on for months. By this time the lighter was right way down flat [*meaning low in the water*]. As I said, I was with the City of Birmingham Squadron, who normally rarely saw the sea or a dockyard, unlike me, coming from a shipbuilding area. The foreman said to me, 'I want the bar to go from there to there' [*Chick pointed*]. So, we got the men to haul it slowly along the pontoon. I fastened it up with a nice clove hitch knot at this end. I didn't bother to fasten that end.

We went to work the next day, and the whole of the harbour was covered in bloody oil [*laughs*]. The tide had gone out, my two clove hitches had held, and the barge was tipped over like that [*demonstrating*]: eight or nine hundred tonnes of oil was all over [*laughs*]! That was my war effort, by the way; that was my big moment! All this oil spilt all over the dockyard, all over the bay, dead fish all over the place. There was absolute pandemonium down there. And the best thing about it, I never saw the foreman any more. I don't know what happened to him, but he went. My other war effort was when I got to the ship early one day, went on board and there was a great big box of tools. I kicked it over the side. Churchill would have been proud of me that day [*laughs*]!

Working Methods
We also built ships. I must say this about the Japanese mind: they don't have 'demarcation lines' in jobs like we have. Compared to the Japanese, you can see why our shipbuilding industry went for a burton.[70] In Japan, workers did all jobs. One day you are shovelling coal, the next day he's welding, the next day he's riveting and the next day after that he's doing a bit of plumbing work. Every job to the Japanese was interchangeable. When there was a shortage of workmen for one task you were just moved from there to there and did whatever job you were told to do. You weld today, you're shovelling coal the next day, you're doing totally different jobs all the time. All the trades were intermixed. As a result, of course, the ship just went up like that [*meaning it got built faster*]. There was no waiting anywhere; nobody was waiting for someone to drill a hole or arguing if the wood was attached to the metal and so on. Might be a bit dodgy some of the time but it got done.

More Sabotage
We were building a landing craft. This is where we came up with another trick by putting sand, which there was plenty of on the beach nearby, in the bearings of the winches. You got some sand from the beach here [*pointing to a photo*], put it in your pocket and when you were on the job you just had to drop the sand in the bearings. Another big war effort!

Examples of POW Money
By the way, I have some Japanese money here. I was told I was coming down

---

70 'Gone for a burton' means something or someone who is no longer functional.

to this Probus Club at South Shields, and I said, I'm going to show them some Japanese money that I had to work for. I was told, we know those people down there and if I were you I'd put the money under glass and count it!

[*laughter*]

So, at great expense I've got this under glass and this is the actual money I worked for, so very, very hard. It's under glass so I know I'm going to get it back from you!

[*laughter*]

The End of the War

The Americans, as I say, had been over, bombing and machine-gunning and all the rest of it. They shot about 40 of us. One morning we got to the dockyard and there was absolute silence. There was a Japanese foreman sitting at the end of this number 4 dock, where we were to work on cleaning out this engine. So, he just sat there all morning, not a murmur. So, it got towards lunchtime – what a lovely word for a bowl of rice! – lunchtime. They said, go down there, Chick, and find out when we can have lunch. I said I'm not going down there, there's something gone wrong. Anyway, it got to lunchtime, and I did go and speak to this foreman, who was quite a docile bloke really, so I said, it's quarter to 12 and before I finished he went rabbiting on. So, I went back to the lads and they said, 'What did he say?' I said, I don't believe it, I said, the only words I got were 'American' and a 'bomb' and '100,000 people'. I said, it's ridiculous that, no, I've picked it up wrong from what he said. Anyway, we went down and had our meal, came back, still no work at all. We went back to the camp; everything was dead silent down there.

As you know, the atomic bomb was dropped on Hiroshima, which is here [*pointing to the map*]. This small island, on the 'Inland Sea', was where we were. It was called Innoshima, which is 30 miles away from Hiroshima, so we were 30 miles away from where the bomb was dropped!

Now, don't ask me how we got away with that. As you know, they dropped a second bomb. Not near us this time. As you know, that led to the capitulation.

The Japanese Emperor and Bushido

Now, here's a situation, where the Japanese emperor, who is a god, wants to capitulate. Now what happens to the spirit of *bushido*? The spirit of the warrior and all the rest of it? These people had been brought up for years to believe that the emperor is a god, absolutely infallible: what he says is right. You die for the emperor, you die for your country, then go to your Valhalla. How does the emperor come out and explain 'capitulation' after all these hundreds of years when the spirit of *bushido* has been forced down the throats of the Japanese?

Here is how we heard the news of capitulation. We went down, and we sat on the dockyard and listened to the emperor on the radio. I can't give you what he said word for word, though one of the lads was writing it down, but basically what he said was that the spirit of *bushido* was still alive in Japan as they hadn't been beaten by force of arms; they'd been beaten by silence. In other words, Japan had not been beaten on the field of battle, so *bushido* was still intact, the spirit was still there, but they couldn't compete with a big bomb. Americans were cowardly for dropping the bomb because it wasn't really a battle. Notwithstanding they [*the Japanese*] had been bombing for years, over and above that, excuse by the emperor was a cop-out, you see.[71]

Japanese Reactions

So, how would the Japanese react to this? Well, we got back to the camp, there wasn't a soul there, everybody had gone, except us: 140 to 180 blokes. Who's going to feed us? Where's the food coming from? So, we broke open the stores. We sat outside with the greatcoats and the boots and the army uniform and all the rest of it. Then a Japanese woman came up and we did a bit of barter, you know, you can have a blanket for this fish and so on. Shoes and boots were being swapped for this and that. That's how we got the food. Then the next thing we got was word from the Red Cross. I've got a copy of the letter here, dated 27 August 1945:

> To prisoners of war from Fritz W Bellfinger, representative for the National Red Cross
>
> The hour of your liberation has come, representatives of the protecting powers, Switzerland, America, Britain, Australia, Sweden, the Netherlands etc, and the undersigned are in touch with the Allied High Command and will assist the Japanese authorities in your evacuation.

'A speedy and comfortable evacuation can only be assured if you collaborate and maintain order to the last,' it said, and we were very concerned about this. 'For this reason, you are requested to follow the instructions of your camp

---

71 Cop-out – a failure to fulfil a commitment or responsibility or to face a difficulty squarely.

representative who will be in contact with us and will receive the necessary information. Therefore, please be patient and do not create any disturbance which may delay your evacuation. Japan should see you leave with all your honour and dignity.'

What everybody was afraid of, here, was which way would the prisoners go, and which would the Japanese go, because here the lads, over three and a half years, had been kicked about from pillar to post, and this could well be payback time. On the other hand, we had been told, in no uncertain terms, that we were insurance against Japan being invaded, and the Japanese had made it perfectly clear that, in the event of any Allied soldiers setting foot on Japanese soil, prisoners of war would be beheaded. This was their insurance policy. So which way do you jump? It was a very tense situation because nobody knew which way they were going to go. We were a bit vulnerable; I mean, we didn't have a rifle between us in order to protect ourselves. The Japanese had guns all over the place; they'd all been in the army. Anyway, we ventured out, two or three at a time into the town of Habu. Well we got all this [*demonstrating bowing*]. We got asked to come and have a cup of tea and all that. One or two of the Jap foremen got kicked about a bit. They had been a bit unkind to us. But that was that.

The Best Meal I Ever Had
We had been advised to put PW on top of the camp rooftops. So, I put PW in big white letters. American bombers came over, the bomb doors were opened and – manna from heaven – all the parachutes came down with the food, the razor blades, Red Cross parcels, meat, corned beef, condensed milk. Oh, wonderful, all this stuff! The best meal I ever had was a tin of corned beef; I had never seen meat for three and a half years, a tin of corned beef with a tin of condensed milk over it – the best bloody meal I've had in my life. I was as sick as a dog, but I didn't half enjoy it [*laughs*]. We were told to be a bit careful what you eat because, you know, you've been on starvation rations all these years: if you start to pack your stomach, things are going to happen.

We Leave Japan
Eventually a ferry came and they took us up to Tokyo. I've never seen so many ships in all my life. It was full of aircraft carriers and battle cruisers and so on. The Yanks were in charge of us. We were told to strip off: whatever we had on, into the fire it went. And the next thing they gave us was a bar of scented soap

[*laughs*]! There was a long passageway to showers with hot and cold water, and you just marched in there… [*mimics washing and laughs*]. We got to the other end, they gave us a great white bath towel, we dried ourselves with this bath towel. That was taken and put into a furnace: it was burnt because they didn't know what we had; I mean, we don't know what we had either. Also, stories had got out that lads had gone a bit, I don't mean *queer* queer, but they'd gone a bit funny in the head and how would they take to eating all this food and so on.

Anyway, we came out of there and we were taken to the stores. We were told we could have what we liked. Typical British, we said, 'We can have what we want?' They said, if you can carry it, you can take it. So, I got army boots and God knows what else, staggered out with this stuff. 'If you could' because, let's be honest about this, I was one of the fit ones and I was six stone seven.

I was 13 and a half stone when I became a POW and six stone seven when I came out. To give you some idea, I had a belt; this is the actual belt [*demonstrates by showing where it was buckled*]. Six stone 7, an hourglass figure. My wife did have an hourglass figure at one time but unfortunately all the sand dropped to the bottom!

[*laughter*]

We got aboard this Australian aircraft carrier, HMS *Ruler*, which took us away from Japan. Up until then the Americans didn't refer to us as prisoners; they always referred to us as 'our guests'. So, we got all kitted out; we were all washed and shaved and looking lovely. Then we heard the speakers say, 'Will our guests please go to hanger one?'. Well, we go to hanger one and they gave us a great big tray with indentations on it for your food. The hanger was full of food! We couldn't believe it: there was custard, there was jelly, meat and so on. Of course, some of the lads, they just went hammer and tongs at it, they just couldn't stop eating. Anyway, the next announcement was, 'Will our guests please go to hanger number four?'. Oh, by this time there was an orchestra playing.

So, we go down to hanger number four, nobody was pushing us, just asking us very gently and very nicely. We were formed into long lines and queued to meet a sergeant at a desk and a bloke with a typewriter taking name, rank and number. Over to one side were what they called a WACs [*Women's Army Corps*] in the American Army over there, and they had a shop with all sorts of stuff: there was chocolate, razor blades, all sorts of things. So, I went over there, and

I said, 'Do you take Japanese money?' and she said, 'No, I don't take that.' I said, 'Well I've got no dollars and no pounds.' I said, 'How do you get hold of this stuff?' She said, 'Well, just tell us what you want, you can have it!' [*laughs*] So I got loaded up with this stuff and came back to the lads; they said, 'Where did you get that, Chick?' I say, 'Over there.' They asked, 'How much?' I said, 'Nothing.' Whoosh! They were all over there [*laughs*].

Then we were taken out to this Australian aircraft carrier, HMS *Ruler*. I knew we were back [*in the British Forces*]. There was a line three times round the ship, sign here for your money, your knife, fork and spoon, nothing's changed [*laughs*]! Anyway, HMS *Ruler* took us down to Sydney, Australia.

In Sydney

We went to the Union Jack club in Sydney. There was another array of girls there. I'll tell you this much, after what we had been through it was food first. If you don't get your food women don't come into it; women are secondary. At the Union Jack club they asked us, 'Where would you like to go?' My pal and I said, 'We'd like to go to a sheep farm.' They said, 'Come back tomorrow morning, seven o'clock'. We got back there at seven o'clock the next morning. They said, here's your railway ticket, your ration ticket and this, that and the train leaves at half past. All at no charge! Well, we got on the train, and soon it came out of Sydney. What did we see? Miles and miles of nothing. Nothing [*laughs*]!

We get to this tiny station and a bloke turns up in a big Buick. He says, 'Mr Henderson and Mr Hornsby?' I say yes, and he says, 'I'm your host.' We get in the car and he takes us to this sheep farm and he gives us a horse each. So, we're riding the range [*laughs*]! He said, 'I was in the First World War and I was wondering what I could do to help the old country [*meaning Great Britain*] and what we are doing now is the only thing I have thought of.' He went on, 'I was wounded in Gallipoli and they sent me back to England and they were very, very good to me, over there,' he says. 'I was in a place called Brighton; do you know it?' I said, 'Oh aye'; turning to my mate I said, 'He comes from there!' Well, after that we could do no wrong! Later, he said, 'We're going to a dance.' I said, oh aye, thinking to myself, where in this place? Well, we went to this place and there were about 50 or 60 people in there. Everyone was sitting round the side of the hall. Well, they live in the back of beyond for years, and they see two young lads from England, prisoners of war, I mean – we were a bit on display. We had a great time and a laugh!

We got back into Sydney after a week. The taxi drivers wouldn't take any money by the way. Shortly afterwards we came back to England. We were put on a train to Cosford[72] near Wolverhampton and got demobbed straightaway, they gave us our back pay for three and a half years. Looking at this book made out in my name I said, I'm never going to be poor again, never be poor again with three and a half years' back pay [*laughs*]! I went home and the girl who I'd left behind me in Sunderland, which is where I come from, she was waiting for me, and we got married and she lived happily ever after [*he said this jokingly and laughed*].

[*applause*]

QUESTIONS FOR CHICK

Forgiveness
Mr Henderson, Chick, could you feel forgiveness towards the Japanese?
I can't do that. I tried to explain to start with what it was like and what these people did to us, and there was no necessity for it really. I mean, I know they were having a tough time trying to feed us, but the brutality, what they did to us for the sake of, well, nothing! As I've said before, they had this *bushido*, it was their culture, right or wrong, but by the same token they were hurting people for no reason at all. We were working, we were doing what we were told... I wouldn't say doing our best, but we worked hard for the most part. I mean these lads on the railway,[73] you know [*there was*] a death with every sleeper that was laid. But we worked in the shipyard and got kicked about. What they did to us, you can't forgive them for that. A few years ago, I bought a Japanese car, which nearly broke my heart. No, I can't, sorry.

Cruelty
Were they equally brutal to their own...?
It's funny you should say that. Yes. In our day, in the forces, if you did something wrong you were on a charge, and ultimately there was the court martial. That was how we dealt with our chaps. If a Japanese soldier did something wrong, the sergeant or whatever, slapped them across the face, or hit them with a bayonet or whatever. So, justice was very swift. They had very few rights at

---

72 This was an RAF station in WWII. It now houses an RAF museum.
73 Meaning the building of the infamous Burma Railway in Thailand.

all, that army. They were always subservient to the next man up the line. They were cruel to their own people. Cruel in our eyes. It's only, what, 250 years ago they were still chasing each other with bows and arrows. You see, Japan was like what England was in 1066: you had the barons and the serfs and no sort of middle class. You had the barons and serfs, and this is why basically Japan never invented anything. You know, when we were kids, oh, 'made in Japan'? Rubbish. The stuff only used to last five minutes and drop to bits. But you see the top brass, the hierarchy, they wouldn't dirty their hands, and the blokes down below didn't have the mental acumen.

To give you some idea, in the camp we used to do guard duty, night picket, you had to walk round with a Japanese guard because the buildings we were in were all made of wood and there was a fire in the middle, so we had to be careful about fire. Well, at every opportunity we used to extol the virtues of being British, and of course this Japanese guard, he used to always say Japan is a lovely place, you know, we've got the geisha girls and the cherry blossom. I would say, 'Go to England and get £20 in the [armed] forces', 'Churchill will be pleased to see us when we get back'. We extolled the virtues of England. This went on and on, back and forth. Then he would say Japan is very strong, have got a good army and we would say, when we go back, everybody will be very pleased to see us, our wives and sweethearts and all the rest of it. Well, that stumped him. You won't believe this, but he looked up at the moon, he said, well, what you said may be right, he says, but you haven't got one of those in England, have you [*laughs*]? That killed that conversation! I gave in!

Clothing
During the winter I've been to Japan, I know it's very cold, did they provide you with anything?
[*Chick shakes his head*] You just had basic clothes all through the year. That's it. They gave us uniforms which were made of compressed paper and they didn't last five minutes, you know, working, I mean you're flogging your guts out shovelling coal and all the rest of it. It was, as you said, freezing cold in winter and that's why we got pneumonia and so on. Then we had the roasting hot summer. From memory they only seem to have two seasons there – winter, summer; the spring and the autumn were short.

VOTE OF THANKS

[*Bill Dixon is asked by the chairman to give the vote of thanks*]
Mr Chairman, gentleman and the gentleman known as Chick… It's been a privilege listening to your recollections of your incarceration in Japan. Looking around at the faces told me that people were enthralled and extremely interested. I speak with a wee bit of background knowledge because my former boss in Dunlop was in the Argyle and Sutherland Highlanders and was actually captured in Singapore. He never fired a shot in anger. Jim could never forgive the Japanese. The Dunlop Company and its counterpart in Japan is a joint effort. One day, as the Japanese walked in the front door, Jimmy walked out the back and never, ever came back. Mr Henderson, thank you very much indeed. I would ask the members of the Probus Club to show their appreciation in the normal way and give you what's in this envelope, and, if you'll excuse me, in the hope that you'll use it to the best advantage. Thank you very much indeed.

[*Chick*] Thank you very much. Thank you.

[*applause*]

SUNDERLAND

This interview was conducted at various places in Sunderland, Chick's home town.

Originally, I am from Sunderland and I was born at 12 Olive Street, Park Lane, Sunderland, in 1920. This was in my grandmother's house because my father to had go off to London to look for work after WWI. I was a big child; I was 14 pounds at birth, which was quite heavy for those days, or at any time for that matter. Strange as it may seem for the time, the house I was living in was owned by my grandmother. She took in theatrical people from the local Sunderland Empire Theatre. At that particular time there was a sea captain staying with us on a long-term basis and we got quite friendly. I was christened Philip after him, which was with one L, which was the Greek way: he was Greek. Unfortunately, the second name was spelt incorrectly by the registrar, we wanted to register Philou as my second name, but the registrar wrote Filou and I've been stuck with that name ever since.

MY FATHER

My father was in the 1914–18 war. When he came home there was no work, so he went off to London to look for work, so this was why my mother was staying with my grandmother when I was born. He'd looked for work in Sunderland but there wasn't any to be had, so off to London he went. He worked for a while down there and when his job finished he decided to come home. His journey was blazoned over all the newspapers, well, *The Sun and Echo* particularly. It described how a Sunderland man, Jack Henderson, had walked all the way back from London to be with his wife and his new-born child. There was quite a lot of publicity about it at the time, apparently, or so I was told. But for someone to walk 250 or 300 miles from London back to Sunderland was quite an achievement, and that after four years of war.

[*Talking about football, Chick added:*] The first match I saw at Roker Park [*one of the former grounds of Sunderland AFC*] was in 1924, which now means I've been a supporter for 80 years. I remember my father taking me there on his shoulders and being dumped down at the front on the straw. It was my first match. I'm still a season ticket holder.

MY MOTHER

My grandfather was a Lloyd's surveyor in Sunderland. He died at a very early age, he took a fever on board one of these ships and my grandmother was left a widow when she was about 20. In those days there was no subsistence [*meaning unemployment and other government benefits*], so you had to do something, and she started up as a dressmaker. When she finished being a dressmaker she bought this house in Olive Street and started taking in lodgers. My elder sister took me around when I was young, at five, six and seven years old. There were plenty of cinemas in Sunderland and doors opened about half past 12 and the performances went on until half past ten, or 11 o'clock at night. It was only about two old pennies to get in. So, my sister and I would go there. Mother gave us a bottle of water and some jam sandwiches and we used to go for the one o'clock performance and sit there and watch the film until half past four or five o'clock. We had strict instructions from our mother to stay there until we saw the king, because in those days, at the end of every performance, a photograph of the king appeared, King George V, on the screen and everybody stood up while the national anthem was being played. And this was always done, and it was always meticulously observed: nobody moved while the national anthem was being played.

SCOUTS AND BOXING

When I was 11 I joined the Boy Scouts Association and got interested in boxing. So, I went for this championship and I finished up as boxing champion in the seven stone and under group. The final was fought in the old Victoria Hall (it was bombed during the war), which was in Towersgate. I got my first medal and it was presented to me by Jimmy Wilde, who was a world boxing champion at that time. This was a great honour and that medal is still in my possession to this day, and very proud of it I am too. So, I did a bit of amateur boxing till I was about 16.

While I was in the Sunderland amateur boxing club word came that there was a competition for the All England Boys' Championship. I fought through one or two preliminary rounds and the semi-finals and finals were to be boxed at Bradford. This competition was run by the Bradford Constabulary. Well, in those days going by motor car from Sunderland to anywhere for that matter was a bit dodgy because of the breakdown of cars, which weren't very dependable. So, five of us piled into this little car to go to Bradford on this particular Saturday morning: no room for me on the seat so I sat on a petrol can. You carried petrol cans in those days because garages were not very frequent down what was the old A1. Well, the car broke down, we had to get another car to get us there, and we finished up getting into Bradford at five o'clock in the afternoon. I had to change into my boxing gear in the car, so I dashed out of the car into the boxing ring, to fight this lad. I fought him, and he knocked spots off me: he was a southpaw, left-handed boxer, and I could not cope with the situation at all. Anyway, he was from Newcastle as it happens, so the blow was a lot more bitter. Anyway, I got a medal from the Bradford Constabulary Association. I went into the office on the Monday and my boss at the time took me to one side and said, well, look, you know, you're now a local government officer, you're in a public office and we can't have you coming to the office with a black eye and broken nose with cauliflower ears, so I suggest you give up boxing for the time being and your appearance will be more presentable to the public. So, I gave up boxing.

OLD MONEY

I used to go dancing and I used to go to the local rink in Holmside, which later became the Regal Cinema, which I remember being built, and it was quite a thing in those days. I used to see two films and a full show. All for sixpence in the afternoons, six old pennies!

ON THE SEA SHORE

[*Standing on the seashore, Chick continues:*] This is the place where I first learnt to swim, I'd be about five years old, I lived up there [*pointing*] at a place called Dock Street. There were no stones here then [*looks down to the seashore and the breakwater*]; there was a mass of sand bags, and we used to dive off the sand bags into the water. We were in woollen bathing costumes. Once you got in the water with your woollen bathing costume on, it absorbed all the water and you'd just sink to the bottom.

There was a time the rockets went up [*signalling a shipping emergency*]. The ship was visible over there. It came in between these two piers here and grounded itself just there. The lifeboat and the breeches buoy[74] were out. The ship itself couldn't be released, it got right into the sand, it was there forever. There's a marker out there where the ship was grounded. You can still see the skeleton of the ship when the tide is very, very low. I remember that very well.

SCHOOL AND SWIMMING

My school teacher, in charge of sports, indicated to me that it would be a good idea for me to apply for my life-saving medallion, which I did. I took this course on life-saving, which took place at the baths at High Street in those days. I eventually finished up and got a bronze medallion. The medal was presented to me at school on one Monday morning at prayers, and this bronze medal was the first medal ever given to the school. The next morning, I was called to the headmaster's study and he indicated that the medal should not have been presented to me because I was too young. I was 14 at the time and the earliest you can receive a bronze medallion for life-saving is at 15 years of

---

74 A 'breeches buoy' is a crude rope-based rescue device used to extract people from wrecked vessels, or to transfer people from one location to another.

age, but in the circumstances I was allowed to keep the medal, and because I'd attained this for the school the reward was a free pass to the swimming pool for a complete year. I was in the pool three times a day – before breakfast, after lunch and at teatime – for 365 days of the year!

RUGBY AND HIGH TEA

I was interested in playing rugby; I played for Sunderland Boys. We got into a final at Ashbrook and we won that match. We played a team from Hartley Boys, I remember, and this was the first time our club had won the cup for 20-odd years and we were all quite pleased. We were all invited to a high tea afterwards and there was a marvellous array of knives and forks and spoons and none of us could understand which one to use first because we'd had no particular training about this! This was the first time I'd seen butter in rolls. We were used to margarine out of the paper!

KNIVES AND FORKS

The other 'dining' experience I had was with a friend of mine; his father was the chef for the Masonic temple. This was a Masonic lodge near the old Central Park, where the school is; now, that was an open space in my day. My friend was having a birthday treat from his father, the chef. He'd mentioned to his father that I was left-handed. We got to this function and there was this marvellous array of food laid out with all the utensils, the knives and forks. I thought, well, I shouldn't be worried about this, I'll just watch and do what other people do. Unfortunately, by virtue of his son telling his dad I was left-handed, he'd moved all the knives and forks over to the opposite side, therefore I was in a bit of a quandary as to which knife and fork and spoon to use!

THE RAF AND THE WAR

In June 1940 I was in the RAF and did my initial training and finished by being posted to an RAF camp in Sutton Bridge in Lincolnshire for further experience, on old Hurricane aircraft. This was a training squadron, and I was there till about April 1941. One evening we went to Wisbech, about seven or eight miles away, on the border of Lincolnshire and Cambridgeshire. There was a dance. It was Christmas time. I had no transport of course. It was pitch black. Luckily a civilian chap offered to loan me his bicycle, so I say great! So, I cycled all the way down to this dance at Wisbech. I locked the bike up and took me greatcoat off and put it on the bike and went into the dance and had a great time. I came out of the dance and found somebody had stolen me greatcoat. Inside me greatcoat was the lamp for the bicycle, my scarf, my hat and the keys to the bicycle. The back wheel was locked. So, I got that off and picked up this bike; it was freezing, perishing cold, I remember, and I walked across the fens back to the camp. I had to walk all the way back, rolling the bike along on the front wheel. Without any greatcoat on I was blue with cold when I got back. I reported the fact that somebody had taken my greatcoat to the sergeant; he says, well, you know what to do, I says, no. He said, well, go back and pinch somebody else's! That was the advice I got in the RAF [*laughs*], which I never did. I had to go to the stores and draw a new coat. In those days you paid for the one that you lost, and you had to pay for the one that replaced it! They deducted six pence a week off my pay until they were both paid for! My pay was three shillings and ninepence a day [*about 19 pence in today's money*] by this time because I was a rigger. So, I learnt a lesson there. After that, everything was nailed down!

They wanted riggers in the Middle East, so I volunteered for the posting. So, they gave us a week's leave and we reported to Liverpool. When we got there our draft had gone. So then we were milling about waiting for a ship. Anyway, eventually we got on board this ship and the convoy sailed from Liverpool, and we joined a convoy to South Africa. Our first shore leave was at Durban. We had a good time there. After this, one part of the convoy went straight up to the north to the desert, and the other half of the convoy, which I was in, that finished up in Singapore. Well, this was about June, July time in 1941, which was before it was attacked by the Japanese.

[*In this interview, Chick then went on to summarise his capture and imprisonment, which is covered in detail earlier in this chapter.*]

MY GIRLFRIEND WAS STILL WAITING FOR ME!

My girlfriend was still waiting for me. We used to work in the transport offices together; she was only 16, 17 when I first met her; I was about 17. We weren't engaged but she waited for me all this time and on 1 May 1946 we were married. We had a son, Philip Keith, and he was born in October 1947. It was quite a homecoming, actually, at Sunderland railway station, the north end as I remember; everybody was waiting, all the friends and neighbours and relatives, and the train was very late in getting in. It must have been getting on towards midnight. And of course I was surprised and amazed at this reception because I was the only POW there, and this lovely young lady came dashing towards me and threw her arms round me and kissed me and hugged me and I remember saying, 'I don't know who you are but you're a bit of alright,' and it eventually transpired she was my younger sister, which was a bit of a blow as far as I was concerned [*laughs*]. That was Ivy, my sister. And my elder sister was Mabel and of course she was there as well; there was the flags out and everything.

My mother was still alive at the time, but my father wasn't there, because they were still separated. They never got back together again. Life wasn't very easy at all in Olive Street. Money was in short supply and you had to find your own entertainment and so on.

DEMOB AND GETTING A JOB

I was demobbed straightaway. From memory, your leave entitlement was a day for every month you spent overseas. So, I had three and a half years' back pay in my bank book and I was getting a cheque every fortnight from the RAF. I thought I was never going to be poor again! I went out to see different people when I got home, friends and relations, and it got a bit boring sitting around doing nothing, so in the January I said, well, I'll go back and start working again. By this time I was, what, 25? I went to get my old job back and the chief clerk of the transport office, he says, look, you went away a boy, you've come back a man, it's very difficult to give you that job back but I have this other job for you, which involves shift work. I had to get up at half past four. The first trams and buses were out at five, and the job entailed seeing the conductors had their boxes with all their tickets in them, seeing the trams went out on time and all the rest of it, and you finished work at 12. There were other shifts involved as well and I didn't like this one little bit, so I looked around and I thought, well, housing is the big thing here, there was a big push about building houses straight after the war, so I started to study to become a housing manager.

MY CAREER IN THE HOUSING DEPARTMENT

In between times I'd applied for a competitive transfer from the transport department to the Sunderland housing department. The housing manager at that time was a Mr Corthorne, who I remember very well. I studied for three and a half years. There were no facilities in those days, no night classes, so it all had to be done by correspondence course, and this was ten old shillings a month, which was a bit of a drain because my wages at that time were £365 a year, I remember. £365 a year! I was buying a house in Ormond Street. It was up by the general hospital. This first house in Ormond Street was £1,000, which was an awful lot of money, and we were struggling, but the mother-in-law came to live with us and she paid for part of the cost by virtue of me giving her two or three rooms in this big Victorian house that I'd bought. Anyway, I eventually qualified and the first job I applied for was with the Middlesbrough Corporation. They had this wonderful idea of putting an estate manager on the estate, giving him a house with an office attached. You had 500 tenants or 500 houses to look after. Well, you were there in the middle of this estate and you're all things to all men; you were known as the 'rent lord' in Middlesbrough. So you collected the rents, you saw your gardens were cultivated, you had to arrange exchanges and transfers, inspect houses, sort out neighbours' quarrels and troubles; you're the only one on the estate, there was only the one telephone, and you were the father confessor up there: you had to do all things for everybody. A marvellous experience. I was there for, what, three, three and a half years? I then applied for a deputy housing manager's job at Tynemouth, Northumberland, and I got this position. The housing manager there was retiring in five years and they wanted some continuity, so they brought in a deputy, which was a new position. I started working there on 1 April 1953 in Tynemouth, then I was made housing manager in 1958, when the other housing manager retired. This went on from 1958 until 1969.

By this time there was new government legislation indicating that local authorities which were too small had to amalgamate with nearby authorities. We had the amalgamation of Whitley Bay, Tynemouth, Walls End and so on. These five local authorities amalgamated eventually, but in between time I thought it would be a good move, as far as I was concerned, to get some more experience, because by this time Walls End Borough was advertising for a housing manager at the centre of a completely new housing department, which appealed to me. So, I applied for this job and I was appointed in 1969 to create this whole new department. This went on till 1974, a very happy time, but come 1974 [*in the actual amalgamation*] the job was advertised, and I didn't get it. So, by this time I'd just about had enough of housing, so in 1974 I officially retired as housing manager. The then borough treasurer asked me to stay on in some capacity rather than lose all this local knowledge, so I went back there for six or seven years as a district ratings officer with Walls End. At the end of that time I retired; that was 1981.

GOING BACK TO JAPAN?

Interviewer: Did you ever want to go back to Japan?

Going back to Japan? I can't see much virtue in it. First of all it's a horrendous journey getting all that way, and the second thing, there's nothing to see, because we were on this little island, as I've said, on the Inland Sea, and the camp that we were in has now been demolished, and I've got that on good authority because one of my contemporaries did go across – there's nothing left of the camp at all; it's just an open space now, so there's nothing there to see. The shipyard is still there but of course all the foremen and so on that were there, they'll all be dead by now. They were in their 30s and 40s when we were there, I was there when I was 20, so unless they're 100 years of age now they've all gone, so there'd be absolutely no point in going back there at all. As far as nostalgia's concerned, I had seen enough of the shipyard there in three and half years. I worked jolly hard there. I was heaving coal and cleaning out engine rooms and dry docks and boiler rooms and all the rest of it, so I've really got no wish to go back to Japan. After they dropped the bomb we went down to the village, which was called Habu. There the Japanese women and men treated us with the utmost respect after they dropped the bomb. They invited us in for tea and tried to give us things and all the rest of it. But we were so pleased just to get away, we'd had three and a half years in this camp and all we could think about was getting on board a ship and getting out of it, getting away from them, leaving them behind. No, I've got no big interest in going back to Japan at all, and I certainly have no time for the Japanese people.

WELCOMED IN SYDNEY

We were taken down to Australia on the Australian aircraft carrier HMS *Ruler*. In Sydney the people knew who we were by virtue of how we were dressed, but because they didn't have the full RAF uniform for us I had to wear the Royal Australian Air Force blue uniform with the 'glengarry' cap.[75] We had to have Great Britain flashes put on our shoulders. And, of course, the taxi drivers wouldn't take money from us and the dance people would let us into dances for nothing and give us a wonderful, wonderful time.

They couldn't send us home the way we were, as we came out of POW camp. I was only six stone seven when I was released, and I was one of the fitter ones: I was on me feet, anyway. But a lot of the lads were in a bad way – they were just put on hospital ships – so they didn't dare send us home at six stone seven. So, they put us on board this aircraft carrier, as I say, fed us on the best food and we could have as much as we liked. In Australia it was the same, so, by the time we got home in December, we'd fattened out, because as soon as we started eating meat and fat and carbohydrates we just sort of all swelled up and we all looked fit and healthy, which of course we weren't.

VERY LUCKY

Figure 7.5 Chick Henderson in RAF uniform.

Back home my stomach was bad for 20, 30 years after that and for the first ten years I could only eat one meal a day because my stomach had shrunk that much. So, at the end of the day, when I look back in retrospect, I was very lucky really, very lucky, especially in consideration of some of the chaps I have met since then. Back in Java, all my squadron got away, except the three of us. We were left because we didn't go back to the camp on the day we should have done. The whole squadron got away to India apart from us.

---

75 The glengarry bonnet is a traditional Scots cap. It is also adapted as a side cap; it is a foldable military cap with straight sides and a creased or hollow crown sloping to the back where it is parted. All ranks of the Royal Australian Air Force (RAAF) are entitled to wear the garrison cap.

CHAPTER 8

Wilfred Batty

WILFRED BATTY (3 APRIL 1918–17 FEBRUARY 2009)

Through the publication of my father's story I've been lucky to have had a number of people contact me with information about the experiences of their own relations during World War II. In this particular case, I'm indebted to Adrian Batty for his information and cooperation relating to his father's experience in the war, and as a POW. Adrian's father, Wilfred Batty, was captured in Java and my father was captured in Hong Kong, but after that their experiences almost mirror each other. They were both taken by ship to Japan and they both ended up in the same POW camp. They also came home together on HMS *Ruler* and then the *Dominion Monarch*. Even though they almost certainly were in different POW groups (RAF and army) in Habu, it's quite clear from the little comments that my father made that they were experiencing the same thing in their sections of the camp, on board

Figure 8.1 Wilfred Batty.
Source: Adrian Batty's photo collection.

HMS *Ruler* and on the remainder of the journey home, right down to the fact that they went out on the town in Fremantle, Australia, on their way home to the UK!

My thanks to Adrian for allowing me to publish his father's story in this book as it fills in the gaps for me regarding my father's experiences.

WILF BATTY BY HIS SON ADRIAN BATTY: PRE-WAR YEARS

My father, Wilfred (Wilf, Bill, Batt, Batty) Batty, was born on 3 April 1918, the only child to survive beyond a few weeks to parents Charles Henry and Mary Ellen Batty, aka Nellie. After birth, Wilf lived with his parents at 1 Cliffe Terrace, Grange Street, Hull, a one-up one-down house with a small kitchen and outside toilet.

Charlie, Nellie and Wilf then moved to 3 Grange Street, Hull, when Wilf's grandfather Daniel Batty moved in with them. Wilf could recall sitting on his grandfather's knee when he smoked his pipe and had a tot of spirits. 3 Grange Street was a big improvement, having a front room, living room and scullery with pantry off. There were two bedrooms with an attic. The toilet was still outside. The living room had a Yorkshire fireplace, with an oven at the side and a boiler at the other side. It had to be black leaded regularly. Bathing was in a tin bath in front of the fire or at the 'wash house' in St Paul Street where it cost a penny for a bath and a penny for a towel. Wilf attended St Paul's Infant and Junior School, although for a short period he moved in with his Uncle Bill (William Batty) at 243 Grovehill Road, Beverley, when he attended St Mary's School, Beverley. While living in Beverley, Wilf attended a corrugated iron church on Sundays, known as the 'Tabernacle', Swinemoor Lane. He was paid a bar of chocolate for pumping up the harmonium!

In the 1920s Wilf's father started a business charging accumulators in a shed in the yard. He also loaned accumulators and large batteries out for 6d a week. Charlie then moved into radio and bicycle repairs and hired out radios and crystal sets, which used earphones in a mug to amplify the sound. Charlie was also an agent for BTH (British Thompson Houston Co. Ltd) selling swan neck speakers and he shared a market stall at the Hull Market with a family friend, Uncle Jim Sykes, who sold gramophones and gramophone records. Wilf worked for his father from the age of 11 carrying out electrical work. He earned five shillings for fitting a light socket and ten shillings for fitting an electrical point (this would have entailed a great deal of work in those days!).

As a boy Wilf learned to swim in Barmston Drain at the rear of Grange Street and learned to dive from the bridge on Fountain Road. The water in the drain was always warm owing to the discharge from the Sculcoates Power Station.

Wilf completed his education at Brunswick Avenue School (now a social services building) in 1933 aged 15. After leaving school, Wilf did not take an apprenticeship but worked for his father. However, he also had a Saturday job working in the market (Charlie, Nellie and Wilf went on market trader trips). He worked for a 'snake charmer' who sold 'snake oil' for the relief of arthritis. Wilf had to make an early trip to Woolworths to buy the ingredients for the snake oil, including ammonia and soap flakes! He would mix the ingredients and pour the mixture into slim bottles, which were sold for 1/6d. The snake charmer would go to the pub for lunch and on his return would sell two bottles for 1/6d. Wilf also had to be hypnotised by the snakes every Saturday and was paid 10/- for the day: a lot of money at that time.

Wilf continued working for his father and in 1933 the business was known as C.H. Batty and Son.

However, Kelly's Hull Street Directory of 1936 reveals Charles Batty was a cycle dealer at 3 Grange Street, Hull, and Wilf was listed under 'Cycle Makers, Agents and Repairers' with a shop at 15 Reform Street, Hull. Wilf stated the shop was chosen to get the passing trade of Reckitt's employees who mostly travelled to work on bicycles. The shop was not too successful, though, and Wilf went to work for the Valiant Cycle Company, based at 11 Hessle Road, Hull. The business was owned by the Gresswell family who bought in bicycles to put their own badges on them as well as bicycle repairs. Gresswell's also arranged hire purchase agreements and Wilf worked Friday nights and Saturdays collecting debts. He said he had many stories to tell regarding debt collection, but never revealed them. Stan Gresswell was my godparent. Wilf continued to live at 3 Grange Street until with war looming he volunteered to join the RAF in January 1940.

JOINING THE RAF

Wilf's work experience enabled him to take an RAF apprenticeship on 'Airframes and Engines', leading to him becoming an aircraftman. His RAF career started at the No. 2 Recruitment Centre, RAF Cardington, near Bedford. Wilf said this was for the basic 'square bashing'. He then moved to RAF Locking, Weston-super-Mare, where the 'Training and Technical Services' were based.

Wilf's next destination was 504 Squadron, RAF Castletown, Caithness, Scotland. However, in error, he first was sent to Castletown, Isle of Man! After much travelling Wilf arrived at 504 Squadron, working on Hawker Hurricane planes, before volunteering for further training at the No. 7 School of Technical Training for Engine and Airframe Fitters, at RAF Innsworth, Gloucester. Following training Wilf was sent to RAF Monkmoor, Shrewsbury, where he worked in the 'Maintenance Unit' salvaging spares, especially guns, from planes that had been shot down or had crashed. Wilf classed this as a 'lousy' job, being reimbursed an allowance of 2/6d for bed and breakfast and 6d for tea. He was expected to scrounge his lunch!

His next move was to No. 1 Echelon, RAF Tern Hill, Shropshire, near Market Drayton (March to May 1941), although no one knew what it was! He serviced all planes that landed for a few weeks and missed a posting to Bermuda as he was ill in hospital with a hernia problem. After running out of money he went to the County of Warwick 605 Squadron, RAF Tern Hill, who were short of fitters.

The 605 Squadron flew Hawker Hurricanes and then moved to RAF Baginton, near Coventry (May to September), and RAF Honily, Warwickshire (September to October 1941). Wilf said that at RAF Baginton he learned more about 'soldiering' (army manoeuvres in case of enemy invasion) but slept at RAF Honily.

At this time Hull was suffering badly from bombing raids by the Luftwaffe, and in March 1941 Wilf received a telegram informing him that his family home, 3 Grange Street, along with houses in Lorne Street and Fountain Road, had been hit by a stick of bombs. Luckily his parents had survived by hiding under the staircase, where they were buried. The neighbours were not as lucky: the occupants of 5 and 7 Grange Street were killed. Wilf was given compassionate leave and returned home to salvage what he could from the wreckage. Wilf rescued a pack of six unscathed eggs and the family nest egg! Charlie and Nellie temporarily moved in with Nellie's brother Harold North (North Timber Merchants) at 5th Avenue, North Hull Estate, before moving back to another house, 52 Grange Street, which was very similar to 3 Grange Street.

Wilf and his fellow aircraftmen spent much of their leisure time in Warwick and Royal Leamington Spa and during a superb day's weather during Easter 1941 Wilf met and followed Doris Gertrude Griffin at the bus terminus in Leamington Spa. Doris lived at 51 Bury Road, Leamington Spa, with her parents.

Wilf was promoted to leading aircraftman – 944068 L/A/C Batty RAF, this being the second rank. He then learned he was to be posted abroad. It appears Wilf and Doris may have become engaged before Wilf left, as Doris states in later letters that she still had the ring. Wilf also left a letter for Doris with his parents; sadly this letter is lost, but Doris stated she was ignoring the contents.

JOURNEY TO THE FAR EAST

The 605 County of Warwick Auxiliary Fighter Squadron left Honily for Gourock, west Scotland, in the early morning of 6 December 1941.

Records show Wilf sailed for the Far East on 9 December 1941 after embarking on the troop carrier HMT Z16, which was formerly the Union Castle Liner *Warwick Castle*, the previous day. He was informed he was going to North Africa to invade Tunisia. However, a significant action occurred which had an impact on what was to follow for Wilf, when the Japanese carried out a surprise attack on Pearl Harbor on 7 December 1941. In a letter to Doris after being released as a POW, Wilf refers to the 'ill-fated Friday morning 5th December 1941 at 6 o'clock', when he said cheerio! (From Warwick, I assume.)

HMT Z16 left Gourock, Scotland, for Malta but the Japanese threat to the Dutch East Indies meant it was diverted and pilots, planes and aircrew were parted. The convoy was reorganised several times but eventually it arrived at Freetown, Sierra Leone, and anchored for four days before leaving on Christmas Day for Cape Town, South Africa, arriving on 5 January 1942, when the men were allowed shore leave. HMT Z16 set sail for the Indian Ocean on 9 January 1942, one half of the convoy leaving for Singapore.

Wilf arrived at Tanjung Priok, Batavia, Dutch East Indies, on the island of Java, on 3 February 1942 and disembarked the following day, to find that Japanese attacks were expected at any time. The squadron was split up at Batavia, the majority departing for Palembang, on the island of Sumatra, on 8 February, arriving Oosthaven, Sumatra, by small boat, then travelling by train, followed by a route march in full kit, to Palembang Town on 9 February and an airfield known as P1, there finding few aircraft or pilots (one person stated there were four Hurricanes, three Blenheims and a dozen assorted light aircraft). There were two airfields, P1 and P2, considered secret forward fighter and bomber bases in the Sumatran jungle, allegedly near-impossible to be neutralised! P2 was about 20 miles south of the river, where they were trying to assemble a bomber force. On arrival all RAF personnel were requested to hand over their weapons to the Dutch Army, apparently to replace the ones they had lost escaping from Singapore. A couple of days later, on 13 February 1942, Wilf said he reported to Wing Commander McCarthy (a doctor) with a painful ear when they looked up to see Japanese parachutes descending, along with Japanese aircraft strafing and bombing the airfield. They decided to escape to Palembang as the airfield was under constant attack, and they were evacuated on 14 February. They procured a lorry, Bren gun, rifle and bayonet and went into the jungle with the intention of going into the mountains but decided not to risk it as the forest around the airfields had swamps, snakes, leeches etc. and they had no medical supplies.

At this time Singapore was under attack by the Japanese between 8 and 15 February 1942, with Singapore surrendering on 15 February, thus releasing more Japanese troops for the attack on Sumatra and Java. The battle for Palembang lasted two days and several RAF personnel were killed protecting the airfield and during the escape to Palembang and Oosthaven. All Allied troops in Sumatra and Java surrendered within two weeks. The Royal Netherlands East Indies Army surrendered to Commander Hitoshi Inamura, capitulating to the Japanese with all Allied troops on 8 March 1942.

It is not known how Wilf escaped from Sumatra to Java, but most escapees appear to have used ferries of some sort. Wilf did state that he procured a motorcycle and rode to the southern end of the island (it's not known if this was Sumatra or Java), where he tried to board an Australian ship, but was refused. So he had to turn around and go back!

In a letter written on 27 October 1945 on his return home on the *Dominion Monarch*, Wilf informed Doris that on his return to Java from Palembang he had written her a letter 'pouring out his heart'; two days later he was pouring gallons of fuel over thousands of letters and putting a match to it!

Wilf's officers met with the Japanese under a flag of truce and with the Japanese promising to allow prisoners to study and work in the fields, they surrendered. (Compare this with the execution of POWs in Singapore.) Wilf was taken prisoner on 20 March 1942 and it appears the POWs wandered around for a couple of days until they were imprisoned. Wilf's war was to take a very different direction!

JAVA – CAPTURE AND IMPRISONMENT

My father rarely spoke of his experiences as a Japanese POW. The following information has been gleaned from snippets he gave, from other POWs, 'Chick' Henderson, George Spink, Terence Kelly, others and the history of the 605 Squadron. I am also very grateful to Vic Ient, the son of a fellow FEPOW, for his research at the International War Museum.

Along with his RAF comrades, Wilf was imprisoned at Boei Glodok, Batavia, on 23 March 1942. Boei Glodok was a Dutch prison for 400 long-term Javanese criminals, who were herded into one corner. Cells for ten criminals were filled with 30–40 POWs. Each cell had one hole for a toilet, not very pleasant when many POWs were soon to suffer from dysentery and were infested with bedbugs, the bites of which could lead to ulceration.

Figure 8.2 Wilfred Batty and fellow POWs. Wilf Batty is 2nd from the left.

A fellow POW, George Spink, informed me that the POWs had been a full day without food or drink and then found out that their officers were sitting on a lot of tinned fruit. Wilf led a protest against the officers. George said Batty (as was my father's nickname) stuck up for himself.

The *Daily Mail* (later called the *Hull Daily Mail*) on Friday, 10 April 1942, reported, under the heading 'AIRMEN MAY BE PRISONERS': *'Reported missing and believed prisoner of war is L/A/C Wilfred Batty RAF of 52 Grange Street, Hull. As a boy he attended Brunswick Avenue School and later worked for a Hull cycle firm.'* It printed a photograph of Wilf and A/C Foster, who was also reported missing.

Wilf had a regular routine of being woken early, breakfast being a pint of steamed rice and cup of hot water, midday meal 3/4 pint of steamed rice plus green vegetable water and evening meal a pint of steamed rice and the vegetables used at lunch! Barely enough to survive on.

One of the first jobs the POWs were given was to be marched to the airfield to fill in the bomb craters in the runways created by the Japanese bombing and the RAF to prevent the Japanese using it. Wilf said he then spent the next six months cutting grass around the airfield with small scythes.

Wilf was to find himself in trouble with the Japanese on several occasions, not helped by the total unpredictability of the Japanese. One day, Wilf noticed a native in the long grass at the edge of the airfield trying to attract his attention. Wilf discovered he was selling Nestle condensed milk stolen from the stores. Wilf was caught by the Japanese, marched to a hut and had his hands tied behind his back and forced to kneel down. A Japanese officer then stood above him and rested his samurai sword on his neck! An American RAF officer thought to be 'Red' Campbell successfully pleaded for his life. Wilf and his comrades were then marched out and stood in line, expecting the worse. However, the Japanese officer then made the native walk along the line of POWs and give a tin of condensed milk to each POW.

Life was difficult in Boei Glodok. Owing to the lack of food POWs soon started to suffer from several diseases/illnesses including dysentery and malnutrition with several dying from their conditions. Some, who could not face the hardships, gave up, lay down and died. Many of the POWs arranged lecture groups and concert parties were organised for Saturday nights to relieve the tedium, but after six months many of the POWs were required to move.

BY HELLSHIP TO JAPAN

Wilf and many other POWs, including many of the 605 Squadron, were embarked on a Japanese freighter, the *Yoseda Maru*, on 21 October 1942. They left TanJung Priok on 22 October with 268 men in the hold of the ship. They had no idea where they were going or what the future held for them. The POWs were undernourished, underweight, suffering from many ailments including dysentery and wearing tropical clothing.

The *Yoseda Maru* sailed to Singapore, arriving on 26 October 1942, where the POWs were herded onto another ageing freighter, the *Dainichi Maru*, later to be nicknamed one of the 'hellships'. The POWs were held in holds in deplorable conditions, having to sit and sleep on the wet iron ore being carried in the hold, along with rats and insects. Toilets were wooden structures on deck accessible only by climbing one steep ladder out of the hold. The *Dainichi Maru* departed on 29 October.

Weather was atrocious for much of the journey and initially the *Dainichi Maru* was in a convoy, but after breaking down ended up on its own. American submarines were active in the area and it was later discovered some hellships had been sunk, with POWs secured by the Japanese in the holds and in one case being shot as they tried to save themselves!

The ship initially sailed to Saigon, arriving and departing again on 3 November, arriving at Takoa, Formosa (Taiwan) on 12 November and departing on 15 November. Many POWs were to die in the disgusting conditions. The first deaths were honoured by the Japanese (a dead POW was given more respect than a live one) with burial at sea along with food to help them on their journey, but as the deaths increased the ceremonies were stopped. Many POWs were now too ill to even climb the ladder to visit the toilets, adding even more to the miserable conditions.

The *Dainichi Maru* finally sailed into Shimoseki, Japan, on 25 November 1942 in a snowstorm. The POWs disembarked on 26 November. It was the Japanese winter and the POWs were ill prepared for it. On disembarking the POWs were given an embarrassing medical including having to lower their trousers in front of many civilians to have a glass rod inserted in their anuses! Wilf was then transported by train to Onomichi and by ferry to the inland island of Innoshima and finally to a shipyard at Habu, an inland dock where they commenced working on 8 December. This was to be Wilf's home for the next three years.

HABU POW CAMP, JAPAN

Habu was (and still is) a dockyard on the inland island of Innoshima, near Zentsuji, Japan, so there was no chance of escape. On arrival at the dockyard, the POWs were split into work teams known as PT gangs. PT was thought to refer to 'painters and transport' but soon became known as the 'physical torture' gang. PT gangs were determined on levels of fitness. PT1 were the fittest, biggest and strongest, known as 'genki boys' (Japanese for strong/good), and were required to do the majority of the heavy manual work. Wilf was in PT1. The last PT gang (byoki) was made up of the sick and weak POWs, who were required to carry out tasks such as sorting nuts and bolts from scrap, sweeping and clearing rubbish etc. All had to work in some capacity. The PT gangs had foremen with nicknames such as 'Hatchet', 'The Bull' and 'Ring piece'.

The camp changed its name several times and was known as Fukuoka 12, then Zentsuji 2, before becoming Hiroshima 5. The dockyard built and repaired ships and Wilf was to spend his captivity in the PT1 gang carrying out this work. This was of course in contravention of the Geneva Convention. However, Wilf and his fellow POWs took any opportunity to sabotage the ships, fitting weak rivets or fitting rivets loosely. A Japanese worker would inspect the rivets and put a cross against any that were faulty. When he had gone the team would remove the crosses and put new ones next to sound rivets. The team also unscrewed oil pipes to the engines and filled them with sawdust and threw any equipment they could find overboard. They tried their best to aid the war effort.

The POWs lived in purpose-built wooden huts, which were very cold in winter, with heating from stoves only allowed for two months of the year. The POWs were in a very poor condition when they arrived and suffered eight deaths shortly after arrival due to deprivations and disease of the voyage there. George Spink, a good friend of Wilf's, was six and a half stone on arrival and seriously ill. He was kept alive with goat's milk for two and a half months. Food was very scarce and became scarcer as the war continued. It does appear that the POWs were a lot better off than many POWs in other camps. Red Cross food parcels arrived four times during the three and a half years and were a great bonus. Clothing was of poor quality and wore out quickly; other essentials such as soap and shaving materials were also scarce.

The day commenced with reveille at 5 am, breakfast at 5.30, roll call 6 am, march to the docks, midday meal 12 noon, evening meal 5 pm, march back to camp and roll call 7.30 pm, bed and lights out 8 pm.

It is hard to imagine exactly what the POWs had to contend with, but one incident confirmed in a book by Terence Kelly gives some idea. Rigor mortis had set in with one of the early deaths and Wilf had to put the body in a small coffin meant for the smaller Japanese. To achieve this he and some others had to break the limbs of the dead POW.

Several of Wilf's fellow POWs stated that officers did not have to work, or had light duties. George Spink stated that the officers expected the lower ranks to act as batmen to them. Virtually all POWs declined!

Wilf developed many skills to survive and became a very skilled thief and lock picker with a set of skeleton keys. Apparently he was the first to do this and made some keys out of flattened bicycle spokes. The only locks he couldn't open were Yale-type ones. Chick Henderson stated that three sets of keys were also made in the workshops. Initially looting was petty thieving, but as food became scarce in Japan the food stores on board ships were padlocked so Wilf and the PT1 gang became an accomplished team of thieves (as did some other PT gangs) who broke into Japanese ships stores, some being lookouts, to steal food etc. Favourite loot included miso, beans, soup flavouring and stock, rice, barley, vegetable oil and noodles. Excess food was bartered for things they needed. Cigarettes were the most important currency. They took enormous risks because a severe beating was the least they could expect should they have been caught. Apparently a guard, 'The Bull', was caught stealing a chicken and was imprisoned! Many POWs were not prepared to take the same risks. The team also went onto ships they were not working on to thieve, pretending to be a working party!

To carry their spoil the PT1 gang made small bags out of material taken from life jackets (the kapok-filled ones) and carried them between their legs suspended from string around their necks. The small size of the bag limited what they could carry and they couldn't carry too much as they were subjected to regular searches by the guards. Apparently they carried the bag in their groin areas as the Japanese avoided this area when carrying out searches. George Spink tells of a Japanese guard protecting bags of rice. Some of the team got him into conversation while others emptied a bag of rice behind his back!

A cartoon drawing kept by Wilf sums the thieving up. One side depicts POWs on watch while another one opens a door and the reverse shows the POWs being marched back to camp with bulging uniforms!

One day, while being marched to the dock, the POWs saw a pile of onions, which they stuffed themselves with on the way to the dock. The next day all of the POWs were ill except for one, who didn't eat any. It turned out the onions were daffodil bulbs!

George Spink told me how the PT1 gang stole most of the contents of a sack of wheat. The sack was hung on a wall guarded by a Japanese. The POWs had cut pieces of bamboo into six-inch lengths, pointed at one end and hollowed out. The POWs struck up a conversation with the guard with his favourite topic: 'what the Japs would do to the English girls when they won the war'! One POW at a time would go behind his back and stick the bamboo into the sack, removing a tube full and emptying the tube into their small pouches. The POWs took turns until the sack was nearly empty. It's not known what happened to the guard.

Wilf did say one of the guards was suspicious and knew he was up to something but could never prove it, so he 'had it in' for Wilf and had many run ins with him. One such occasion was when Wilf asked for a new shirt as his was falling apart. The guard went to the stores and offered Wilf a shirt in a worse condition. Wilf laughed and the guard threw a punch at Wilf, which he ducked and then laughed again. Wilf then received a severe beating. At this time the camp commandant was away; when he returned, Wilf received another beating, ending up in the hospital. Phil 'Chick' Henderson, another genki boy, confirmed that Wilf had done something to upset the Japanese, although he didn't know what and was singled out and given a bad time including beatings and hard work.

In the later years of his life, Wilf had to wear a leg iron to correct a damaged ankle. The damage occurred when Wilf and fellow POWs were pushing a truck along a railway track: Wilf trapped his ankle in the points, causing the damage.

On another occasion, when Wilf's shoes fell apart and he refused to work, the guard left and returned with a pair of sandshoes from a dying POW. Wilf refused to wear them, stating 'he didn't work in sandshoes', and received a severe beating. However, the guard later returned with a new pair of size nine boots (no one knew from where). The guard said, 'Now you work.' Wilf replied, 'Yes, now I work.'

On 23 January 1943, 100 Hong Kong Defence Volunteers arrived at the camp as POWs. Two, Hal Halsall and Vic Bond, were put into Wilf's PT team and became good friends (they lost touch in the 1950s). Hal Halsall became my godparent in 1950. Hal Halsall was reported to be a very tough little guy. One day Japanese teenagers started throwing lumps of coal at him, so he thumped one of them. His punishment was to be put in a five-foot-high cell for seven days and fed three rice balls a day. When released he was in a very poor condition and was unable to stand.

The Japanese had many rules including POWs having to bow to everyone, when they could smoke and eat and having to look away and avert their eyes when a Japanese battleship came into the dock for repair. Failure to comply meant a beating even if the POW was not aware a Japanese was present or if he was occupied with other matters.

The POWs had bamboo identification tags on chains around their necks, each with a number. Wilf was number 31. I remember the tags when I was a young lad (in the 1950s) in the shed, thrown in a box of nuts and bolts along with some unknown medals. Now they are sadly lost.

The PT1 gang and others were given difficult jobs. One particularly nasty job they had to undertake was on an oil tanker in midwinter, in Eight Dock. The job took several months to complete. As oil was becoming short in Japan, every drop was important to their war effort. The oil tanker had leftover oil in its tanks that could not be sucked out. It had also solidified in the cold weather. The PT1 gang had to work in the tanks, warming up the oil little by little and transferring it to four-gallon drums, which were passed up in big iron buckets. These drums were then hoisted onto the dockside and emptied into a lighter moored alongside. The only way the POWs could clean themselves at the end of the working day was to rub themselves down with handfuls of sawdust, hence the comment on the cartoon depicting 15 August 1945: 'They were grim days. Freezing days on oil in Eight Dock.' Perhaps the POWs had the last laugh though as the Japanese tied the lighter up wrongly one night and when the tide went out the lighter tipped over.

Sometime around June 1943, Doris received an 'intimation' that her fiancé was a POW in Japanese hands and wrote to the Red Cross Society to inform them. The Red Cross wrote to Doris on 16 July 1943 with details of how to transmit letters to Japan. Doris and Wilf's parents wrote to Wilf as soon as they knew he was alive and a POW. I'm not sure how many got delivered, although several are in the family records. Several cards were sent from Wilf also during 1945 and some were delivered. One card from Wilf that was received on 4 August 1945 stated 'Happy to know everything is OK. Congratulations to Jack, Tommy and Erk.' When I asked Wilf who these people were, he informed me that Jack meant Navy, Tommy meant army and Erk meant Air Force (erk, airc or aircrew) and it meant the POWs were aware of the success of D-Day and VE (Victory in Europe) Day, which was on 8 May 1945.

Perhaps one of the better days was 10 October 1944, when the Japanese allowed the distribution of Red Cross food parcels, which had arrived on 5 October. Twenty-two and a half parcels were shared between 185 men.

Reserved for the sick POWs were: 16 tins of milk, 30 tins of ham and eggs, 30 tubs of chocolate, five tins of ham, one packet of raisins, 45 tins of butter, 23 packets of soup, ten packets of cheese, 16 packets of sugar, 15 tins of pork loaves and four packets of prunes.

Reserved for the cook house were: 75 tins of milk, 19 tins of jam, 26 tins of bully, 63 tins of pork loaves, 20 packets of prunes, 13 tins of ham and eggs, 27 tins of butter, 13 tins of cheese, 24 tins of rose patty, two tins of spam and 25 tins of salmon.

On top of this, 10 October was granted a Yasumi (rest) day.

One of the cartoons depicts Room Two's First Yasumi Eve Guest night on 9 October, with a menu. Another cartoon celebrates Victory Dinner on Tuesday 24 October, with a menu and signed by many of the POWs. This dinner was presumably celebrating the release of the food parcels.

An interesting story about the thieving was recounted by 'Swede' Moulstone:

> When one thinks back to those days in the camp, the break-ins into ship's stores and general stealing from the Japs, it makes one's hair stand on end. The leaders like Batty, Foster, McGuire etc. they were as cool as cucumbers and as skilled as locksmiths. I'm afraid I went on only a couple of break-ins; I just didn't have the nerve that these sorts of fellows had. I went on one such break-in to a ship's store (led by McGuire). Opening the door was child's play. They had a look inside then stood in the doorway and said 'There's a good variety in here. What do we need?' You would have thought they were in a supermarket, picking up the week's groceries.

And he goes on to recount a break-in he was involved in, in the smaller Mitsunosho dockyard, when it was decided to raid a Japanese naval vessel despite there being an armed guard on the gangway. They went on board carrying a pole and a five-gallon can with just sufficient rubbish in it to provide cover over their intended haul, broke into the store and discovered a huge quantity of eggs, theirs for the taking. They made several trips on and off the ship collecting them; they hid them temporarily in the nut, bolt and rivet store ashore and then took them back into camp in the three buckets which had brought the rice and soup lunch ration to the dockyard! (Not Batty but Mick McGuire and Tom Foster.)

George Spink made an interesting comment when he stated Wilf was instrumental in their survival!

Following this comment by George Spink, I was surprised to discover in my research that one of the POWs, a pilot, had written several books after the war, recounting his experiences. The author was critical of the Genki boys, Wilf in particular, for their thieving activities. The Genki boys I spoke to explained the enormous risks they took in stealing food. Many of the POWs also carried out many acts of sabotage. Hence the POWs were not passive captives but actually engaged in supporting the war effort.

The criticism of the Genki boys appears to centre on what they did with their excess stolen food. Essentially they bartered their excess food for supplies they did not have and set up a 'black market'. This was not unusual in camps where food could be stolen. Cigarettes were the currency of the camp.

The Genki boys did inform me they made sure those who were sick received extra food. Any POW unfit to work was put on half rations by the Japanese, which did nothing to help their recovery. One POW who later thanked Wilf for saving his life, was 'employed' by Wilf: as what, I do not know.

Every morsel of food stolen was a morsel less for the Japanese and more for the POWs. Every nut and bolt tossed into the dock was a nut and bolt denied to the Japanese. Following on from George Spink's comment, it is interesting to note the deaths of the POWs while at Habu. There were eight initial deaths on arrival at Habu from the conditions endured on the Hellship. There were no more deaths in the camp until 1944, when four members of the Hong Kong Volunteer Defence Corps died. It has to be remembered that this was despite the rations supplied by the Japanese being repeatedly reduced. Quite an extraordinary record when compared to other Japanese PoW camps.

THE TIDE OF WAR TURNS

Eventually the war turned against Japan. The POWs were able to watch huge formations of Allied aeroplanes, including B-29 bombers, flying inland to bomb Japan. Allied planes also bombed the Habu dockyard and Wilf obtained photographs of the damage caused. Chick Henderson stated that the Genki boys were working on a ship when it was bombed and they were lucky to escape without injuries, running to a cave for shelter. Food rations were reduced further, with less and less food available to maintain strength.

Following a meeting in Potsdam on 26 July 1945, to spare Japan from utter destruction, the Allies issued an ultimatum calling on the Japanese to surrender or face the consequences. The Japanese were offered the chance to surrender on 29 July. They refused and on 6 August the first atom bomb was dropped on Hiroshima. Still the Japanese refused to surrender and the second bomb was dropped on Nagasaki. The Japanese surrendered on 15 August 1945, although many of the Japanese military still wanted to continue fighting. It was later found out that the Japanese intended to execute all POWs if they were invaded, and some were. Apparently the POWs found the capitulation difficult to comprehend and they carried on as normal until 3 pm, when Wilf and the PT1 gang lit a fire under a damaged boat and roasted some beans! There is a cartoon of this event, signed by many POWs.

Many years later, fellow POW Ted Read informed me that he was in the 'Plating Gang', putting steel sheets into place for ships hulls. He spent two years doing this to build a landing craft. It was never finished.

Wilf and his fellow POWs were not aware of the atom bomb dropped on Hiroshima even though they were only 30 miles away as there was a mountain between them and they were becoming used to the sound of explosions in the distance. However, my sister Avril recalls Wilf stating they were aware something had happened as they could see something over the mountains.

On 23 August the POWs received orders to paint letters 20 feet in length on the roof of their billet for identification by Allied aircraft dropping supplies. Two weeks after the Japanese capitulation a B-29, *The Uninvited*, dropped food supplies for the POWs. One pack of condensed milk landed on a peasant's house, destroying it. Apparently the POWs enjoyed a meal of condensed milk and corned beef, one of the best meals they had.

An American naval medical team arrived to assess which POWs were fit to travel, with those too ill being transferred to hospital ships. The fitter ones were transferred to Tokyo Bay, where they were showered, their clothes destroyed and given American fatigues. All possessions were disinfected.

WILF WRITES HOME AS A FREE MAN!

Wilf wrote to Doris of these final events from HMS *Ruler* anchored in Yokohama Bay and it is best to repeat his account (in his words) written on 14 September 1945:

> I am writing you once more a free man and on a British Aircraft Carrier anchored in Yokohama Bay… I will try and give you some idea of what has happened in the last month or to be exact from the 15th August. Well here goes. On the 15th August the Emperor gave a speech over the radio which was broadcast throughout Japan announcing the capitulation of the country. We were at work in the dockyard cleaning up the debris from the last raid we had, by the way it was our own people not yanks which dropped it on us. The British Major who planned the raid was in Yokohama to meet us and was pleased to hear no prisoners were hurt. He knew we were imprisoned on the island but did not know the exact location of the camp. They sure plastered the dockyard sinking 4 ships wiping out the workshops putting the yard completely out of commission, but making plenty of work for us. Anyway on with the story, we got hold of the gist of the Emperor's speech and downed tools immediately and refused to do anything at all. We were then marched back to our camp, told a pack of lies and finished by telling us we would not have to go to work the following day or until they received official information. We stayed quiet for a few days and then got fed up of eating rotten rice and soups so we set off for the village, commandeered all the stores and lived merrily ever afterwards. The Nip police got in touch with our officers and promised plenty of food if we would stop looting the village stores etc. so we gave up looting and settled down to a life of idleness, sun bathing and swimming. I forgot to mention that our camp was situated 2 yards from the sea. We stole a launch and had some good picnic trips to the surrounding islands. The days marched by very good weather and everyone was happy for the first time in 3 years. And now we pass onto the 2nd September, a Gala day for us, the signing of the Peace Treaty and also a B.29 dropped us our first relief food supplies, what a day: fags, chocs, oh everything that mattered. What a feast I nearly made myself ill. That many fags even I couldn't have smoked them all in 3 months. After a few more days we received a visit from the Swiss Red Cross delegate and was told the conditions of the surrender. All about the atomic bomb and bomb damage throughout the whole of Japan and did we cheer for after all we had not suffered in vain. The Japanese

are now starving, they have nothing which pleases all POWs immensely. On with the story for the airmail is getting less and less. We left our island in the inland sea on 12th August [I think Wilf meant September] passing through Fukohama, Osaka and other big towns. You may believe it or you may not but it is true of these towns, there is nothing, when I say nothing I mean NOTHING if I had not seen it I would not have believed it myself. For 2 hours at 45 miles an hour in the train we passed through what must have been a thickly populated area. So for about 90 miles long and as far as the eye could see on either side of the train there was nothing but charred wreckage. We arrived in Yokohama and received a marvellous reception from the Yank army of occupation. Silver bands to play us in and out during dinner, a Yank dance band playing to us the slow swing which I understand is all the rage now. To cut the story short we boarded the HMS *Ruler* last night and now once more we are under the British Flag.

GOING HOME

The aircraft carrier HMS *Ruler* entered Tokyo Bay on 31 August 1945 in preparation of the signing of the Japanese surrender on 2 September. It left Tokyo Bay on 13 September for Sydney, Australia, carrying nearly 450 ex-POWs, including Wilf and various friends: George Spink, Chick Henderson, Vic Bond, Hal Halsall etc.

The *Sydney Morning Herald* on Tuesday, 25 September 1945, carried a report stating the:

> HMS *Ruler* was due in Sydney Thursday 27th with nearly 450 Ex POWs from Tokyo [269 UK Nationals]. Food for passengers was as varied as possible with the emphasis on meat and vegetables so much needed to make good deficiencies of diet in the last few years. Ships carpenters also made wooden toys for children who had never had any since capture 3 years ago. 'Passengers' received a cash advance of £5.00 each and were allowed a ration of bottled beer every day. The condition of the 'passengers' improved rapidly.

HMS *Ruler* arrived in Sydney and was greeted by the Duke of Gloucester, governor of Australia. The POWs were given more medicals and supplied with RAF uniforms. The POWs were then settled into HMS *Golden Hind*, a Royal

Navy barracks set up on Warwick Farm, one of Sydney's racecourses, 15 miles from the city. Here they were allowed to recover from their ordeal.

In a letter dated 30 September, Wilf stated that his weight was back up to 13 stone and a letter dated 4 October stated he was more settled mentally and he had had a two-day holiday in the Blue Mountains. He had tried to get flown home, though without any luck. There was plenty of food and no shortages, he could have as many beef steaks and eggs as he could eat and they were swimming in milk. He did say there was a shortage of booze, although he could buy 'fancy stuff' such as gin slings and whiskey highballs, which 'made him frightfully ill if taken in too large a dose'.

Wilf decided to stay at the barracks as he thought he would get home earlier. I believe Chick Henderson went to a sheep farm for two weeks and some POWs, including 'Swede' Moulstone, decided to stay in Australia. It appears reading between the lines that this may have been a good time, with a ratio of '12 girls to every male', although allegedly it was his friend Alf who took advantage of this! The *Hull Daily Mail* on 2 October carried the news of 'RELEASED POWS – News of Hull and District Men', in which L/A/C Wilfred Batty was mentioned.

In a letter dated 4 October 1945 Wilf wrote to Doris from Australia:

> Many thanks for your letters whilst I was a POW. You have no idea what they did for me; they gave me new faith in life and helped me win out on the right side. I only had 4 letters and 2 cards from you but I read them every night before going to sleep, they were a good relaxation from the routine of PoW life.

In an earlier letter, dated 17 September 1945, Wilf wrote to Doris:

> I have lived over and over again the times I have spent with you, this most of all along with you waiting for me, has kept me alive. It was only too easy to give up and die like many of my comrades did. I am not brave, many has been the time when I have been on the verge of doing it myself, but my thoughts of you and home have always kept me plodding along. We always knew we should win some day.

Wilf and his fellow ex-POWs boarded QSMV *Dominion Monarch*, a liner converted to a troopship, on 17 October 1945 and sailed for the UK the next day via Fremantle and Suez arriving in Southampton on 15 November 1945.

Wilf was writing letters to Doris almost daily, it appears, some of which survive.

In one of his letters Wilf tells a story of going out on the town with some 'Jacks' in Perth, when they docked in the nearby port of Fremantle. One of the Jacks got drunk and took his 'one-night girlfriend' back on board with him, who was discovered 100 miles out to sea! The *Melbourne Argus* did report on 26 October that a female stowaway had been found on board the ship.

It appears that Wilf was not impressed with the ship. On 20 October he wrote that the ship was horrible. On 27 October he said that the ship was rocking and rolling and he was green with envy; fortunately there were plenty of portholes! It was hot and Wilf stated that 'he was browned off in more ways than one, what with the usual service red tape, out of bounds there, don't do this, don't do that, it is just barely possible to exist on this ere ship'. He did get a daily allowance of chocolate and cigs, though.

HOME AT LAST

It's not known if anyone met Wilf when he sailed into Southampton as he requested them not to, owing to red tape; he wanted to visit Doris at her home and then travel to Hull to see his parents. However, on arrival in Southampton, the arrivals were greeted with banners stating 'To Our American Friends – Good Luck'! Some very indignant Wrens made a big fuss and eventually the Mayor of Southampton turned up.

Wilf was at Cosford Camp on 27 November 1945 when he received back pay of £422, 15 shillings and nine pence, entered into a Post Office savings bank book on his behalf. He also paid income tax on his earnings while a POW too!

Wilf was finally home after a very difficult four years. It is not known what he thought of conditions at home, bomb damage, rationing etc., especially as he had just spent a few weeks in the land of plenty! In total, 5,102 men of the Royal Air Force had fallen into the hands of the unsympathetic Japanese, of whom 1,714 did not return home. Wilf was one of the 'lucky' ones.

Wilf brought home some memorabilia including postcards, letters, drawings, a piece of paper signed by most POWs in the camp, a sketch of Churchill also signed by most of the POWs and a photograph of Doris, which he had kept throughout his incarceration. It appears Wilf met up with Doris immediately on his return and they were married very quickly on 23 December 1945 at the Parish Church of St John the Baptist, Royal Leamington Spa, Warwickshire. The marriage certificate stated that Wilf was a corporal in the RAF, aged 27, living at 52 Grange Street, Hull, and Doris Gertrude Griffin was a machine operator, aged 24, living at 51 Bury Road, Royal Leamington Spa.

The married couple moved into 52 Grange Street, Hull, with Wilf's parents for nine months while Doris visited the council's housing department every day looking for their own property. Housing in Hull was however in short supply due to the intense bombing Hull suffered at the hands of the Luftwaffe, 95 per cent of houses having been destroyed or damaged. Eventually, in September 1946, they were offered a requisitioned hairdressers shop at 128 Great Thornton Street, Hull, not far from the Valiant Cycle Company on Hessle Road, Hull, where Wilf had resumed his career on leaving the RAF. They bought a German shepherd dog to 'protect' Doris and called it 'Dominion Monarch'! But they had to rehome it when it became too protective of Doris.

Avril (7 April 1948) and Adrian (29 January 1950) were born at 128 Great Thornton Street and in May 1950 the family moved to a new council house at 219 Anson Road, Bilton Grange, Hull. Doris didn't want to buy a house in Hull as she always expected to move back to her beloved Leamington Spa.

In the early 1950s Wilf successfully applied for a job at Blackburn Aircraft, Brough, East Yorkshire, starting on 6 April 1954, where he was to remain until he retired early in 1982. He helped in the design of the Blackburn Buccaneer and the Hawker 'jump jet' vertical take-off plane. He made and tested models in the low- and high-speed wind tunnels and rose to the position of head of precision engineering, aerodynamics laboratory. On his retirement, Doris and Wilf bought a lovely detached bungalow in Newport, East Yorkshire.

I have some interesting memories. Wilf could and did smoke his favourite cigarettes, plain Park Drive, down to a sixteenth of an inch while still attached to his lip and he could transfer his cigarette from his lip to the tip of his tongue and hide it in his mouth. He also carried on stealing for some time! Sadly all his teeth were removed in the 1950s due to malnutrition/vitamin deficiency and he had to wear false teeth. Wilf also shrank five inches in height in his later years, which the medics put down to the same reasons.

As stated, Wilf rarely spoke of his experiences and it was a surprise to him when he found out Doris had been in touch with the FEPOW Association in around 1994, having read an article in the press. At first Wilf resisted any attempts at a reunion but relented and after several chats on the phone with other surviving POWs he agreed to attend the FEPOW fiftieth anniversary weekend celebrating VJ Day. Here Wilf met many fellow surviving POWs including a tearful reunion with several fellow 'Genki' boys.

The reunion was very good for Wilf: he was able to arrange a twice-yearly visit from an armed forces psychologist to help with his mental health issues and found out he was eligible for a war pension! The ex-POWs also received an ex gratia payment of £10,000 each from the British government on 7 November 2000.

As mentioned, Wilf did carry on thieving for some years, silly things like packets of razor blades: it must have become a way of life! He was very good at it though, for he was never caught. After the fiftieth anniversary meeting, many POWs were surprised that Wilf had surfaced after so long and he received a letter from 'Swede' Moultsone in Australia, which started:

> Dear Wilf, well after all these years you finally surfaced. We often wondered what happened to you when you got back. We couldn't get a lead on you at all. I hope you don't mind this joke, but the standing joke about you was that you were so damned good at breaking and entering Jap boat stores that you may have taken it up full time!

Wilf did agree to a chat with a reporter from the *Hull Daily Mail* and a short article and photograph of Wilf and Doris was published on 25 January 1995, when he stated he weighed six and a half stone on his release and described how he was beaten unconscious by five Japanese soldiers when caught bartering with a native, an attack he related to the War Crimes Commission in 1946. Wilf stated he still felt bitter towards his former captors.

One final point of interest occurred in the mid-1960s, when Wilf was in The Crown public house on Holderness Road, Hull, when he was approached by a man he didn't recognise. The man shook Wilf's hand and thanked him for saving his life. Apparently he had given up all hope and had lain down to die, but Wilf had harangued and kicked him back into reality until he had changed his mind. Wilf had then 'employed' him to give him focus. Sadly we no longer know his name.

This brief history of my father's early life has been put together from several sources. Any errors are entirely mine.

Adrian Batty.

CHAPTER 9

Visits to the Far East

Like many others who write up their family history, I started too late. In this chapter I record the somewhat accidental nature of my 'field trips' to corroborate what I was writing at home about the wartime period.

My continuing search for information about what happened to my father during World War II was greatly helped when I was given the opportunity, through working for Ericsson, to go to China. On my way back I went to Hong Kong, which was a significant part of my parents' life, and of course, that is where Dad was captured. When I returned I carried on my research and, through my brother John, I discovered the work of Terence Kelly. The possibility of a trip to Hong Kong came as a complete surprise and it 'kicked off' my interest in expanding my family history to include my mother and father's experiences in the Far East and what was to befall them in World War II. Like my trip to Japan, visiting Hong Kong was a seminal moment for me. My various trips to Singapore, starting in 2009, were useful in corroborating Terence Kelly's experiences both before and immediately after his capture. Looking into the history of the fall of Singapore gave me a good grounding in understanding how dramatic the collapse of British influence in the Far East was. As I worked on the story of my family's experiences leading up to and during World War II, and especially my father's capture and imprisonment as a POW, the need grew in me to visit the POW camp in Japan where he had been incarcerated. The year 2010 was the perfect time to make this trip and whatever I write nothing will replace the emotions I felt when visiting the actual POW camp

1999 – VISIT TO HONG KONG

Dad had been posted to Hong Kong in 1938. This far-flung outpost of the British Empire was seen as one of the plum postings in the army. Later that year, Mum and my three brothers joined him. Things seem to have been going right for Mum and Dad. I have always wanted to see this place. When I was a kid, it seemed to have a magic and mystique about it in our family.

What sparked my WWII history project off came just before my mother died in October 1999. I was working for Ericsson, the international telecommunications company, and an opportunity came up to travel to Beijing in the early months of 1999. I grabbed this with both hands! I was very excited at the possibility of my first visit to the Far East and China, but I was especially pleased to be able to visit Hong Kong, where Mum and Dad had some of the best and worst days of their life. It was in Hong Kong on Christmas Day 1941 that Dad, along with his fellow servicemen, were told to lay down their arms and surrender to the Japanese Army.

Once the trip was agreed with the company, I scooted off to see my mum in Aldershot to tell her all about it and to ask what I should go and see when in Hong Kong. So, we sat in Mum's cosy lounge surrounded by the clutter of ornaments and furniture one afternoon and she revealed the magic of the Far East to me. Although this visit to Mum was tinged with sadness, Hong Kong was where my brother Tommy had died in 1940, she was so excited that I could see the gleam in her eye when we talked about all the places I should see. Even after all these years she clearly remembered the place in some detail. It was lovely revisiting Mum's memories of the place. We talked about where Dad was captured on that Christmas morning in 1941. I really wanted to know where this was, and Mum helped me, saying that she thought it was in Mount Austin Road at the Peak.

So, in March 1999, I went off to Beijing. I asked the Ericsson travel office to allow me to return via Hong Kong. My stopover in Hong Kong gave me a full weekend. During our visit my feet didn't touch the ground. I went everywhere and anywhere I could in the 48 hours I had available.

It's easy to get to the Peak – you just take the funicular tram up from the central area of Hong Kong. The tram soon brings you to its destination near Victoria Peak, which rises up above the mass of urban development including high-rise blocks above Victoria Harbour. In the 1930s and '40s the scene would be much the same, looking out across Victoria Harbour to the New

Territories on the mainland. The only difference is that the high-rise blocks wouldn't have been there, and the harbour would have been full of shipping, including junks and sampans.

This is the view that my father would have witnessed in the closing stages of the Battle for Hong Kong. The frightening addition would have been that the whole of the scene below them was laid out in a real-life battle scene, with Japanese aircraft strafing and bombing the British positions, along with cannon fire causing explosions as bombs hit buildings and smoke billowed up.

I walked up to Mount Austin Road from the Peak tram station and soon found Mount Austin Road, which itself winds up the hill towards Victoria Peak.

The Peak stands out, along with the range of hills covered with a carpet of green trees, bushes and grassy slopes contrasting to the mass of urban development at this western end of Hong Kong Island. This road leads away from the luxury low-rise houses up towards Victoria Peak. Further up the road you are away from the houses. I came across an old bunkhouse, which certainly dated from the wartime period. I imagined my father having to lay down his rifle along with his fellow soldiers outside the bunkhouse after they had been given orders to surrender. I don't know if this was the place or whether it is further over on the other hillside, but the location seemed spookily right to me. My father had said they were up at the Peak. My mother mentioned Mount Austin Road and here I was looking out across Hong Kong and Victoria Harbour towards the New Territories. In the week leading up to Christmas Day 1941 my father would have known that the Battle for Hong Kong was coming rapidly to an end as the Japanese Army had already taken the New Territories and fighting was going on across into Hong Kong Island. The Peak today is an historic hilltop district atop Victoria Peak, known for its panoramic city and harbour views. There are tree-lined trails which wind around the mountain and into what is now a country park.

I had come to the most significant place in my father's life. His capture and imprisonment as a POW changed his life forever. He would not walk freely again until September 1945, when he arrived in Australia after his rescue from Japan. He would not see his wife, Toby, again until November 1945, when he arrived back in England. Dad had been parted from Mum and his sons when they were evacuated from Hong Kong in July 1940, over five years previously.

My weekend visit to Hong Kong was very busy. It was wonderful to visit the places that Mum and Dad enjoyed so much, including Stanley Bay, Temple

Street market and the floating restaurant at Aberdeen Harbour to name just a few. I visited Happy Valley, where Mum and Dad lived, and I visited the beautifully kept graveyard where my brother Tommy was buried in 1940 after a terrible accident early in 1940.

All in all, it was a seminal visit and I shall never forget it.

2009 – SINGAPORE

My son, James, had moved to the Far East a few years before my visit to him in 2009. James has lived there permanently since 2007 and over the past few years I've been able to visit Singapore a number of times. I've also been able to visit Jakarta in Indonesia. The National Museum of Singapore and the Singapore History Gallery has helped me put into context the background to the events leading up to the fall of Singapore, which has been very helpful in studying the history of war in the Far East.

In writing about the war in the Far East it would be wrong to leave out any comment on the war in Malay and Singapore. One can't ignore the massive military defeat that the British suffered in Singapore. Singapore and Hong Kong are tiny islands, but they were supremely important strategic locations for the British Empire.

The Japanese attack on the Malay peninsula began on the same day as the invasion into the New Territories in Hong Kong, 8 December 1941. On this day they also began their attack on the Dutch East Indies, which is largely part of modern-day Indonesia. These attacks were synchronised with the Japanese naval attack on Pearl Harbor on the same day. In the case of the British territories, the Japanese swept down the Malay peninsula and eventually onto Singapore island. Surrender in Singapore occurred on 15 February 1942 and in the Dutch East Indies a month later, on 15 March 1942.

However, apart from my son living there and apart from my interest in wartime history, Singapore had come onto my radar from another direction. In 2004, I'd interviewed Terence Kelly, who had been in the same prisoner of war camp as my dad. His story didn't start in Hong Kong but in Singapore and the Dutch East Indies as an RAF flight sergeant. So, I was intrigued to know more as to why he was so critical about the British military at the end of 1941 and the beginning of 1942. Going to Singapore brings into sharp focus the geography of the place. Visiting Fort Canning, which was the British command headquarters in the Battle for Singapore, enables one to ponder on the wartime situation because you are actually in the place where the British were making their fateful decisions.

Although I didn't know it at the time, Singapore and the Dutch East Indies (now Indonesia) were to figure significantly in the wartime experiences of my father's fellow POWs. Apart from Terence Kelly, Philip (Chick) Henderson and Wilf Batty who were captured in Batavia (modern-day Jakarta).

In fact, there is a direct connection between one of the POWs I write about in this book and modern-day Singapore. If you visit the National Museum of Singapore and the Singapore History Gallery, there is an excellent exhibition that takes you through the history of Singapore from early times right through World War II and up to the time it gained independence. In one of the audio descriptions of the Battle for Singapore I discovered that you can listen to the words of Terence Kelly describing his situation in Singapore and later on in the Dutch East Indies during WWII. Amazing!

2010 – VISIT TO JAPAN

In 2010 we arranged another visit to see my son in Singapore. This time we were going on to Australia. I also had in mind a long-term ambition of mine, which was to visit the place in Japan where my father had spent most of the war in captivity as a POW. Thankfully my wife was up for it and we made arrangements for our trip to have an extra week so that we could fly on from Australia to Tokyo.

I had no idea where the Habu POW camp was and, so far, I hadn't yet researched the location – I hadn't googled it! I knew from talking to my father before he died that it was near a dockyard on the 'Inland Sea' on the island of Innoshima. Dad had described the location on this island as being surrounded by hills on this island and other islands across the water. The Inland Sea is dotted with islands, as I later found out. Dad had mentioned how in the spring all of the hillside was covered with beautiful cherry blossom. Clearly had it not been for the war one might have thought this a beautiful place.

Also, I was armed with Terence Kelly's book *Living with the Japanese* (later retitled *By Hellship to Hiroshima*). He describes arriving at Habu Camp: 'finally, we, the second hundred, were transported by tugboat to the island of Innoshima which is in the "Ken"[76] – of what the near English equivalent is a county of Innoshima'. He continues: 'I remember the first walk through Habu dockyard. I can still see the skeletons of half-built ships, the flashing of welding, the piles of wood and scrap, the curious faces, the dry docks and the slips. I can see the dumpy travelling cranes and hear the harsh clang of hammers on metal plate and the woodpecker sound of riveting.'

I also knew what the prison huts looked like. The pen-and-ink drawing made by a fellow POW, Geoffrey Coxhead, that my dad kept on his wall at home showed the large wooden hutments next to the quayside and below some low hills.

It was easy to search on the Internet and find Innoshima. It was a little more difficult to actually find the word Habu. The descriptions of minor places are not always in English. After some time, I established roughly where I thought the POW camp was. The next thing was getting there.

Through Rotary International, I had mentored several overseas postgraduate students at the local university here in Sussex. One of the students was Kumiko from Japan. She returned to Japan in about 2004 but we stayed in touch. In 2009, when planning the trip, I got in touch with her and she replied that she would be very pleased to help us find the POW camp. I'm not sure if we would have found the place without her help. For those who don't speak Japanese, travelling to the main towns is pretty simple, but to explore further on and ask questions about specific obscure places like Habu it would have been pretty difficult. None of the signs are in English, which is fair enough, but also there are many people in the non-tourist areas who speak no English.

Kumiko was fantastic! We flew to Tokyo and got ourselves tickets for the bullet train to travel down to Kobe, a city located on the southern side of the main island of Honshu. We knew we had to travel in this south-westerly direction via Kobe to get to Innoshima Island, so it was very convenient that Kumiko lived in Kobe. The day after meeting up we all travelled down to Onomichi, firstly via a high-speed train and then via a local train.

At Onomichi, Kumiko enquired about the bus service to Innoshima Island and Habu port, which we had found on the map. We were quickly aboard a local bus service and off we went. Kumiko thought it was best that we head for the council offices or the centre of the town of Habu. None of us had any idea exactly where we were going or who could help us. When

---

76 The counties which Terence Kelly refers to as 'kens' are the prefectures of Japan. There are 47 in all and we were heading for the prefecture of Hiroshima.

Figure 9.1 Onomichi bus station. The railway station is just behind it. This is where my father started his journey, firstly by train, home after the end of the War in the Far East.

we got there, we realised we were in the middle of a chain of small industrial ports along the west coast of Innoshima Island looking in towards the Inland Sea. I immediately felt we were in the right place as low hills rose up behind us. There were still some cherry blossom trees in flower, just as my father had described. I don't think many tourists come here, I said to myself. However, Kumiko quickly found her way to the council offices and she spoke to some of the staff. It was quite clear that this was only a small council office and I think we were lucky to have found it staffed on that late April morning. From the conversation between Kumiko and one of the older members of staff it was quite clear that he was directing us further along the coast if we were to find where the Habu POW camp was sited. He wasn't sure, but he felt it was in that direction and he suggested we go to the Buddhist temple located just above to get further directions. We took a taxi from here and, as directed, we carried on along the coast road through the dockyards and out to a little-used small marina. Here the road turned inland so we couldn't continue along the coast. The taxi took us up a short drive through a hamlet of single-storey and two-storey wooden houses, some of them quite ancient and rundown.

I knew we were in the locality of where the POW camp was. My father had

Figure 9.2 Habu village.

Figure 9.3 A derelict house in Habu village - probably dating from the wartime.

described these wooden houses quite near to the POW hutments of the prison camp rising up into the low hills. Just as we cleared away from the small hamlet, we came to the turning for the Buddhist temple. There was a young monk in charge and we realised we were lucky to see him since he wasn't always there.

(Left to right)
Figure 9.4 At the Buddhist Monastery above Habu village. The monk was very helpful in recounting his father's memories of wartime.
Figure 9.5 At the Buddhist monastery graveyard above Habu village. We are looking down the valley to the sea where the POW camp was.

Kumiko explained our mission and he said his father knew of the POW camp and he pointed down the hill where we could see a quayside and a small, virtually empty marina. He said that his father knew the POW camp had been on that quayside.

Wow! We had found Habu! I can't tell you how important this journey was and to know that I had come to this place. This quest had been in my mind for years and I never thought that I would actually get here. Everything fitted in. The description of the hillsides by my father and the POW hutments by the quayside, the march each day to the dockyards came into sharp focus. It was all there and confirmed by Geoffrey Coxhead's pen-and-ink drawing of the prison camp.

The monk turned to the subject of the remains of a group of British soldiers (POWs) who had died in the POW camp. He took us to a large memorial in the graveyard. He said the ashes of some 30 unnamed POWs were interned here. This was a very emotional point for me, standing there looking at this memorial. What more can I say?

I thanked the Buddhist monk, saying I was very grateful for his help. The

 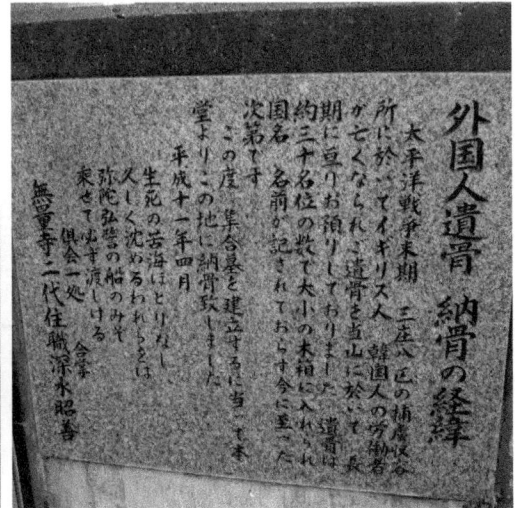

(Left to Right)
Figure 9.6 At the Buddhist monastery graveyard above Habu village. The monument to the 30 POW dead who are buried here.
Figure 9.7 The inscription to the 30 POW dead who are buried here.

taxi took us back down the hill to the quayside by the small marina. There were no hutments there, of course, but standing there I imagined the buildings on the edge of the quayside and tried to imagine what life was like for my father and the other POWs.

I looked out to sea towards the headland and remembered my father's words when he described how overjoyed he was to see a British Navy motorised launch flying the Royal Ensign coming around the headland to their camp in September 1945. The officer in charge had said that they would be rescued very soon. Dad said he was only there a few minutes.

The taxi took us back through the shipyards. This whole coastline is dotted with small ship repair yards. We went through the one which I'm sure my father worked in. I got the taxi to stop and I took photographs through the fencing. It seemed exactly as my father described: ships in dry dock being repaired; great sheds where other ships were being repaired or fitted out.

I was at the place where my father laboured as a prisoner. The photographs I'd seen when researching information about this camp and those in Terence Kelly's book were absolute proof of where we were.

Figure 9.8 Here I am on the quay where the POW huts stood.

Figure 9.9 Looking out to the Inland Sea.

Figure 9.10 My photo of the current-day dockyard.

The rescue in September 1945 had taken the prisoners by boat from here to the main railway station at Onomichi and on to Osaka, where my father and his fellow POWs had boarded the British warship HMS *Ruler*. So they left the POW camp on Innoshima Island, only 35 miles (55 km) over the hills from Hiroshima, where the first atomic bomb was dropped on 6 August 1945.

Postscript

The most shocking fact about war is that its victims and its instruments are individual human beings, and that these individual beings are condemned by the monstrous conventions of politics to murder or be murdered in quarrels not their own.

Aldous Huxley

Acknowledgements and Thanks

My thanks to those POWs who have allowed me to publish their stories and to Adrian Batty for allowing me to publish his father's story, and for persuading me to go to the Java Club meeting in Stratford-upon-Avon in 2013. If I hadn't gone I would never have met Chick Henderson and this record of valiant men who survived POW camps in the Far East would be all the poorer for it. Just as this book is published, I've heard that Adrian Batty has sadly passed away. This book, therefore, is, I hope, a lasting tribute to his efforts to remember those who fought for our freedom in WWII. A special thank you to Lizzie Spinks for allowing me to use the recording of her father where he and Monty Truscott are interviewed in Hong Kong and for the copies of the photos and memorabilia. My thanks also to Kumiko Kiuchi for her help in accompanying us in Japan to help us find my father's POW camp at Habu. My thanks also to Dr Tony Banham for writing the foreword to this book.

Thanks are also due to Hugh Jackson who has done an excellent job in proofreading this book and to Alistair Hill who put me in touch with Hugh.

A special thank you goes to my wife, Carol, for her help in proofreading the early versions of the book and for her patience over the years during my research work.

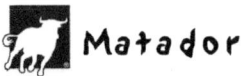

For exclusive discounts on Matador titles,
sign up to our occasional newsletter at
troubador.co.uk/bookshop